GROUP
LIFE AND HEALTH
INSURANCE

Other Authors

Isabelle Branschofsky

A. Charles Bredesen

John Cartmell, FLMI

Charles H. Cissley, FLMI

Daniel D'Andrea, FSA

Charles A. DiFalco

Richard M. Heins, Ph.D.

Bernard F. Kalb, CLU

R. Werner Lederer, FLMI, CLU

Charles H. Meyer, CLU

G. R. Minns, FIA, FCIA, ASA

Arthur E. Nolan

Craig R. Rodby, FSA, MAAA

John H. Tweedie, FSA

GROUP
LIFE AND HEALTH INSURANCE

VOLUME 2

by
**Robert W. Batten, George M. Hider
and others**

FLMI Insurance Education Program
Life Management Institute
Life Office Management Association
100 Colony Square, Atlanta, Georgia 30361

The Life Office Management Association is a research and educational association of life insurance companies operating in the United States, Canada and a number of other countries. Among its activities is the sponsorship of an educational program intended primarily for home office and branch office employees of these companies.

The FLMI Insurance Education Program is comprised of two courses—Course I (Parts 1 and 2), "Fundamentals of Life Insurance," and Course II (Parts 3 through 8), "Advanced Life Insurance." Upon the completion of Course I, the student is awarded a Certificate. Upon the completion of both courses (eight parts), the student is designated a Fellow of the Life Management Institute (FLMI) and is awarded a Diploma.

ISBN 0-915322-31-5

Library of Congress Catalog Card Number: 78-71257

Printed in the United States of America

CONTENTS
Volume 2

Part 3 Other Forms of Group Insurance

Part 4 Administration of Group Plans

Part 5 Group Insurance in Canada

Part 6 Government Insurance Programs

PART 3

OTHER FORMS OF GROUP INSURANCE

CHAPTER 18

CREDITOR GROUP INSURANCE

INTRODUCTION

Creditor insurance is that form of insurance which, in the event a debtor is unable to repay a debt because of death or disability, pays the outstanding indebtedness to the lender. In the most common insuring arrangement, the creditor purchases a group policy covering a specified class of debtors. In general, if a debtor dies, the insurer pays the creditor the unpaid balance of the indebtedness. If the debtor becomes disabled, as defined in the contract, the insurer pays the creditor either the unpaid balance of the indebtedness in the event of total and permanent disability, or the amount of the debtor's monthly installments for the duration of a temporary disability, but not beyond the point the indebtedness is extinguished or its maturity date is reached.

Creditor insurance may be written on both individuals and groups. However, in 1973 it was estimated that approximately 86 percent of all creditor insurance is written on a group basis.[1] Therefore, this chapter discusses group creditor insurance primarily.

The hazards insured against are death and disability. The disability coverage is commonly attached to the credit life policy for administration purposes. While there are many similarities in the provision of coverage for these two hazards, there are also significant differences, particularly in administration and in policy provisions.

This chapter has two major sections. The first presents creditor group life insurance. Although emphasis is on the life coverage, much of the discussion also applies to the disability coverage because of their similarities. The second section discusses those features of creditor group disability insurance that are different from the death coverage. The discussions of both creditor group life insurance and of creditor group disability insurance include brief descriptions of their

---

[1]"Credit Insurance Statistical Review," *Spectator*, Vol. 181 (October 1973), p. 57.

by
RICHARD M. HEINS, Ph.D., *Professor of Risk and Insurance, University of Wisconsin; Executive Vice President, Capital Management and Planning, CUNA Mutual Insurance Society, Madison, Wisconsin.*

origins and basic characteristics, their administration, and their major policy provisions.

CREDITOR GROUP LIFE INSURANCE

Origin: The Morris Plan

Until the early 1900s, the majority of lenders required negotiable instruments and easily accessible assets as security before granting a loan. However, in 1910, Arthur J. Morris, a Norfolk, Virginia attorney, founded the Morris Plan Bank. Its primary purpose was to offer installment credit to borrowers who had nothing more than the potential ability to repay. As a result of the less stringent loan requisite, many who previously did not qualify for loans became eligible.

Since both the untimely death of the debtor and the subsequent inability of the survivors to repay the loan would place the creditor in a difficult position, Morris sought to develop an insurance plan to protect against this contingency. He attempted to interest several insurance companies in the idea of providing short-term life insurance of small amounts on borrowers, but because no mortality experience on borrowers existed and because short-term small amount policies would involve a high expense ratio, the idea had little appeal at that time.

Morris therefore decided to provide such protection through his own efforts and founded the Morris Plan Insurance Society on September 18, 1917. The New York stock company was predicated upon the philosophy that "no man's debt should live after him." In the first year of operation, 1,432 individual term life insurance policies were issued, amounting to $170,950 of insurance.[2] In 1946, the name "Morris Plan Insurance Society" was changed because a number of banks that were not Morris Plan Banks requested and were granted permission to use the original company's insurance facilities. They suggested the present name, "Bankers Security Life Insurance Society," instead of limiting it to the original name and to Morris Plan Banks. Under the present name, the company has more than $130 million of creditor group life insurance in force.[3]

Development and Growth

Table 18-1 and Diagram 18-A show the growth of creditor group life insurance in force since 1935. The exceptionally high percentage increases between 1945 and 1955 reflect the surge in consumer credit insurance purchases after the easing of the World War II credit restrictions. Since 1956, the yearly percentage increase in force has averaged approximately 10.8 percent.

[2]D. P. Kedzie, *Consumer Credit Insurance* (Homewood, Ill.: Richard D. Irwin, Inc., 1957), p. 18.
[3]"Credit Insurance Statistical Review," *Spectator*, Vol. 183 (September 1975), p. 47.

TABLE 18-1
Growth of Group Creditor Life Insurance

Year	Group Creditor Life Insurance in Force (000,000)	% Increase from Previous Period
1935	75	
1945	264	72
1950	3,169	92
1955	12,371	74
1960	25,715	52
1965	49,303	48
1970	74,232	34
1975	112,032*	34

SOURCE: Institute of Life Insurance, *Life Insurance Fact Book* (New York: 1973 and 1976).

*Includes individual contracts. Group alone not available.

REASONS FOR GROWTH

There are at least four additional plausible reasons for the sustained growth of group creditor life insurance. They are the increase in outstanding credit, inflation, the increase in the number of insurers, and an increasing concern with financial security in American society.

Increase in Outstanding Credit. One obvious reason for the growth of creditor group insurance is the increase in outstanding credit. Installment credit is the type of credit most readily insured under a creditor group policy because typically it is small in amount and thus repayable in a relatively short period of time. Table 18-2 shows the history of total and outstanding installment credit along with the corresponding growth of creditor group life insurance covering the outstanding credit. It may be said that "as outstanding installment credit goes, so goes the creditor group life insurance in force." Table 18-2 also shows the percentage of outstanding installment credit that is insured. As Diagram 18-B illustrates, this percentage has increased dramatically from a low of 1.4 percent in 1940 to a rate of about 70 percent in 1975. Not only has creditor group life insurance grown along with outstanding credit, but the proportion of outstanding installment credit that is insured has increased steadily as well. This trend reflects an increasing demand for, and appreciation of, credit insurance in our society.

Inflation. Inflation has intensified the demand for installment credit, which has led to an increase in credit insurance purchases. Because of the rising prices of consumer goods bought on the installment plan, the amount of credit insurance purchased has also increased.

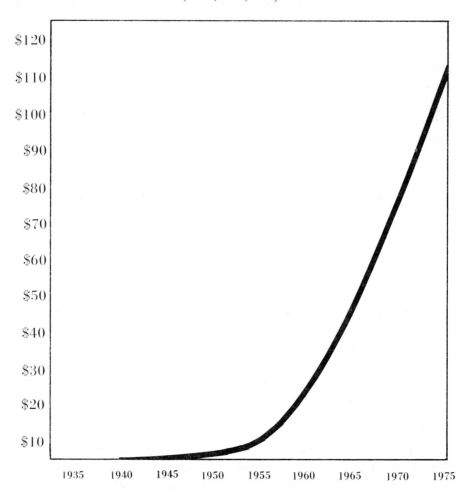

DIAGRAM 18-A
Group Creditor Life Insurance in Force in the United States
Insurance in Force
(000,000,000)

Increase in the Number of Insurers. The increase in the number of companies providing creditor group life insurance has probably contributed to its continued growth. In 1930, only three companies wrote credit insurance. By 1946, about fifty companies wrote some form of credit life insurance.[4] Today, there are more than 270 companies providing creditor life insurance on a group basis.[5]

Security-Minded Society. The quest for financial security has become an increasing concern not only among individual borrowers, but also among large corporations. Insurance is the primary vehicle by

---

[4]Institute of Life Insurance.

[5]"Credit Insurance Statistical Review," *Spectator*, Vol. 183 (September 1975), p. 46.

TABLE 18–2

**Comparison of Growth of Installment Credit and
Creditor Group Insurance**

Year	Total Installment Credit Outstanding	Group Creditor Life Insurance in Force	% of Installment Credit Insured
	(000,000)	(000,000)	
1940	5,514	75	1.4
1945	2,462	264	10.7
1950	14,703	3,169	21.5
1955	28,906	12,371	42.8
1960	42,832	25,715	60.0
1965	70,893	49,303	69.5
1970	102,064	74,232	72.7
1975	161,819	112,032*	69.2

SOURCES: Institute of Life Insurance, *Life Insurance Fact Book* (New York: 1973 and 1976); *Federal Reserve Bulletin* (various issues).
*Includes individual contracts. Group alone not available.

which such security is attained. The growth not only of creditor insurance, but also of other forms of insurance, is part of the trend in American society to minimize uncertainty and exposure to loss.

There are, of course, many other possible reasons for the growth of creditor group insurance. Whatever the preferred explanation, it is apparent that the availability of credit insurance has allowed an increasing number of people the opportunity of securing credit, and thus enabled the high American standard of living to be within the reach of virtually anyone willing and able to work.

Master Policy Provisions

The master policy establishes the insuring agreement between the insurer and the creditor covering the creditor's outstanding loans. Although differences between the master policies issued by different group credit insurers exist, there are several policy provisions that are common to most master policies.

GENERAL CHARACTERISTICS

The following discussion provides a general idea of the characteristics of a typical group creditor life insurance master policy and its provisions.

Insuring Agreement. The master policy provides that upon due proof of death of the insured debtor, payment will be made to the creditor in the amount for which the debtor was insured at the time of death. The policy further provides that the proceeds received by the

DIAGRAM 18-B

Insurance as a Percentage of Installment Credit Outstanding

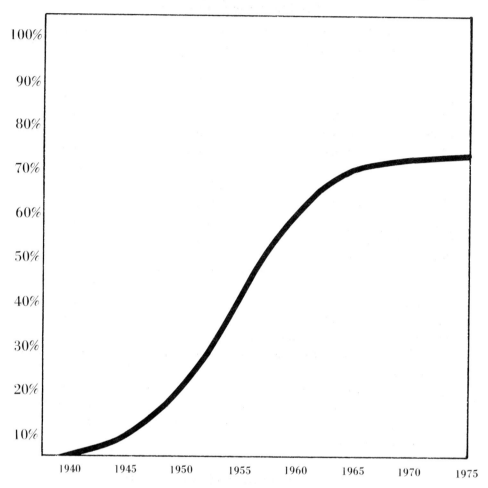

creditor will be applied toward the discharge of the insured's indebtedness.

Inception of Coverage. The inception of coverage for each debtor depends on whether the premium payment is based on a contributory or noncontributory plan. In the contributory situation, the debtor becomes insured only after premium payment arrangements have been made with each individual debtor. Under the noncontributory plan, each eligible debtor usually becomes automatically insured as of the date the loan agreement is signed, since no premium paying arrangements with each individual debtor is necessary.

Statement of Insurability. One simplifying aspect of creditor group insurance is the elimination of the evidence of insurability under normal circumstances. However, the insurer reserves the right to require that any insured debtor furnish evidence of insurability satisfactory to the insuring company.

At-Work Provision. This provision stipulates that an eligible debtor may be insured only if the debtor is actively at work and regularly performing all of the usual duties of the debtor's occupation at the time the insurance is to become effective. The primary purpose is to make certain that the insured debtor is earning an income from which to repay the loan and thus minimize the adverse selection effect suffered when insured debtors who are not "at work" as defined in the policy become unable to repay the loan. Although many states still allow this provision, the trend is toward disallowing it, based on the argument that depriving nonworkers of the opportunity to be insured under a creditor group policy discriminates against borrowers who either cannot or do not work yet have income from other sources. Nevertheless, inclusion of nonworking debtors in the insurable group tends to have an unfavorable effect on the loss experience of the group as a whole. This results in a seemingly inequitable practice of having to charge a higher premium to all group members, most of whom work and faithfully repay their loans.

Risks Not Assumed. This typical standard provision states that no benefit will be paid for a loss occurring within the first six months of coverage if the loss was caused or contributed to by an accident. Nor will there be payment if the loss was caused by sickness or disease which was contracted or for which the debtor received treatment within six months preceding the initial date of coverage. The primary purpose of this provision is to minimize the insurer's exposure to deliberate antiselection, as in cases where an individual, upon learning of some personal disease or illness, takes out a loan and has it insured knowing that imminent disability or death will result in repayment of the loan via the insurance.

Misstatement of Age. The misstatement of age provision states that the insurer has no liability other than to refund premiums for the period during which the debtor was ineligible for coverage because of the debtor's actual age. Since most creditor group policies charge the same premium rate regardless of age up to a maximum of 65, this provision generally applies only in situations where the debtor has exceeded the maximum age restriction.

Termination. The master policy may be canceled by either the lender or the insurer. The lender may terminate the policy by giving written notice of whatever time the master policy specifies, say, 15 or 30 days, to the insurer. The insurer may likewise terminate the contract, giving 30 days notice to the lender. Reasons for termination of the master policy by the insurer include continually late payment of premiums, nonpayment of premium, fraudulent claims filed by the lender, or failure to fulfill any underwriting requirements.

In addition, there are four events that result in termination of the individual debtor's coverage under the group master policy. These include: (1) repayment of the loan either prior to the maturity date or in accordance with the original repayment schedule; (2) debtor default on the scheduled repayment of the indebtedness; (3) assignment of the debt by the lender to a creditor not included in the policy, unless the assigning lender continues to service the debt and retains adequate equity to justify continuation as beneficiary of the insurance; and (4) voluntary termination of the master policy by one of the contracting parties.

Underwriting

There are four general aspects of underwriting that must be considered in the underwriting of creditor group insurance. These are the eligibility of the lending institution, the eligibility of the loan, statutory underwriting requirements, and the rates to be charged.

ELIGIBLE LENDING INSTITUTIONS

The list of institutions eligible to have their debtors insured is a long one. The list includes commercial banks, finance companies, credit unions, savings and loan associations, trust companies, sales finance companies, small loan companies, colleges and universities, credit card companies, mutual funds, production credit associations, and Federal Land Banks.

Credit of the installment type is most readily insured under a creditor group policy. Table 18-3 shows the leading types of installment credit lenders and the amount outstanding for each. As the figures indicate, commercial banks lead in providing installment credit and at least 90 percent are users of credit life insurance.

ELIGIBLE LOANS

Most installment loans normally granted by lending institutions are eligible for creditor group insurance coverage. If the criteria used by banks in evaluating a loan request are based on sound lending

TABLE 18-3
Total Installment Credit Outstanding
(000,000s)

Year	Total	Commercial Banks	Finance Companies	Credit Unions	Retail Outlets	Other
1940	5,514	1,452	2,278	171	1,596	17
1945	2,462	745	910	102	686	19
1950	14,703	5,198	5,315	590	2,898	702
1955	28,906	10,601	11,838	1,678	4,508	281
1960	42,968	16,672	15,435	3,923	6,295	643
1965	70,893	28,962	23,851	7,324	9,791	965
1970	102,064	45,398	27,678	12,986	13,900	2,102
1975	161,819	75,710	38,932	25,354	18,328	3,495

SOURCE: Federal Reserve

principles, it is generally assumed that the loan meets the major underwriting requirements of the insurance company. Only loans granted to natural persons, as opposed to corporations, are eligible under the group master policy. Generally, only one person may be insured under each loan, although there are provisions for "joint spouse credit insurance" wherein death or disability of the husband or wife is the risk being insured under the single loan coverage. Among the kinds of loans most commonly insured are those for automobiles, residential mortgages, mobile homes, home improvements, revolving credit accounts, education, and leases.

STATUTORY UNDERWRITING REQUIREMENTS

In addition to the general eligibility characteristics just described, there are statutory requirements established by each state as part of the regulation of creditor group insurance. Although the specific requirements vary among the states, the following requirements are typical of statutory underwriting requirements.

Maximum Amount of Coverage. The amount most commonly accepted as the maximum insurable loan balance is $10,000. Setting a maximum reduces the potential for antiselection, because the maximum limits each group borrower to a definite maximum amount of insurance coverage and thus limits the insured group to a stated maximum loss. The result is to minimize wide fluctuations in the group's loss experience.

Maximum Loan Duration. If the loan is insured under a contributory premium payment plan, the usual maximum loan duration allowed for a loan to be eligible for inclusion in the group policy is 60 months. Under a noncontributory plan, this statutory restriction does not apply, and the maximum repayment period may be as long as 20 years. However, primarily because of inflation, it is becoming increasingly difficult under the contributory plan for consumers to repay some types of loans within the statutory 60-month limit. In response to this problem, the trend is to increase the 60-month statutory limit to 120 months.

Maximum Age. The most common maximum insurable age for the death coverage is 65, although in some states coverage may be granted up to age 70. The primary purpose for this maximum is to reduce the adverse effect of including debtors who because of their advanced age have a high risk of death.

Minimum Participation. For the creditor group insurance contract to keep operating costs, claims costs and premiums low, there must be a minimum number of eligible debtors insured under the group master policy. Under the contributory plan, statutes generally require that 75 percent of the eligible class of debtors be insured under the group master policy. The contributory method is voluntary in the sense that even though debtors may be in the insurable class, they have a choice as to whether they want the loan insured under the group master policy. It follows that there exists a greater chance for adverse selection against the company because of the tendency for borrowers in high risk classes to seek insurance more readily than others. The minimum participation requirement is designed to reduce this adverse effect. Under the noncontributory method, all eligible debtors automatically become insured at the inception of the master policy, and thus participation is 100 percent.

The underlying purpose of these statutory requirements is to ensure that the experience of the group will be such that the insuring company will be able to charge relatively stable premiums and still cover the expenses and claims as they arise.

RATING

Rating Criteria. In addition to rating criteria common to all forms of insurance (mortality rates, reserve requirements, acquisition costs, and administrative expenses), there is information unique to group creditor insurance that is utilized in determining risk classification and the group rate for creditor insurance. This information includes the size of the lender's operations, the interest rate charged debtors, the kinds of indebtedness to be insured, the current volume of loans as well as the anticipated growth, and whether the premium payment plan is contributory or noncontributory. Once the information has been considered, the rating can be applied. The two most common methods of rating creditor group policies are the prima facie and deviated rates method and the prospective rates method.

Prima Facie and Deviated Rates. One common rating procedure applied under a contributory premium payment plan involves the application of a prima facie rate and a deviated rate. A prima facie rate is essentially the standard rate recommended by state regulation. The insurance company initially is allowed to charge a rate that is either equal to or less than the prima facie rate. Then, based on the experience of the particular insured group, the insurance company can seek approval from the state insurance commissioner to charge a higher rate. This higher rate is known as a deviated rate, since it deviates from the prima facie rate. Criteria used to determine whether a deviated rate will be allowed include (1) evidence of loss experience, (2) the amount of time the group has been insured, (3) the credibility of the premium and claims experience, and (4) the type of indebtedness insured. The purpose of the regulatory procedure is to assure the insureds that they are being charged equitable rates, particularly under a contributory plan where they are paying directly for the insurance.

Retrospective Rates. Another common rating procedure is retrospective rating, which is usually applied under a noncontributory premium payment plan. It is based on the common practice among insurance companies to return to the lender that portion of the paid premium that remains after all expenses and claims have been paid for one particular operating period. This is comparable to a mutual company's policy dividend.

Under this procedure, the insurer sets a base rate that is to be charged on initial business. At the end of an operating period, usually one year, if the difference between the total premium less the expenses and claims is positive, the amount of the difference is returned to the lender. Conversely, if the difference is negative, the lender must absorb the loss. This is usually accomplished in one of three ways.

First, the lender may have a reserve account from which the necessary deficit is extracted and paid to the insurer. Second, the lender has the option to allow the insurer to charge an additional predetermined premium known as a "retro premium." For example, at the beginning of a period, the lender and insurer will agree on a base premium of, say, $.65 per $1,000 per month, and a retro premium of $.85. During the operating period, the $.65 base premium is used. If at the end of the period there is an underwriting loss, the insurer can retroactively charge the $.85 retro premium, which means up to an additional $.20 on the prior period business in an attempt to offset the loss. Third and finally, if the first two procedures are inadequate or unavailable, the lender can carry the loss forward to the next period, usually a policy year, as a liability. This will then be added to the next year's premium.

Administration

Although some aspects of creditor group insurance administration are common to all insurance companies and lending institutions, each insurer or lender may also implement administrative policies that are unique to that firm. It is beyond the scope of this chapter to deal with all of the possible variations. However, some procedures are common to most companies. The following discussion focuses on these common administrative procedures.

GENERAL CHARACTERISTICS

Compared with other forms of group insurance, the administration of creditor group life insurance is relatively simple and economical for most insuring companies. There are several reasons for this. First, the group creditor policy is written so that the amount of insurance is limited to the indebtedness by using a decreasing term contract. If the loan is for $1,000, it is unlikely that so small an amount of decreasing term coverage will be available to the purchaser through any other form of life insurance; but if so, it would most likely be more expensive. In addition, no evidence of insurability is normally required for consumer credit insurance; the premium rates are the same for all ages up to age 65 (through the same lender); and the premium is most often added to the loan payment. Routine record keeping and paperwork are thus minimized and administration is simplified. Some of the administrative duties rest with the lending institution through whom the insurance is sold to the borrower. These duties are created when the insurer issues a master policy to the lending institution.

MASTER POLICY

Creditor group insuring plans require the lending institution to complete an application form before being granted coverage. Once the application has been approved, a master policy is issued to the lending institution. Basically, this policy sets forth the insuring agreement between the insurer and lender and activates a decreasing term insurance contract on all eligible debtors of the lender-policyowner. The issuance of the master policy makes the lender not only the policyowner but the beneficiary as well, a distinction unique to creditor group insurance. In addition, the lender receives compensation from the insurer for the business generated through the lending institution. Among the general administrative duties assumed by the lender under this agreement is the issuance of a certificate of insurance to each individual debtor. Its purpose is to spell out the essential elements of the coverage. Other duties include making certain that only eligible debtors and classes of loans are insured, reporting any change in the amount of insurance in force, and making notification of termination of insurance by the individual debtor.

PREMIUM PAYMENT PROCEDURES

Premiums are paid either under a contributory plan or under a noncontributory plan.

Contributory Plan. Under the contributory method, the debtor is charged an identifiable amount for coverage. The debtor pays this amount directly to the lender, who in turn passes the premium amount on to the insurer. There are generally two ways by which premiums can be paid under a contributory plan: single premium and monthly outstanding balance.

Under the single premium method, the debtor is charged a single premium amount at the inception of the loan. This premium is based on the amount and duration of the loan. Assume that a loan for $1,000 is issued, and that the appropriate total premium to insure that loan is $15. The borrower may pay the entire $15 premium to the lender at the inception of the loan. Alternatively, the $15 premium can be added to the $1,000 principal, making the total loan $1,015. The premium is then included in the periodic loan payments made by the borrower to the lender. This latter procedure is the more commonly used single premium payment procedure. The lender then accumulates all the premiums received during a given period, usually a month, and pays a lump sum to the insurance company.

Under the monthly outstanding balance method, the lender applies the appropriate premium rate to the outstanding insurable loan balance of each debtor at the end of each month. For example, if a debtor has an outstanding loan balance of $1,000 at the end of a month, the appropriate premium for that amount for one month, say $.75, is added to the outstanding loan balance owed to the lender. The lender transfers the accumulated premiums to the insurance company as payment for the insurance. This type of premium collection procedure is most widely used in such open-end credit situations as department store revolving credit accounts.

Noncontributory Plan. Under this method, the cost of the insurance is absorbed by the lender as an operating expense. The amount of the premium is based on the outstanding loan balance of the entire insured class of loans. Payments are made regularly, usually monthly, to the insurance company. This type of premium payment method is restricted almost exclusively to credit unions.

The use of either a contributory or noncontributory premium collection method depends on the type of lending institution, the kind of insurance being offered (life or disability), and the premium level for the insured class of debtors.

CLAIM AND BENEFITS ADMINISTRATION

When a claim is reported, the lending institution is required to submit proof of death to the insuring company, along with the master policy number, date of the loan execution, the amount of original indebtedness, and the outstanding balance to be repaid. Some insurance companies may require the lender to forward original promissory notes or account cards in addition to the proof of death to further verify the existence of the loan. When a claim is paid, the draft is usually drawn in favor of the lender, who in turn credits the insured account and notifies the survivors of the settlement of the account.

Under a creditor group life insurance decreasing term contract, the amount of insurance on the debtor's life declines as the debtor makes loan repayments. There are two ways to reduce the amount of insurance. Under one method, the amount of insurance is the unpaid balance of the insured loan. Under the second method, the amount of insurance is reduced by an equal amount each month. The amount of the monthly reduction is equal to the original amount of insurance divided by the term of the indebtedness in months. Thus, if the principal sum and interest amount to $1,000 and a loan with a 20-month repayment period is issued, the original amount of insurance would be $1,000. This amount would decrease by $50 each month ($1,000 ÷ 20 months = $50 a month) for 20 months. If the unpaid balance exceeds the scheduled amount of insurance, the debtor is insured for only the maximum permitted under the policy. Although there are provisions for level term insurance where the amount of insurance remains constant for the duration of the loan period, decreasing term coverage is the type most often used.

PREMIUM REFUNDS AND DIVIDENDS

Most noncontributory group contracts provide that a premium refund shall accrue to the lender-policyowner if the insurance company agrees and lender experience so warrants. The dividend may be paid in cash to the creditor or applied toward the payment of any premium at the lender's option. In some cases, the dividend is left with the insurer at a stated rate of interest.

Regulation

Creditor group insurance was originally regulated by the state standard provisions and laws applicable to other forms of group insurance. The primary objective of this regulation was to make certain that the coverage was provided on a sound underwriting basis. Consequently, the degree of regulation was no more stringent for creditor group insurance than for other forms of group insurance. However, the unique relationship among the insurer, lender, and borrower, where the lender assumed the dual role of policyowner and beneficiary, gave rise to practices by lenders and insurance companies that were not governed by the initial regulation.

MAJOR ABUSES

Among the abuses discovered as group creditor insurance became more popularly accepted were instances of coercion, overcharging for premiums, pyramiding, requiring more insurance than needed to cover the indebtedness, and failure to refund unneeded premiums.

Coercion. The first major abuse discovered involved the lenders coercing the borrowers into purchasing insurance. Because the borrower was considered to be in an inferior position in seeking a loan, some lenders granted a loan only on the condition that the borrowers purchase credit insurance through them.

Overcharging and Reverse Competition. Another major abuse was overcharging. Borrowers were overcharged by being required to pay higher premiums than were warranted by the benefits provided. The phenomenon of "reverse competition" is closely associated with the increased premiums. This is a practice whereby lenders, because they received compensation from the insurer in the form of commissions and premium refunds, seek to insure with companies who charge the highest initial premium rates. In doing so, the lenders profit by higher commissions and refunds. Insurers, in turn, would tend to charge higher premiums to attract more business. Thus, instead of insurers competing for business by offering the lowest rates possible, they would compete for business by offering high rates, or by reverse competition. This practice resulted in the cost of high rates being passed on to the borrower.

Excessive Insurance. In addition to being overcharged for the proper amount of insurance, some lenders sold excessive amounts of insurance to consumers. This abuse involved selling insurance to the debtor in an amount greater than the loan amount that was being insured. While the excess would go to the insured's estate if the insured died, most insureds were paying for unneeded coverage.

Pyramiding. Pyramiding occurs in cases where a loan is refinanced prior to its maturity. Some lenders would issue credit insurance policies on the new debt without canceling the already existing insurance. The effect was to pyramid insurance and coverage in amounts in excess of the actual indebtedness.

Lack of Disclosure. Because the master policy was issued to the lender, the borrower often was not fully informed of the essential elements of the coverage. Although certificates of insurance were made available by the insurer to the lender to be distributed to the borrower, the borrowers were not always provided with or made aware of the contents of such certificates.

Failure to Refund Unearned Premium. Another major abuse discovered was the failure of the insurer to refund to the debtors the unearned portion of the paid-in premium upon termination of the coverage.

THE NAIC MODEL BILL

Eventually, these and other abuses made it apparent that additional regulation specifically designed to cope with these problems was needed. Consequently, in the early 1950s, legislators, insurance executives, and trade organizations responded to the growing concern over abusive practices and inadequate regulation. Much of the subsequent regulation is based on the 1957 model bill developed by the National Association of Insurance Commissioners (NAIC). Although the NAIC Bill is only advisory, it has been substantially adopted in the model form in 45 jurisdictions and most insurance commissioners have promulgated regulations under it.[6] There are, however, some who still feel that federal regulation is necessary to monitor the credit insurance industry. Thus, legislative bills promoting uniform regulation have been introduced in Congress.

The model bill, and the legislation patterned on it, tried to correct the abuses mentioned above by requiring disclosure of the rates and conditions of coverage to the borrower, by giving the borrower an option to provide insurance from another source, and, in some states, by promulgating premium rate standards.

The creditor was required to provide the borrower with a cer-

[6]Paul F. Boyer, "The Regulation of Consumer Credit Insurance," *Spectator*, Vol. 181 (October 1973), p. 23. Legislation (other than insurance legislation) dealing with the operations of creditors, such as banking laws, small loan laws, retail installment sales law, etc., may also impose some limitation on the use of creditor group insurance.

tificate describing the coverage, to inform the borrower of the charge for the insurance coverage, and to allow the borrower the option of providing the coverage through existing policies or the purchase of a policy insuring himself or herself for the amount of the loan from another insurance company. The laws also stated that any unearned premiums must be refunded to the borrower if paid for by the borrower, and that borrowers could not be charged more than the premium paid by the creditor to the insurance company.

Schedules of rates, policy forms, and certificates had to be approved by the insurance commissioner of the state concerned who could, in some states, require that a certain benefit to premium ratio be maintained to prevent overcharging. Of the states that adopted this last requirement, most use a 50 percent loss ratio, that is, the premium charged cannot be more than twice the benefits paid out.

EFFECT OF REGULATION

The enactment of regulations by many states largely eliminated the abuses that had taken place prior to the 1950s. However, there is continuing controversy over the effectiveness of the present regulations, particularly in coping with coercion abuse and excessive rates produced by reverse competition.

Two significant studies bear on the effectiveness of the regulations in dealing with these problems. The first revealed that on a yearly average, out of 66 valid credit insurance complaints per state, less than one-half of one complaint involved coercion.[7] The second study, the 1973 Ohio University Study of Consumer Credit Insurance, concluded that "the charge of coercion, either overt or subtle, in the selling of CCI is not substantiated," and that "allegations of coercion in the marketing of credit insurance appear to be exaggerated."[8] A follow-up study of premium rates revealed that in 48 states, credit life insurance premium rates had either been reduced or had remained level over the ten years from 1963 to 1973. Thus, the allegations made in support of the reverse competition theory of increasing rates would not seem to be supported by the facts.[9] Although there may be isolated incidents of abuse, this evidence indicates the overall effectiveness of credit insurance regulation.

CREDITOR GROUP DISABILITY INSURANCE

The disability coverage provided by creditor group insurance is commonly combined with the death coverage to provide complete

[7]NAIC Staff Study, *A Background Study of the Regulation of Credit Life and Disability Insurance* (November 1970).
[8]Charles L. Hubbard, *Consumer Credit Life and Disability Insurance* (College of Business Administration, Ohio University, July 1973), pp. 73, 88.
[9]Donald R. Quackenbush, "The Myth of Coercion, The Fallacy of Reverse Competition," *Spectator*, Vol. 182 (September 1974), p. 56.

credit insurance protection to the debtor. Because of this combined feature, there are many similarities in providing both coverages. Consequently, much of the previous discussion about the administration and policy provisions of the creditor group life insurance applies as well to the disability coverage. However, there are several characteristics of creditor disability coverage that distinguish it from death coverage. These distinguishing characteristics are described below.

Origin and Basic Characteristics

Creditor disability insurance originated in 1930, and thus is more recent than the life coverage, which originated in 1917. Originally disability coverage was written on an individual basis because statutes expressly prohibited its being written on a group basis. However, since 1930, creditor disability insurance has been offered on a group basis along with the group life coverage.

In general, creditor group disability insurance is a group coverage that repays the indebtedness to the lender in the event a debtor becomes disabled and subsequently unable to repay an indebtedness because of lack of income. Two basic kinds of disability are covered under creditor disability insurance: total and permanent disability, which implies a disabling condition from which there will be no recovery; and total and continuous disability, which temporarily renders the debtor unable to work. The significance of the permanent-temporary distinction will become evident when the policy provisions and claim and benefit administration features are discussed below.

Policy Provisions

Just as there are two kinds of disability, permanent and temporary, there also are two basic policies to deal with each kind of disability. Distinct problems arise when insuring a permanent loss as opposed to a temporary loss, so it is necessary to provide separate insurance policies to successfully implement the insurance coverage. The essential policy provisions of each type of coverage provide a basic understanding of the differences between the two creditor group disability coverages.

TOTAL AND PERMANENT DISABILITY POLICY PROVISIONS

The total and permanent disability provision is commonly attached to the life policy itself. The basic provisions included in the policy that apply to the permanent disability are outlined below.

Insuring Agreement. The insuring agreement provides that when disability of a total and permanent nature is incurred, the insurer will repay the amount of the outstanding loan in a lump sum. Further, it provides that no additional premium payments for the insurance are required of the borrower.

Definition of Total and Permanent. The policy necessarily includes a provision defining the nature of the disability that is insured against. As previously defined, the disability, mental or physical, must be total and permanent for the insurance to take effect. Qualification for such insurance claim depends on the insured's acceptance of all reasonable medical and surgical treatment that would provide a reasonable probability of removing the disability.

Total and Permanent Disability Benefits. Similar to the death benefit previously discussed, the disability benefit consists of the unpaid loan balance of the insured debtor at the time the disability commences. Thus, as in the death coverage, the insurable loan balance is paid in a lump sum. However, some policy plans reserve the right to liquidate the debt in installments, with the payments made only upon receipt of due proof indicating a continuation of total and permanent disability.

TOTAL AND CONTINUOUS DISABILITY POLICY PROVISIONS

The total and continuous disability insurance coverage is commonly provided by a policy separate from the life policy. Even though many of the general policy provisions of the creditor group life insurance policy apply to the separate disability policy, there are policy provisions that apply exclusively to the temporary disability coverage. The following basic provisions are representative of those found in most total and continuous disability coverages when applied to creditor group insurance.

Insuring Agreement. The insuring agreement provides that upon proof of total and continuous disability of a temporary nature, the insurer will pay the amount of the insurable loan balance in monthly payments equal to the monthly loan installment payments for the duration of the total and continuous disability or until the loan is repaid, whichever comes first.

Definition of Total and Continuous. All policies contain a definition of the total and continuous disability that is covered. Total and continuous disability is defined as a medically determined sickness or accidental bodily injury, or both, the result of which makes the insured debtor unable to perform the duties of which his or her occupation and prevents gainful employment in any other occupation for which substantially equal remuneration is received.

Waiting Period. Most total and continuous policies require that the insured be disabled for a waiting period before any benefit payments are made. The waiting period is usually 14 or 30 days. There are two kinds of waiting period plans. One is an elimination plan, which provides that no benefit payment be made for the elapsed waiting period. Instead, benefits become due on the first day following the waiting period. The second plan is the retroactive plan whereby the benefits are payable from the initial day of disability provided the waiting period is exceeded.

Total and Continuous Disability Benefits. The benefits under the total and continuous policy are made in monthly installments equal to the loan installment payments, but only so long as the disability continues. This constrasts with the lump sum benefit payment made under the total and permanent disability policy. Monthly benefits are most commonly limited to $250.

Administration

In general, the administration of creditor group disability insurance is similar to that of creditor group life insurance, with the exception of the claim and benefit administration. The primary reason for the exception lies in the differences in the nature of the loss for which the claim is made. In the event of death, the extent of the loss is definite and determinable, and thus the claim administration procedure is relatively simple. The benefit is usually paid in one lump sum. However, in the event of an insured debtor's disability, particularly one that is temporary, the character, extent, and duration of the loss are not always so readily determinable as in the event of death or of obvious total and permanent disability. Thus, the claim procedure as well as the benefit payment method differ from those of the death coverage. The distinctive features of the disability claim and benefit administration are discussed below.

CLAIM ADMINISTRATION

Upon disability of the insured debtor, proper proof of loss and/or an attending physician's statement confirming the insured's disabled condition has to be forwarded to the insurer. In addition, some insurers may request a statement from the insured's employer verifying the existence of the disability. These documents, especially the physician's diagnosis, are heavily relied upon by the insurer in the decision to accept or reject the claim. Because of the wide variety of potential disabilities and the variation in the degree to which any one individual may be affected, the physician's opinion often determines the nature of the disability and thus whether the claim is justified. This means that there is some potential for abuse and fraudulent claims through collusion between unscrupulous doctors and insured debtors. Once a claim is approved for payment, the disability benefits are administered according to the policy provisions.

BENEFIT ADMINISTRATION

For the most part, the disability benefit administration is similar to that of the death coverage discussed previously. However, an obvious difference is that in the death situation the loan is paid in a lump sum; by contrast, in a disability condition, particularly a temporary disability, the benefits are usually distributed periodically for the duration of the disability. Therefore, once the debtor has recovered, the disability benefits can be terminated, leaving an outstanding loan balance to repay. In total and continuous but temporary disability cases, each monthly benefit payment made to the lender must be preceded by proof of continuing disability in the form of an authorized statement from a qualified medical professional. This statement is necessary to make certain that the debtor is indeed qualified for the disability benefits, although the determination as to the extent of a disabled condition is in many cases difficult to assess. Clearly, the continuing benefit payments and proof of disability requirements, and questions about the extent of the disability in disability cases, particularly temporary disability, make the disability benefit administration different from the administration of the death benefits. Although the temporary disability benefits are commonly distributed periodically, some insurers have the right to "commute" the benefits. This means that even though the disability may be considered temporary, the insurer may elect to extinguish the debt in a lump sum payment to avoid the administrative expense of many small installment payments.

SUMMARY

Historically, creditor group insurance has performed an essential function by providing security on installment purchases to borrowers and their families. The trend, since the inception of creditor group insurance in 1917, has been one of impressive growth and increasing popularity, as witnessed by the in-force statistics. This trend reflects the social and economic customs of the present era. A majority of individuals as well as businesses consider it imperative to borrow, and banks (and other financial institutions), manufacturers, and merchants are all willing to extend credit. Creditor group insurance has provided and will continue to provide loan protection to the many consumers who have adopted the system of time purchasing.

This chapter has described the principal types of creditor insurance, which pay the outstanding indebtedness to the lender if a debtor is unable to repay a debt because of death or disability. The origins of creditor group life insurance in the 1917 Morris Plan and its subsequent rapid growth were described. Among the major aspects of creditor group life insurance discussed at length were administrative practices, underwriting characteristics, master policy provisions, and problems of regulation. The two basic kinds of creditor group disability insurance, total and permanent disability and total and continuous disability, were distinguished and their basic characteristics presented.

CHAPTER 19

ASSOCIATION GROUP INSURANCE

INTRODUCTION

This chapter will concern itself with association group insurance, tracing its origin from the early 1900s to its present-day status. The regulation of this form of insurance by the 50 states through amendments to the various state insurance laws is detailed in a special table showing the specific association groups eligible for group life insurance in each state jurisdiction.

Attention is given to groups such as trade associations, associations of individuals, public employee associations and professional associations. The special considerations for each particular group for eligibility in association plans are carefully outlined.

ORIGINS OF ASSOCIATION GROUP INSURANCE

At its inception in 1911, group life insurance was intended solely for sale to employer groups of at least 50 lives and was limited to a maximum of $3,000 on any single life. In the years since then, group insurance coverage has been expanded in four ways:

1. The minimum number to qualify a group has been steadily reduced, to a point where many companies underwrite small groups of even ten members;
2. Eligibility of groups has been extended to include many associations not originally permitted;
3. The protection available now includes not only life insurance, but also hospital, surgical, medical, dental and disability insurance, and old-age pensions; and
4. Maximum benefits have risen to include death benefits of

by
DANIEL D'ANDREA, FSA, *Vice President and Assistant Actuary, The Prudential Insurance Company of America, Newark, New Jersey.*

several times annual earnings on life insurance policies. In addition, group health plans offering major medical benefits of $1 million and even unlimited benefits are not uncommon.

The expansion of eligibility to include more types of associations has not been without some controversy. Concern has been raised about the soundness of underwriting some types of groups; also, some agents have expressed concern that the expansion of group insurance to associations intrudes into the market for individual policies. Nonetheless, the trend has been toward a liberalization of the definition of eligible associations. This liberalization has been attractive for two major reasons: (1) carriers have been able to expand sales of their group products to persons who might otherwise not be reached; and (2) conversely, a larger part of the population is able to participate in programs of insurance on a group basis and therefore purchase insurance at a lower cost.

Today, the insurance industry offers a full range of products to various associations. Life insurance is customarily sold on the basis of one-year renewable term; very little is permanent insurance. Although plans are often flexible in the amounts of benefits that are available to the purchaser, the policy often restricts amounts by age of the insured and often has a terminal age beyond which no coverage is available. Health insurance—medical, hospital, surgical, dental, and disability income—is also offered, as are annuities and pensions.

In summary, whatever is sold to single employers is also available to members of associations. However, companies differ in their willingness to offer different plans to various types of associations. For example, a company might underwrite health insurance for a trade association, but not for a charitable or religious association. Such a distinction can be the result of regulatory restrictions or the company's own underwriting practices in determining the eligibility of associations for group insurance. A decision on whether or not to offer hospital, medical and dental coverages may also be affected by the variations in costs by geographic area. Such variations present actuarial and marketing problems not present with life and disability income coverages.

Regulation

In 1917, the National Convention of Insurance Commissioners adopted a model bill defining group life insurance. It restricted group insurance to employer-employee groups of 50 or more lives. The model bill underwent several revisions and by 1956 the bill finally recognized four types of eligible groups: (1) employer-employee, (2) debtors of the same creditor (creditor group insurance), (3) members of a labor union under a policy issued to that union, and (4) employees of two or more employers in the same industry or members of one or more labor unions under a master policy issued to a common trustee.

These four types of groups remain the most common ones for which group life insurance plans have been underwritten. However, since the adoption of the 1917 Model Bill and its several revisions, the various states have amended their insurance laws to extend eligibility to a wide variety of groups not included in the original model bill. Some states' laws are so broad as to permit group coverage of any association not formed or maintained for the purpose of providing insurance. Most states, however, specifically define eligible groups, which may include teachers, police, members of the National Guard, veterans, depositors of a bank, clergymen, and associations of students. In two states, New Jersey and Texas, there is a discretionary provision under group statute whereby coverage of association groups is subject to the approval of the state insurance department. Table 19-1 shows the types of associations eligible for group life insurance in 35 states and Puerto Rico.

TABLE 19–1
States That, Under Varying Conditions, Specifically Permit The Issuance of a Group Life Policy to Associations or to Trustees of an Association Fund

Jurisdiction	Types of Association Groups Eligible for Group Life Insurance as of June 1978
Alaska	Public employees association
Arkansas	Public employees association
California	Trade association Public employees association Association of private employees of common employer
Delaware	Public employees association Professional association
District of Columbia	Professional association Trade association Association of federal employees National veterans association
Florida	Professional association
Georgia	Association of governmental or public employees Association of employees of common employer Trade association Professional association

TABLE 19–1 (Continued)

Jurisdiction	Types of Association Groups Eligible for Group Life Insurance as of June 1978
Hawaii	Public employees association Professional association Occupation, industry or trade association Mutual benefit society
Idaho	Public employees association
Illinois	"Associations"
Indiana	Voluntary industry association, but only for executive, supervisory, sales and professional employees of members and the employees of such association
Iowa	Nonprofit industrial association Teachers, lawyers, voluntary firemen Fraternal society and similar groups
Kansas	"Association groups"
Kentucky	Public employees association Industrial and professional association
Louisiana	Organization or association groups
Maine	Trade association Municipal employees association Professional association
Maryland	Professional association Public employees association
Massachusetts	Charitable or religious association Public employees association
Michigan	Nonprofit incorporated industrial association covering executives only State teachers association Postal clerks association
Montana	Public employees association
Nebraska	Public employees association Professional association
New Hampshire	Nonprofit industrial association Public employees association
New Jersey	State police benevolent association Religious and charitable association National scouting organization Discretionary

TABLE 19–1 (Continued)

Jurisdiction	Types of Association Groups Eligible for Group Life Insurance as of June 1978
New Mexico	Professional association Agricultural association
New York	Employer trade association Association of civil service employees or teachers State police, policemen or firemen's associations Professional association
North Carolina	Professional association
Ohio	Veterans association Agricultural or horticulturists' organizations Professional association National Guard, naval militia and defense corps association
Oklahoma	Professional association Nonprofit industrial association
Pennsylvania	Police and firemen's fraternity Teacher association
Puerto Rico	Cooperative association Professional association Public employees association Trade association
South Dakota	Association groups
Texas	Public employees association Nonprofit service and community organizations Discretionary
Vermont	Public employee association Employer association
Virginia	Public employees association Professional association Association of employees of common employer
Washington	Public employees association Employer association Depositor groups
Wyoming	Public employees association

ELIGIBLE GROUPS

After state insurance laws, company underwriting practices are the major factor in determining the types of associations eligible for group insurance. The theory of group insurance is based on underwriting groups of persons which in the aggregate will yield a certain predictable rate of mortality or morbidity. The selection of an association as a risk unit is only as theoretically sound as the size and the homogeneity of the association is sound. To ensure this soundness, the underwriter must ascertain that certain essential features are either inherent in the group itself or, if any are lacking, that adverse selection by group members can be avoided.

To achieve that end, underwriting considerations for associations usually involve the following three criteria:

1. Determining that the association is a bona fide group, formed for some purpose other than the opportunity to gain low-cost insurance. If the group has no common interest other than the gaining of insurance, it would likely be comprised mostly of poor risks seeking insurance. Consequently, company underwriting standards may require that the group have been in existence for a period of time, such as two years, prior to seeking insurance for its members.
2. Assuring a flow of persons who will be joining the association in the future. This growth is important so that the outflow of aged group members is offset by an inflow of younger members, thereby keeping mortality and morbidity rates (and, hence, premium rates) fairly stable.
3. Insuring a high percentage of the eligible persons in the association. Only in this way can a carrier offering nonmedical insurance gain a safeguard against adverse selection by association members. Lacking a high degree (say, 75 percent or more) of participation, the underwriter may impose some degree of individual underwriting on a medical basis.

In addition to these general underwriting guidelines, companies apply other factors in analyzing the eligibility of associations. The types of associations can be divided into two categories: trade associations and associations of individuals.

Trade Associations

A trade association is an association of employers formed for purposes other than obtaining insurance. The range of membership in an association may be quite large, with both giant employers and small firms as members. In other cases, the trade associations may consist of firms that have members of more similar size.

As a general rule, large firms which are members of a trade association would not be interested in participating in insurance obtained through the association for two reasons: association plans lack flexibility and employers have less control over the plans.

An employer that constitutes an intermediate or larger size group, such as 50 or more members, can often obtain whatever plan design it desires through negotiations with insurance companies. By contrast, participation in an association group forces each employer to accept the plan that is being offered to all association members. It is quite possible that such a plan may involve features that are not to the best advantage of the largest employers in the association.

By purchasing their own insurance programs, large employers have full control over choice of carrier and administrator. If an employer is not satisfied with service or with premium rates, it can take its business elsewhere. Participating through a trade association, however, commits each employer to the decisions made by association trustees.

For these reasons, the firms most likely to participate in trade association insurance are those that do not have a sufficient number of employees to qualify for group coverage on their own, or those firms whose unionized employees are covered by collectively bargained welfare plans. In this latter situation, the remaining nonunion employees, such as office and supervisory personnel, may be covered by association insurance.

Trade associations range from local to national in scope. In evaluating such an association, an underwriter usually seeks assurance of its stability and the availability of one or more persons, preferably officers of the association, to promote enrollment of members. Because there is a natural tendency for participation by small firms, with the attendant risk of adverse selection, most carriers require minimum participation by *all* firms in the association. In addition, carriers often require that the employers contribute at least 50 percent, or possibly more, of the premium cost to encourage participation in the plan and to assure a high degree of membership. Some insurers will not underwrite medical or disability benefits unless they also carry the life insurance of the trade association.

Plans originally produced by brokers are often administered by that same broker. The broker collects premiums from members and remits them to the insurance company. The broker may also pay health insurance claims and attempt to exercise some control over these claims.

Associations of Individuals

The eligibility of associations of individuals for group insurance varies from state to state. All states recognize labor unions as legal groups for obtaining insurance and most states recognize associations of public employees and professional associations. Many other types of individual associations, as shown on Table 19-1, are eligible in one jurisdiction or another.

LABOR UNIONS

Labor unions sometimes act as policyowners of a group policy for their members, without any employer participation. When the union is the sole policyowner, premiums are paid by union members, sometimes at a reduced rate with the difference being paid from the union's treasury.

Underwriting Considerations. To an insurer underwriting union group insurance, the future growth of the union is an important consideration. If the union is growing in membership, the average age of insured persons can be expected to remain fairly stable, or even decline. This situation permits premium rates to be held level. On the other hand, some unions are declining in membership, due to the impact of automation on the industry in which they work. This decline means that there is a much smaller flow of new members into the group, which results in a growing average age. The insurer is then forced with the need to raise premiums, sometimes substantially. This increase, in turn, may lead the more insurable risks to drop the insurance coverage.

These factors result in a situation where, in general, union group coverage is limited to life insurance only and to comparatively small benefit amounts—less than a year's annual earnings on each active member. If larger death benefits or health benefits were issued to unions, these would usually require premiums that are difficult to include in the union dues because of member resistance. The more insurable members would find it less expensive to purchase coverage on an individual basis, resulting in further deterioration of the insured group.

Insurance for Retirees. Another important underwriting consideration for association group insurance is the degree of coverage for retired workers. Continuation of coverage to retired members substantially increases the cost to the group. On the other hand, failure to provide for retirees may cause dissatisfaction among current workers, resulting in reduced participation. One solution to this underwriting problem is to reduce the amount of group life insurance on retired members to a portion, such as one-fourth, of the amount on active members.

PUBLIC EMPLOYEE ASSOCIATIONS

Groups of individuals employed by a governmental unit, usually a state, county, city or school board, form public employee associations. In the earliest policies, written during the 1920s, premiums were paid at an equal rate by each member of the association, regardless of his or her age. When the depression times of the 1930s arrived, there was a scarcity of jobs in the government. This meant a reduced influx of younger persons into the groups. The average age of a group rose, necessitating premium rate increases. Since everyone in the group paid a flat rate, the cost of insurance for the younger employees was greater than that for individual insurance, leading to withdrawal of the favorable risks from the plan.

This led to changes in the design of life insurance plans, whereby either premium rates are graded by age, or else plan benefits are reduced at older ages. Grading of premium rates is also done with medical and with disability income insurance. However, the grading is usually less sharp than with life insurance. The effect of all this revised grading has been to encourage the participation of younger members of the group.

Underwriting Considerations. Although in the early plans the employees paid the entire premium, today the employer most often pays all or part of them. One underwriting consideration must be the legal authority of the employer to purchase such insurance. There must be specific legislation enabling the employer to contract for the insurance, to pay part or all of its cost, and to make any salary deductions. Determining that such statutory authority exists may require research and legal counsel, particularly in cases involving small local units. In addition, underwriting is sometimes complicated by the need to rate groups engaged in hazardous occupations, such as police and fire personnel.

As was the case with union groups, most insurers will not underwrite medical and disability coverage unless they also have the life insurance business of the public employees association. The segment of the total group market represented by these associations has been increasing as a result of the growing number of public employees. Many of the workers are covered by regular employer-employee group contracts, with the employer paying the entire cost of the insurance. However, public resistance to increased taxes is a significant factor contributing to the growth of association insurance as an alternative to employer-paid plans.

Persistency of public employee association insurance is often poor, for any of several reasons:

1. Shifts in political fortunes may result in newly elected officials who seek a change in carriers.
2. Fixed-budget appropriations may not provide for premium increases, forcing the association to seek a change in carrier.
3. In some jurisdictions, statutes require each contract to be put up for competitive bidding at time of renewal.

Insurance for Retirees. Under the first written association group plans, retired public employees lost their coverage at retirement. Now, many plans call for additional premiums which are placed into a special fund to provide for continuation of insurance beyond retirement. These additional premiums help reduce the cost resulting from the higher mortality and morbidity of retired members. In addition, many private plans reduce benefit amounts on retired public employees, thereby reducing the cost load on active members of the association.

PROFESSIONAL ASSOCIATIONS

One basic similarity that professional associations have with labor unions is that both are comprised of individuals who share a common occupation. Beyond that, however, there are wide differences between these two segments of the group insurance market. Professional associations embrace such occupations as physicians, attorneys, engineers, and accountants. These persons are usually highly paid and highly motivated. They recognize the need for insurance, both during their lives and after for estate purposes. Since professionals generally enjoy a comparatively high standard of living, they are receptive to plans that provide large amounts of life and disability income insurance.

Underwriting Considerations. Insurance companies differ widely in their practices of providing guaranteed issue,[1] either on an initial enrollment or for subsequent solicitations. Among those offering guaranteed issue some have limited amounts, such as $10,000, available to new members; others have guaranteed issue amounts available to all members but with a reduced benefit during an initial period of from one to several years; still others provide a variety of different constraints, such as guaranteed amounts that vary by age and membership status. Usually, plans sold to professional associations do not provide guaranteed issue. Participation is usually too low to protect against antiselection. Hence, the insurers tend to utilize a degree of individual underwriting.

A common group term life maximum available to association members, subject to insurability, is $100,000. However, maximums in excess of that amount are often available in larger associations. The contribution rate per $1,000 of insurance paid by association members is almost always graded upward by age.

The experience of insurers with life insurance sold to professional associations has been generally favorable, due in large part to the fact that the insured persons, being well paid, are able to afford good medical care and are motivated by good health habits. This background makes life insurance a desirable product to this market segment. The situation is quite different, however, with health insurance.

---

[1]"Guaranteed issue" refers to the practice of not denying a person coverage for medical reasons as long as he or she is a member of the group.

Health Insurance for Professionals. Professional individuals tend to experience higher medical costs, because the care they receive usually costs more than that for the average individual. This is due to several factors: more frequent utilization of medical services; a preference for high quality services; traditional pricing practices of physicians, which take into account the recipient's income; and the concentration of a large proportion of professionals in work and residential areas of high price levels. The problem of offering health insurance to professionals, then, is not one of increased morbidity, but of increased costs.

For this reason, many insurers who offer life insurance to professional associations do not offer these same groups medical insurance. Those insurers who do offer medical insurance are faced with the need to adjust premium rates upward fairly often, reflecting the constantly rising costs of medical claims. As is true with unions, the carrier must obtain the acceptance of each participant, on an individual basis, to continue coverage at the higher rate. However, the general affluence of the professionals means that a typical premium increase is far less likely to be a burden, and so the loss of insureds is a smaller problem than with union groups.

Professional persons have long been aware of the need for disability income coverage, because continuation of their incomes is often closely related to their ability to engage in their professional activity. Accordingly, plans written for professionals generally involve relatively higher benefit levels and longer benefit periods than do plans for other types of groups. Benefits to age 65 are common, and some plans provide lifetime disability income benefits.

Marketing Methods. The role played by the professional association is an important factor in determining the ultimate success of the amount of professional insurance business sold to members. Professionals join an association in order to obtain services not obtainable elsewhere, such as professional publications, continuing education, and legislative lobbying. Membership in the association requires payment of dues, often of a large amount. The association, then, is important to the professionals and its promotion of an insurance program is perceived by members as an endorsement of that program. The insurance company therefore tries to obtain the maximum support possible from the association.

This support can be given in various ways. If the association has a publication, the plan can be advertised in it. At meetings and conventions, the plan can be promoted and discussed. Representatives of the carrier can be invited to attend local meetings, to explain the plan, to answer questions, and to distribute application blanks. The association's membership records can be used as the basis for a special mailing.

If the carrier offers guaranteed issue, members of the association typically have a limited period of time from the inception of the plan (such as 60 or 90 days) in which to enroll without evidence of insurability. Beyond that initial period of open enrollment, members who decide to enroll must furnish evidence of insurability. However, persons who join the association subsequent to the open enrollment period are usually given a specified period of time to enroll during which evidence of insurability is waived. After that period, the new members must furnish such evidence. In either instance, the evidence of insurability is normally limited to a simple health statment with no examination required.

As with other types of groups, the insurer desires a high level of participation of eligible persons in the plan so as to reduce the chances of adverse selection. In order to achieve this goal, some companies use their career agents for soliciting professional enrollments. Names of association members, taken from membership records, are given to agents for subsequent personal contact. This method of enrollment is costly, but it results in a comparatively high rate of participation.

In most cases, however, the low premiums charged for group insurance preclude personal sales calls upon individual members. An exception might be situations where a member of a professional association is also a partner in a firm, such as an attorney or an accountant. That type situation might warrant a personal sales call because of the chance of obtaining several enrollments from within the professional firm.

Other than this selling situation, most companies utilize direct mail for solicitation and enrollment. One, and sometimes several, mailings are sent to each eligible member of the association, describing the plan and containing an application blank. This method is also used to reach new members as they join the association and become eligible for participation. In later years, the insurer may utilize the same method to promote additional enrollments among association members who had originally declined participation.

Criticism. It was mentioned earlier that the extension of the group concept to associations of individuals has caused controversy, with some agents claiming that it represents an intrusion into the market for individual products. This argument has been most strongly directed toward professional association group insurance. Because they are attractive prospects for insurance, professionals represent a potentially lucrative market segment for career agents, particularly those agents who are skilled in assembling packages based on estate planning or on an overall analysis of the prospect's insurance needs.

Agents' organizations are quick to point out that the expert counseling that is available in individual sales situations with professionals is not possible through the group marketing method. They suggest that professionals will be attracted by the lower premiums of group insurance to the detriment of individualized insurance programs. On the other hand, the condition of underinsurance which is typical of the public at large also applies to professionals, although in less degree. Therefore, it seems fair to say that despite the availability of some amounts of group insurance, professionals continue to need additional insurance on an individual basis.

OTHER ASSOCIATIONS

In a number and variety of types, other associations exist that are eligible for group insurance. In most states, miscellaneous associations of individuals having no common bond except membership are ineligible for group life insurance. A few states, however, have no restrictions at all on types of eligible groups. With group health insurance, the situation is reversed; most states have no restrictions on eligibility on types of groups. Although it would be possible for an insurer to write a master contract in a state with no restrictions, problems could arise if any members resided in other states that did not regard the association as an eligible type. For this reason, major insurance companies have tended to avoid underwriting types of associations such as farm associations, members of a credit union, or veteran associations. As alternatives, these insurers are more likely to write wholesale and franchise insurance for life and health benefits, respectively.

Examples of various associations for whom group contracts have been written include: alumni groups, fraternal societies, savings account depositors, customers of retail organizations, and credit card holders. Each of these types of groups is characterized by some common bond among its members, other than the intention to purchase insurance. Many times, the membership rosters of such associations constitute preferred lists of prospects for individual insurance.

In soliciting members of such "miscellaneous" associations, the sponsorship of the association itself may be quite helpful, or it may be worth very little. Groups such as alumni and fraternal organizations may be able to impart an incentive to purchase the product, much as was true with professional associations. However, associations formed of retail customers and credit card holders have a more commercial relationship as their bases. Solicitation of these individual members by those types of associations is more likely to be received with greater skepticism. Therefore, the insurer must provide some incentive for purchase of the insurance. That incentive is the reduced group premium made possible by lower marketing costs.

On the other side, the insurer must be able to cite some advantage to the associations themselves to warrant use of membership lists for solicitation. One such advantage is the opportunity the association has to offer low-cost insurance as one benefit of membership in the association. This benefit can be especially important in associations

that do not ordinarily seek to provide tangible benefits in direct proportion to costs of membership. In other situations, such as those involving associations of retail customers or credit card holders, the advantage to the association may be a fee received by the association from
the insurance company for use of the association's mailing list.

A number of group insurance plans covering members of miscellaneous groups also exist in fields other than group term life insurance.
For example, one contract covers the cost of prescription drugs incurred by the members of an association of persons investing in a
retired citizens' real estate development. Another contract provides
substantial death benefits to members who die in aircraft accidents.
Other policies provide accidental death and medical expense coverage
on school children and on school and college athletic teams.

ADMINISTRATION OF ASSOCIATION GROUP INSURANCE

The distinguishing characteristics of association group insurance
are the result of two factors. First, many associations lack a strong
administrative core; second, the insureds usually pay the entire premium. These characteristics influence the marketing, underwriting,
administration, and tax aspects of such plans.

Marketing

The search for new business among eligible associations is ordinarily performed by an insurer's group representatives or by brokers
and is accomplished through referrals, business and social contacts,
and ordinary unsolicited calls. Transfer business accounts for perhaps
90 percent of new business, as it does for group business generally.
Opportunities here usually occur at the time of policy renewal, when
the association or its broker decides to put the business out for competitive bids. The role of the soliciting agent in prospecting for new
associations is usually limited to occasional leads that are referred to
the group department for follow-up.

Underwriting

In contrast to the situation found in laws concerning individual
insurance, there are a number of underwriting restrictions found in
state statutes for group policies issued to associations. These restrictions may prescribe minimum size and characteristics of eligible groups,
and minimum percentage of participation by eligible persons.

The purpose of minimum participation requirements, whether set
by law or by underwriting policies, is to guard against the effects of
adverse selection. There are substandard risks in almost any group

who tend to take advantage of open enrollment, or guaranteed issue. In association cases, where the members pay the entire cost of benefits, this means the healthy lives must pay a higher rate to balance the cost of the unhealthy (substandard) participants. If only a small percentage of all eligible members enroll initially, the rates might be inadequate because of the disproportionate number of unhealthy lives. This inbalance would lead to a premium rate increase, which would tend to drive out healthier participants. The resulting chain of premium increases and withdrawals of healthy participants would lead to the destruction of the entire program.

Minimum participation may be expressed as a percentage of eligible members, or as a minimum number of participants, or both. For example, New York's professional association law requires 75 percent participation or 400 lives, whichever is less, but in no event can there be fewer than 100 participants for a group policy to be issued to an association or to the trustees of a trust formed by one or more associations.

Administrative Functions

The normal administrative functions of servicing association group insurance include: determining member eligibility; collecting premiums; processing changes to names, addresses and beneficiaries; reporting withdrawals from the plan; processing claims; and preparing governmental reports. In most cases, the associations themselves are neither prepared to, nor desirous of, accepting administrative responsibility for the plan. Sometimes the carrier provides the services; more often, however, administration is taken over by a third party that specializes in such work.

Tax Aspects

Premium payments made by employers belonging to a trade association that is the owner of a group policy are deductible by the employers, and within limits do not represent taxable income to the insured individuals. Under Section 79 of the Internal Revenue Code, there may be imputed income to employees for life insurance in excess of $50,000 provided by employers. For groups with fewer than ten lives, there may be imputed income for even small amounts of life insurance if certain plan and individual underwriting constraints are not met.[2] In other types of associations—that is, those not involving employer contributions of premiums—payment of life insurance premiums must be made by the participants in after-tax dollars; that is, the payments are not tax deductible by the participants.

---

[2]The tax aspects mentioned here are naturally subject to change with revisions to the tax code.

FUTURE OF ASSOCIATION INSURANCE

The expansion of group insurance to market segments not originally envisioned has greatly broadened the ability of private insurers to provide security against losses from death, disability, medical expenses, and old age. This expansion has served to benefit both the population at large and the insurance companies selling the products. In addition, the expansion has undoubtedly helped the private insurance sector provide protection that might otherwise have been provided through social insurance programs.

Because of this, existing association group insurance will likely remain an important part of the group product line. Companies will continue to seek new groups whose legal and underwriting status make them eligible for group coverage. There will continue to be controversy over the impact of such group insurance on sales of individual insurance. However, in most cases the group protection will continue to provide a basic floor of benefits, standardized for all members of the group, with additional amounts of benefits being provided through the sale of ordinary insurance.

SUMMARY

This chapter has reviewed the history of association group insurance, outlining its expansion and acceptance in the United States. Four special types of groups from the wide variety of groups eligible for association group insurance were singled out for consideration. These were trade associations, associations of individuals, public employee associations, and professional associations. The marketing, underwriting, administration, and tax aspects that are characteristic of association group insurance were also discussed. The chapter concluded with a look at the future for all association group types.

CHAPTER 20

TAFT-HARTLEY WELFARE TRUST FUNDS

INTRODUCTION

Shortly after the conclusion of World War II, the U.S. Supreme Court ruled that pensions and health insurance were conditions affecting employment and, hence, proper subjects for collective bargaining. This ruling had the effect of extending group insurance to union members who worked for small employers not previously eligible for group coverage. In 1947 such employer-union plans came under provisions of the Taft-Hartley Act, which provided for special trust funds for such plans. This legislation introduced, for the first time, regulation of such plans at the federal level. This chapter describes the background of Taft-Hartley plans, their provisions and regulation, and their future.

DEVELOPMENT OF TAFT-HARTLEY FUNDS

Taft-Hartley welfare trust funds are the descendents of the welfare funds established by labor unions in the late 1940s.

Background of Union Welfare Funds

Prior to the late 1940s, group insurance had usually been available only to employers having 25 or more employees. Although this requirement permitted coverage of much of the work force, two segments were left ineligible. The first involved industries such as upholstering and garment manufacturers, where the employer units were traditionally small and comparatively unstable. The second involved industries such as construction and shipping, where workers remained within the same industry but tended to work for any one employer for only relatively short periods of time.

by
ARTHUR NOLAN, *Vice President, Group Marketing and Sales, The Union Labor Life Insurance Company, New York, New York.*

To provide group insurance for workers in these two segments of the labor market, two approaches were possible. The first approach was to have the union itself purchase a policy covering its members, with premiums being paid out of members' dues. Although this approach permitted the sale of economical group insurance to union members, it had strong disadvantages. Some insurers were unwilling to underwrite union groups at all. Moreover, the reluctance of many union members to pay premium increases resulted in relatively low benefit levels.

An alternative mechanism for furnishing group coverage to these market segments was the union welfare fund. Here, the union negotiated welfare contributions from employers, typically on an industry-wide basis. These contributions were paid by the employers to the union, which then deposited them in a welfare fund. Among the first such welfare funds were those established by the Amalgamated Clothing Workers, the Fur and Leather Workers, the International Ladies Garment Workers, and the United Furniture Workers.

These initial welfare funds were administered solely by the unions; employer participation was limited to payment of the negotiated contribution. Most of the funds provided benefits through group insurance contracts issued to the unions. However, some, such as that of Local 65 Department and Drug Store Workers, paid benefits directly from the fund, with no insurer involvement.

The bargaining process between employers and unions for these welfare funds was and remains significantly different from that of single employer bargaining because of structural differences in the industries involved. In some industries—such as steel, automobile and aluminum—each local plant of the employer has a distinct identity. Workers in one plant typically remain with that plant; there is little mobility from one location to another. The workers in a given plant belong to the local of the union, and that local union deals with a single employer.

In such industries, unions typically bargain on the basis of a level of benefits for their members. That is, bargaining is over the amount of the benefits to be provided by employer-financed coverage. This "level of benefit" approach to employee benefit bargaining is traditional with large employers. By contrast, the structure of such industries as construction, printing, transportation and garment manufacturing precludes the "level of benefit" approach. Bargaining in these industries involves many employers, a large percentage of them small firms, unable to provide benefits in the way of a large employer. Such an industry structure is conducive to the "cents-per-hour" formula, whereby each employer contributes to the union welfare fund an amount determined by a negotiated formula.

The union welfare funds are established for the purpose of providing benefits to employees and to their dependents in the event of death, disability, incurrence of medical expenses, or retirement. Prior to 1947, some union welfare funds involved formal trusts; others did not. No laws required formation of a trust to administer the welfare funds. However, other legal considerations sometimes favored formation of a trust. Then, as now, in the absence of permissive statutes, an unincorporated association, such as a union, could not sue or be sued in the association name, and enforcement of association contracts required personal service of legal process on all its members. The device of a trust was therefore often insisted on by insurance companies.

Influence of the Taft-Hartley Act

During World War II, the National War Labor Board had frozen wages and salaries, but it had not restricted employer contributions to employee benefit plans. As a result, employers had turned to group insurance and pension plans as a means of attracting and retaining workers. Unions, unable to obtain wage increases for members, began to bargain for welfare benefits.

Shortly following the end of World War II, federal courts ruled that pensions[1] and group insurance[2] were conditions affecting employment and, hence, proper subjects for collective bargaining. These decisions gave added impetus to industry-wide bargaining of welfare benefits by unions and spurred the growth of group insurance as an employee welfare benefit.

With the lifting of wage controls at the end of World War II, unions attempted to make up for the constraint of the war years. Hard bargaining led to a period of labor turmoil, featuring several nationwide strikes in key industries. The concern of Congress was manifested in the Labor Management Relations Act of 1947, the "Taft-Hartley Act." This act, which applies to labor situations where employees are engaged in activities affecting interstate commerce, pertains to a wide range of collective bargaining functions. One section of the act, Section 302, made it unlawful for any employer to pay money or anything else of value to any representative of any of its employees.

Unmodified, that provision would have prohibited employer contributions into union welfare funds. However, the Taft-Hartley Act permitted welfare payments, provided they were made to trustees of a prescribed insurance trust fund. Specifically, the Taft-Hartley Act requires that:

1. Payments must be placed in trust to purchase insurance;
2. The detailed basis of the payments must be contained in a written agreement entered into by employer(s) and union;

---

[1]*Inland Steel Co. v. N.L.R.B.*
[2]*W. W. Cross & Co. v. N.L.R.B.*

3. The employer(s) and union must be equally represented in the administration of the fund;
4. The trust fund must be audited annually; and
5. Payments intended for purchase of pension annuities must be placed in a separate account under a trust that prohibits the diversion of those payments for any other purpose.

The Taft-Hartley Act has resulted in the extensive use of insurance trust agreements under which the trustees are authorized to purchase, hold, and administer group insurance policies.

RESPONSIBILITIES OF THE TRUSTEES

As the collective bargaining process involves welfare funds, virtually the sole issue is the amount of the contributions to be made into the fund by the employer. All other factors concerning the plan—benefit structure, employee eligibility, selection of insurer, administration of the plan—are the responsibility of the board of trustees.

The legal document formally creating the trust is known as a "trust indenture" or "trust agreement." It is executed jointly among employers, union and trustees. The trust agreement authorizes the trustees to:

1. Collect employer contributions, according to the negotiated formula;
2. Purchase insurance contracts, or otherwise determine and provide welfare benefits;
3. Establish a fund reserve and manage the reserve monies;
4. Obtain data from participating employers regarding employee eligibility;
5. Provide for the inclusion of new participating employees and the withdrawal of terminating employees;
6. Establish and maintain administrative offices;
7. Provide for annual audits;
8. Determine eligibility of employees; and
9. Provide for disposition of funds in event of termination of the plan.

The trustees are designated by the parties creating the trust. In most cases, the trustees will be otherwise fully employed either on the union or employer's side. If employed on the union side, the trustees may be union officers or business agents. If employed on the employers' side, the trustees may be owners or managers of participating firms. In a few cases the trust agreement calls for one or more neutral trustees; more commonly, trusts provide for appointment of an impartial umpire in event of a dispute between the labor and management trustees.

The size of each board of trustees varies, according to the particular situation. If many union locals are involved, as with a statewide or national fund, the board may number 20 or more members. Most often, however, the board consists of six or eight members. As evidenced above, the trustees bear considerable responsibility for the functioning of the trust. The trust agreement invariably attempts to limit the personal liability of trustees, but the fiduciary nature of the position imposes certain obligations.

The test most frequently applied by the courts is referred to as the "prudent man" rule. This rule provides that a trustee shall administer the affairs of the trust just as a prudent man would administer his personal affairs. The trustees are not expected to be expert in matters of welfare benefits; instead, they are expected to call upon other experts for advice, as warranted, and to protect themselves against the results of poor advice. This fiduciary responsibility, plus the growing complexity of benefit plans, has led most boards of trustees to utilize the services of consultants.

Trustees typically meet formally once a month. In the time between such meetings, they are occupied by their other obligations in the unions or in the companies. Because of other commitments, turnover among trustees is fairly common. It is the consultants who bring both expertise and continuity into the operation of a trust.

FEATURES OF TAFT-HARTLEY PLANS

The trusteed welfare funds created under the Taft-Hartley Act provide a number of benefits to union members. Some of these are furnished directly, others through group insurance policies purchased by the trustees with funds contributed by employers to the welfare fund. Because of the nature of many of the industries involved, the determination of the contribution formula and the eligibility rules is sometimes quite complicated.

Benefits

As already noted, welfare funds are most often found in industries in which collective bargaining is done on a cost, or contribution, basis, rather than on a benefits basis. This means that the structure of employee benefits is a responsibility of the plan trustees. A full range of group products is available, including life insurance, health insurance, and annuities.

Group term life insurance benefits for Taft-Hartley plans are commonly far smaller than those for regular group insurance. Where a single-employer policy may provide death benefits of one or two years' earnings, similar benefits in policies provided to Taft-Hartley trusts are often less than $2,000, with few plans providing more than six months' earnings as the face amount. Medical benefits in some Taft-Hartley plans compare favorably with those of regular groups, even to including major medical benefits with a limit of $100,000 or $200,000 on top of basic medical benefits. However, only about 25 percent of the trusts have either dental or vision benefits, and fewer still provide prescription drug benefits.

CONTRIBUTION FORMULA

In designing a plan of benefits, trustees work from the given formula of employer contributions. This might be a simple formula, such as 20 cents contribution per worker hour. However, the formula might be a more complex one, with a scale of contributions. In principle, the plan of benefits should be designed so that an employee working an average number of hours a year will earn enough employer contributions to finance the plan. For example, assume an average of 1,000 hours worked per year by each employee, with employer contributions set at the rate of 20 cents per hour. The fund would then receive $200 for this worker. If administrative expenses were estimated at an average of $25 per worker, there would be a remainder of $175 to be used to provide benefits. Assuming that the eligibility rules do require 1,000 hours per year to qualify for coverage, the fund would not be in a deficit position. Actually, there would likely be a surplus in the fund because some employees will work more than the average number of hours, generating additional contributions, while still other employees will not work sufficient hours to qualify for coverage.

BENEFITS FOR RETIREES

Some Taft-Hartley plans provide benefits for retired employees. When this is the case, several problems arise. The first concerns the question of whether or not an employee has actually retired. Because of the nature of employment in some industries, a worker who has retired and who is drawing retirement benefits may return to work, drawing both wages and benefits and accruing additional eligibility benefits. As a safeguard, eligibility rules for retirees may require that they relinquish all rights to future eligibility as active employees, regardless of the hours they may work.

A second problem arises when there is an industry where some of the plans do not provide retirement benefits. In such a situation, union members approaching retirement age may seek to move into areas covered by plans providing retirement benefits in order to be eligible for them. Trustees can protect against this movement by requiring a minimum period of participation in the plan before workers become eligible for retirement benefits.

Finally, the mobility of retired persons may present an administrative problem in plans requiring employee contributions. If the retiree is covered by a pension-plus-insurance plan, administration is not so much of a problem because the amount of the contribution can be deducted from the regular pension checks. If, however, there is no pension benefit, the trustees must maintain contact with each retiree in order to collect the contribution for life insurance, and, in some cases, for health insurance.

Eligibility

Eligibility rules define the conditions that must be met by an individual to be eligible for welfare benefits. Decisions of the National Labor Relations Board have affirmed that welfare benefits are negotiated for all members of a bargaining unit, not only for those persons who are members of the union. Theoretically, it is possible to have no requirement for eligibility other than employment; that is, with no minimum period of employment required. This approach has the appeal of fairness, with each worker sharing in the amount of the employer's contributions.

In practice, however, most union welfare trust plans define minimum standards for eligibility. The amount of employer contributions is the same, regardless of whether there are minimum eligibility requirements, because the contributions are based on total hours worked by all employees. Eligibility rules based on a minimum work requirement thus provide higher benefits for the eligible employees than would be the case if all were eligible.

ELIGIBILITY FORMULAS

In practice, eligibility formulas are of three basic types: minimum employment, prior period accumulation, and reserve bank accumulation. The *minimum employment* formula requires a given number of days, weeks or months of employment, either with a particular employer or within the industry. It is comparable to the definition of a "full-time employee" under a single-employer plan. This formula is appropriate for those multi-employer funds where employment is comparatively stable, with limited shifting of employees from one employer to another.

The second and third types of formulas are particularly applicable to industries where employees are hired for particular projects and have no permanent relationship with a single employer. Both of these formulas are based on the accumulation of credited hours of employment. The *prior period accumulation* formula determines eligibility on the basis of hours worked during a prior period, called the "accumulation period." For example, this formula might provide eligibility during January, February and March if sufficient work had been performed during October, November and December. As a variation, there might be an intervening, or "lag," month between the accumulation period and the coverage period, to permit processing of the necessary data. In some cases, the formula provides that hours worked during the accumulation period in excess of the minimum required can be applied to subsequent accumulation periods to improve the probability of eligibility. This feature is particularly appropriate in industries that are subject to seasonal fluctuations in employment because of weather or other factors.

Under the *reserve bank accumulation* formula, all hours worked by an employee are credited to his or her "hour bank." For every month that the worker is provided coverage under the welfare plan, a specified number of hours (sufficient to pay the cost of the benefits) is withdrawn from the bank. If the number of credited hours is insufficient to provide for the monthly draw of hours, coverage is terminated. As a practical rule, the size of any worker's bank accumulation is often limited to the number of hours required to provide coverage for three or six months.

In considering the differences between these two accumulation formulas, the prior period method is less complex and, hence, easier to administer. However, the reserve bank method is easier to explain to workers, who are able to see direct relationships between their work and the resultant benefits that can be purchased.

ELIGIBILITY RULES

The trustees of the fund are responsible for determining its eligibility rules. The following principles are commonly applied to the drafting of such rules:

1. There should be an initial waiting period (say, three to five months) between plan inception and the effective date of benefits in order to provide initial operating funds and accumulation of necessary employment data.
2. Eligibility should be based upon work already performed and which has already produced income for the fund.
3. Each worker should earn sufficient employer contributions to pay the approximate share of benefit costs.
4. Eligibility should cease when the worker fails to earn sufficient employer contributions to cover his or her share of fund costs with the exception that, insofar as feasible, workers who are "regularly" employed should have sufficient continuation of coverage to cover normal employment fluctuations without coverage interruptions.
5. Surplus, resulting from workers who fail to meet eligibility requirements and workers who work more than the minimum hours required for eligibility, should be allocated (at least initially) to reserve accumulation, rather than to benefits.

6. Eligibility rules should be considered in light of their administrative complexities and cost.
7. Eligibility rules should provide for credits during periods of disability, so that eligibility may be maintained and coverage continued.
8. Eligibility rules should be initially conservative, to be later liberalized if conditions permit.
9. During periods of unemployment, the trustees should be able to extend coverage to unemployed workers or reduce eligibility requirements.
10. Employees returning to work following service in the armed forces should be immediately eligible for coverage, provided they have returned to work within 90 days of discharge from the service.

Occasionally, the problem of permitting otherwise ineligible persons to contribute premium costs directly into the fund in order to gain coverage has arisen. These persons may be self-employed, or they may be ones who have failed to maintain eligibility. At first glance this seems to be a desirable feature of welfare plans, because it extends benefits to additional members of the union, making the union that much more valuable to its members. However, this invites a high degree of adverse selection. In some plans where information has been available, benefit payments to direct contributors have been found to be 10 to 14 times those for regular employees.

Reciprocal Agreements

In some industries, there is a high degree of mobility of workers from the jurisdiction of one local union to that of another. The construction industry is a prime example. Workers may move from an area where work is slack to another area offering immediate work. At other times a contractor who has obtained work in another territory may assign some regular employees to the project, which will take them into the jurisdiction of a different local of the union. In the construction industry, both unions and contractors favor such mobility, and in some industries, such as structural steel, it is essential.

However, such mobility causes problems insofar as welfare benefits are concerned, because employer contributions to the fund are governed by the labor agreements applicable to the area where the work is performed, not those of the area where the contractor's headquarters are located. If the worker is away from his or her home territory very long, eligibility in the home welfare fund may be terminated. On top of that, the worker may not yet have been able to qualify for the plan in the new territory. The problem is most acute when the various work assignments are short-term ones and the frequency of movement out of the area is high.

One approach toward solution of the mobility problem is through reciprocal agreements between separate funds. These agreements usually provide for transferring credits from one fund to another. In some cases, money is transferred from one fund to another, depending on the equality of employer contribution rates negotiated in the various areas and the balance of flow between the funds. That is, if there is a reasonable balance of movement between the funds over a reasonable period of time, the funds would probably transfer credits. On the other hand, if there is not a balance of movement, the only workable solution would be an agreement that provides for the transfer of money.

Most reciprocal agreements involve adjacent territories. The Hotel and Restaurant Workers' Union provides national portability of credits, but such an arrangement is an exception. Some other unions have attempted centralized administration of funds, with national portability of worker credits, but have made participation in such a fund voluntary to the local unions. In any case, the authority of the trustees to enter into reciprocal agreements must be specified in the trust agreement.

Underwriting

Underwriting of Taft-Hartley trust business involves many of the same considerations as ordinary group underwriting. In both cases, the underwriter must analyze the effect of claims on premiums and be concerned with the ability of the fund to generate enough income to support the promised benefits in the future, even in case of adverse experience.

However, there are special considerations in underwriting Taft-Hartley plans. One is the fact that premium increases may be more difficult to negotiate than with regular groups, because of possible resistance from union members. A request by the insurer to raise premiums because of unfavorable experience may result in the plan's being put up for bids from other insurers. Furthermore, small unions are more vulnerable than large employers to economic fluctuations. Downturns in the economy may have a severe effect on employment, and hence on premiums collected. Some unions face declining membership because of the effects of automation. Shifts in the location of industry, from one part of the country to another, may adversely affect the union in the older territory. All of these are considerations in underwriting a Taft-Hartley plan, in determining the cost of plan benefits, and in establishing a reserve for the plan.

Reserve

The operation of a Taft-Hartley plan is complicated by several factors already discussed: mobility of workers from one plan to another; varying amounts of employer contributions because of variations in employee hours worked; interruptions in work due to seasonal, or other, factors. These complications make it more difficult for trustees to predict accurately the fund's annual income, expenses, and benefit costs.

Therefore, trustees usually find it advisable to allocate a part of forecasted fund income to the accumulation of a reserve. In addition to the amount of the allocation, the reserve will be increased by the amount of contributions received between the period the plan initially commences and the effective date of first benefits. The reserve may also be increased by adding to it subsequent refunds from the insurance company as a result of experience rating.

Trustees face two decisions regarding the reserve: its size, and the period of time during which it will be accumulated. The size of the reserve will be influenced by several factors, such as the desire of the trustees to continue coverage during periods of high unemployment, the terminal liability of the fund under the eligibility rules, or the stability of employment in the particular industry. Typical examples of reserves include one year's annual fund income in the construction industry, and six months' fund income in the printing industry.

Accumulation of the reserve should be accomplished over a period of several years, rather than in the first year or two. To allocate a high percentage of fund income for the reserve in the first few years would deprive the workers of a sizable portion of the benefits they would otherwise be receiving. A reasonable period for accumulating the desired reserve is five years. Once the desired reserve has been attained, the amount previously allocated for accumulation can be used for additional benefits.

Experience Rating

There is no basic difference between the experience rating of a welfare fund and that of a single employer case. Funds are handled by insurance companies on a "retention" basis. That is, at the end of a plan year, any excess of billed premiums over the sum of incurred claims plus the expense charge is refunded to the welfare fund. Such a procedure is commonly accepted by single-employer policyowners, but is less acceptable to trustees of welfare funds. This situation is due to a fundamental difference between the role of trustees and the role of corporate executives.

Corporate executives involved in administering employee benefit plans are likely to take a longer view of the plan. Such persons typically are involved with the plan for many years. A refund of premiums at the end of the plan year does not pose any problem, since there are many uses to which a company can put such a fund.

By contrast, trustees of a welfare fund must constantly recognize their fiduciary responsibility to administer the fund for the benefit of the workers. In addition, the trustees are likely to remain in their position a shorter period of time, and are therefore more likely to prefer short-range planning, preferably for a year at a time.

Consequently, most fund trustees feel an obligation to utilize fund income completely for benefits plus administrative expenses. Premium refunds due to favorable claim experience may be regarded as desirable during early plan years, for the refunds can then be used to increase the fund reserve. In later years, however, such refunds present a problem in conversion into benefits. There are two methods by which year-end premium refunds can be avoided. One method is for the trustees to overspend during the year, in anticipation of the refund. However, this course of action runs counter to the fiduciary responsibilities of the trustees.

As an alternative solution to the problem of premium refunds, the trustees can seek to have the insurer base premiums on rates that contain little or no margin for claim fluctuation. The lack of a margin in the rating structure is incompatible with retention experience rating. Nonetheless, some insurance companies do it as an accommodation to the trustees. Other insurance companies have developed special contingency reserves into which refunds and dividends are paid in years of favorable experience and which can be used to absorb deficits in years of unfavorable experience. Use of such contingency reserves makes it possible for the plan to be administered on a very tight cash flow basis, while still providing a margin for claim fluctuations.

Administration

The administration of a Taft-Hartley trust is under the direction of the trustees. However, as noted previously, the trustees invariably have other obligations, either with their own companies or unions. Therefore, the trustees themselves rarely become involved in the day-to-day administrative functions of the plan. Instead, they rely upon one of two alternatives: (1) hiring personnel to perform the necessary administrative services, or (2) utilizing the services of a third-party administrator.

Hiring its own administrator is a choice normally available only to the largest plans. When this is done, the administrator is often someone connected with the local union and is also someone acceptable to the employers. If the fund lacks the resources to hire an administrator, the trustees may turn to banks, insurance companies or professional administrators. Banks and insurance companies offer the advantage of greatest stability and continuity of service; however, insurance companies, in general, are not active in providing administrative services for Taft-Hartley trusts. Insurers do perform such services as preparing plan booklets and processing claims, but they tend to leave other administrative functions to third-party administrators.

Regardless of the type of administrator, these functions must be performed:

1. Receiving employer reports and contributions and maintaining records of hours and contributions;
2. Maintaining individual employee records of hours worked;
3. Identifying employers who are delinquent in their contributions and reporting them to the trustees;
4. Processing claims by determining claimant eligibility, forwarding claim forms to the insurer (or paying directly from the welfare fund), forwarding claim drafts to claimants;
5. Maintaining records for claim control;
6. Maintaining records of employees and supplying data annually to the insurance company;
7. Handling complaints and grievances; and
8. Preparing periodic reports for the trustees and for regulatory agencies.

Following establishment of the trust, the method of administration should be one of the first decisions of the trustees. A substantial amount of work is needed to commence operation of the plan: employee statistics need to be gathered so that benefit costs may be estimated; forms and procedures must be prepared for employer contributions; reciprocal agreements must be negotiated; and procedures must be set up for transferring credits or money. A failure to process employer reports promptly can lead to a costly catch-up effort and may result in loss of some payments that should have been made by employers.

REGULATION OF TAFT-HARTLEY TRUSTS

The original Taft-Hartley legislation did not provide for regulation of such trust expenditures as commissions, fees, and expenses in installing and administering a plan. While most joint union-management funds were administered fairly, several major scandals were uncovered by Congressional probes in the mid-1950s. These disclosures led to regulations in several states regarding disclosure of activities of such trusts. In 1959 the Landrum-Griffin Act was passed providing penalties for misdeeds by union officials acting as trustees of Taft-Hartley funds. This was followed in 1960 by the NAIC's adoption of a "Code of Ethical Practices with Respect to Insuring of the Benefits of Union or Union-Management Welfare and Pension Funds."

The code laid out practices to be followed in payment of benefits, commissions, fees, and other allowances. It required that the amount of fees bear a semblance to the fair value of the work performed. It also set forth principles governing the relationship between trustees and insurers, methods of acquiring new business, and methods of handling business once it had been acquired.

However, the Employee Retirement Income Security Act now takes precedence in the regulation of Taft-Hartley funds. ERISA requires filings to the Department of Labor and to the Internal Revenue Service for all employee welfare plans, both those of single employers and those of joint union-management funds, ERISA specifically excludes the individual states from regulation of such funds; however, the states continue to regulate the carriers that insure such funds.

The Internal Revenue Code does not make specific mention of Taft-Hartley welfare funds. However, in its rulings, the Internal Revenue Service has afforded such plans the same tax treatment as those of single employers. That is, employer contributions to the fund are regarded as a reasonable and necessary business expense and are, therefore, deductible. The employer contributions are not regarded as taxable income to the employees.

SUMMARY

Ever since the Supreme Court decisions that made pensions and group insurance subject to collective bargaining, joint union-management welfare trusts have been recognized as an advantageous vehicle for covering many employees who would otherwise not be eligible for the low costs of group insurance. In the intervening years, Taft-Hartley trusts have been installed throughout the country, to the point where most of the eligible market has been reached. The potential for expansion of such plans now lies not so much with new groups as with the extension of benefits to existing groups.

Passage of national health insurance would affect existing trust plans, just as it would other health plans issued by insurers. Such legislation might, at one extreme, render unnecessary the health benefits currently purchased by the trusts. The question then becomes one of deciding what to do with the employer contributions that had financed the health insurance. At the present time, it appears unlikely that the unions would give up that contribution, for which it had bargained energetically. Instead, the unions are more likely to use the contributions toward the purchase of additional insurance coverage, such as automobile or homeowners' insurance.

Taft-Hartley trusts are significant for two reasons: they provide coverage for many union members who might not otherwise qualify for employer-union coverage, and they represent the first regulation of benefit programs by the federal government. Taft-Hartley trusts constitute an important part of negotiated benefit programs and are likely to remain so. Future growth seems likely, not so much in reaching additional union members, but rather in expansion of benefits to currently insured workers.

CHAPTER 21

HEALTH MAINTENANCE ORGANIZATIONS

INTRODUCTION

Before comprehensive insurance for health care expenses became prevalent, physicians and their patients were often forced to base decisions about the patient's health care needs on both medical and economic criteria. The physician and the patient carefully weighed the medical advantages of a testing or treatment procedure against the financial disadvantages of having to pay for those procedures. In doing so, both parties included economic feasibility in their definitions of medical necessity.

The ever-growing availability of third-party reimbursement for medical expenses, however, changed this decision-making process. Some claim that the consequences of paying for medical care became so remote that neither the physician nor the patient could easily identify any relationship between their actions and the resulting effect on the cost of care for the population as a whole. In addition, medical care has been increasingly perceived as a right, and attempts at involving the patient in the cost of care (through coinsurance or deductibles) have sometimes been considered violations of this right. Labor unions bargained for 100 percent health insurance coverage paid for by the employer. Management often agreed to provide a set of benefits rather than a predetermined amount of money to pay for health care expenses. Thus, many came to believe that their employers should pay any and all of the costs of providing health care.

At the same time, medical care was becoming less accessible to some people as medical providers left rural and inner-city areas and relocated in more attractive environments. The distribution of doctors and hospitals was, therefore, uneven, creating shortages of medical care in some areas and surpluses in others. Normally, such a situation

by
A. CHARLES BREDESEN, *Executive Vice President, Nicollet/Eitel Health Plan* and **CRAIG R. RODBY, FSA, MAAA,** *Associate Group Pension Actuary, Northwestern National Life Insurance Company, Minneapolis, Minn.*

would resolve itself through the usual economic mechanisms of the free market. However, the noncompetitive pricing nature of the health care industry, where few people buy their health care on a price basis, prevented these economic levelers from working. The maldistribution of health care services continued to worsen.

Long before these problems became acute, prepaid group practice plans existed. However, few, if any, of the early prepaid plans in the United States were developed with the intention of serving the general community, and prepaid plans remained relatively unknown for many years. When new plans did develop, opposition from the medical community posed obstacles that clouded (and still cloud) the issues. In the last few years, however, attention has been focused on prepaid plans as one way in which health care delivery problems can be solved in the private sector without the need for massive government involvement.

One reason for this attention is the urgent need for cost containment measures in the health care delivery system. Because prepaid group plans integrate the delivery of medical care with the financing of that care, many feel that prepayment programs are better able to contain costs than the traditional fee-for-service health care system.

HISTORICAL DEVELOPMENT

The first prepaid plans in the United States were developed in order to provide medical care for certain people who would not otherwise have had access to such care. One of the first group practice plans was organized by the North Pacific Railroad in 1883 to provide care for employees building the transcontinental railroad. Recognizing that these employees would otherwise have no access to medical care, North Pacific built hospitals accessible through their rail systems and employed physicians to staff these facilities. In the late 1880s members of the sizeable French community in San Francisco, concerned that their needs were not being met by the existing medical care delivery system, developed the French Mutual Benevolent Society. Physicians were recruited to work for the society. Members paid for the physicians' services through regular fixed payments to the society.

Prepayment Plans

The Kaiser Foundation Plan, perhaps the best known prepayment plan, was established in the early 1930s to provide health care for a group of Kaiser employees building an aqueduct in the Mojave Desert. Because the location of the work made it impossible to obtain health care through the traditional health care delivery system, Kaiser built a 15-bed hospital and hired a small team of physicians to care for these employees.

In 1938 when the Kaiser organization assumed responsibility for the construction of the Grand Coulee Dam, a similar problem was solved in like manner. The Kaiser organization also utilized the prepaid plan to provide medical care for the hundreds of thousands of defense workers employed in the Kaiser Shipyards during World War II. Immediately following the war, the Kaiser Plan was expanded to include members of the general population.

During the post-war period, two other important plans were organized. On the East Coast, concern over the health care needs of city employees led Mayor Fiorello LaGuardia to initiate the organization of the Health Insurance Plan of New York. On the West Coast, a group of consumers and physicians joined together to form the Health Cooperative of Puget Sound in Seattle, Washington.[1] All three plans have thrived; they are currently the three largest prepaid plans in the country.

CHARACTERISTICS OF PREPAYMENT PLANS

Although no two of the prepayment plans developed in the last two decades were identical, certain similarities have emerged.

First, the plans provide a comprehensive set of services with emphasis on preventive care, early detection of medical problems, and the expanded use of outpatient facilities whenever possible.

Second, in many of the plans, the physicians are organized into group practices. This creates a vehicle by which physicians participate in the financial risk of providing medical services on a prepaid basis. Without the pooling of risk among several physicians, the possibility of unforeseen and lengthy hospitalizations makes such participation nearly impossible.

Third, many of the plans first established own their own out-patient medical facilities. By doing so, the plans can improve access to care by locating the facilities near the population to be served. Expensive equipment that is otherwise available in the community need not be duplicated at the plans' facilities until the utilization of that equipment by plan members becomes great enough to warrant a purchase. Spending for other programs can also be controlled by ascertaining the appropriateness of any given spending request from both economic and medical standpoints, rather than attempting "to keep up with the medical Joneses."

Fourth, members of the plans (the consumers) have input into the plans through membership on the board of directors or through serving in an advisory capacity. This new path of communication is intended to assist medical providers in setting medical care priorities and in receiving more cooperation from their patients in following medical advice.

---

[1]Center for Research in Ambulatory Health Care Administration, *The Organization and Development of a Medical Group Practice*. (Cambridge, Mass.: Ballinger Publishing Co., 1976).

These early programs demonstrated that it was possible for a group of people to arrange for their health care in such a way as to provide access to health care services where none had existed previously, and to finance this care by making regular fixed payments to the medical providers who, in turn, agreed to provide the needed care. The medical providers were assured a regular income, and could make health care decisions on the basis of the long-range savings that would result from prompt and regular treatment.

GROWTH OF PREPAYMENT PLANS

In the 1950s prepayment plans were developed to serve a broader community. These programs were often initiated by community groups who felt that their health needs were not being met by the medical establishment and the insurance industry. Though the growth of these plans was hardly explosive, their numbers have steadily increased. Prior to 1965 there were 26 prepayment plans in the United States. By 1975, their numbers had increased to 170.[2] By 1978 there were 195 such programs.[3]

The success of the Kaiser plan in California made prepaid group practice fairly well known to residents there. However, prepayment plans did not receive significant national attention until the late 1960s, when the federal government began to feel the effects of the cost overruns in both Medicare and Medicaid programs. These two health care financing programs infused massive new purchasing power into the health care system from segments of society that had in the past been almost entirely outside the medical care system. This increased demand, coupled with the trend toward 100 percent medical care coverage that was being provided to many employees through group insurance programs, created such demands upon the medical community that there was little or no concern about fee increases.

Increased medical costs were not the only problem facing health care consumers and providers. During the 1960s, the trend towards educating physicians in specialty care as opposed to general practice accelerated. Medical schools encouraged physicians to continue their training beyond what was needed to ensure good quality primary care. General practice was held in such low esteem that physicians were almost required to become specialists if they wanted the respect of their colleagues.

Specialized physicians were also inclined to believe that they should command specialists' fees even when they were providing primary care, which still remained the major source of activity for most physicians.

---

[2]*HMO Program Status Report*, U.S. Department of Health, Education and Welfare (May 1975).

[3]Health Systems Demographic Center, Interstudy, *HMO Growth: 1977–1978.* (Excelsior, Minn.).

Two main schools of thought developed in response to what many considered as a "crisis" in health care. One school thought that only a major (if not, in fact, a complete) infusion of government control could create meaningful changes in the current system. The other school argued that while modifications did have to be made, health care would suffer unless left to the private sector. Popular support appeared to be with the private sector advocates since previous experience showed little success by the government in its attempts at providing direct control over the delivery of health care. Furthermore, most people were inclined to trust the opinion of the medical community, which strongly and vocally opposed government intervention in the health care delivery system. The strategy that prevailed called for the government to provide incentives for modification in the private sector. The Health Maintenance Organization Act of 1973 (Public Law 93-222) was one such effort.

THE HEALTH MAINTENANCE ORGANIZATION ACT OF 1973

By 1973, prepaid group practice plans had been operating successfully for several years and had shown ability to control health care costs more effectively than both the fee-for-service and insurance reimbursement systems. First the Nixon Administration, and later Congress, became convinced that these prepaid group practice programs offered promise. A strategy for enlisting support for prepaid practice was developed. One of the first steps in proceeding with this strategy was to rename prepaid group practices as health maintenance organizations (HMOs), a politically more attractive term that could also be used later to include a variety of organizations.

The Health Maintenance Organization Act as passed in 1973 was designed to encourage the development of HMOs by providing financial assistance, preempting restrictive state laws, and mandating that employers covered by the Fair Labor Standards Act offer an HMO option. Thus, the three major components of the act were:

1. The sum of $375 million dollars was provided to be used over five years for feasibility studies, grants, contracts, and loan guarantees for initial operating costs. This was necessary because many private sources of capital were reluctant to risk the large amounts of money needed for start-up costs for these "new" programs—the HMOs.
2. State laws that effectively prevented the development of HMO programs were overridden by the legislation.

3. Employers covered by the Fair Labor Standards Act employing 25 or more persons and offering a health benefits plan were
   required to offer an HMO option to their employees, provided
   that an HMO meeting the act's organizational, operational,
   and service requirements (as described below) was serving the
   area in which the employer's employees resided. According to
   the act, no employer offering the "dual choice" is required to
   pay more for the health benefits plan than would otherwise be
   paid. However, failure to offer dual choice was considered a
   willful violation of the Fair Labor Standards Act.

The dual choice provision was included at the urging of HMO
advocates who felt that unless the business community could be in-
duced to offer HMO plans as options to their regular group health
insurance, HMOs would never have a chance to succeed on a major
scale. The dual choice provision was designed to enhance the chances
that HMOs would succeed.

Provisions of HMO Act of 1973

To qualify for financial assistance under the 1973 Act, an HMO
was required to comply with an exhaustive set of organizational and
operational requirements. One major provision was that the HMO
must provide each member with basic health services for a fee that
was (a) paid on a periodic basis without regard to the dates on which
health services are provided, (b) fixed without regard to the frequency,
extent, or kind of health service, (c) fixed under a community rating
system, and (d) supplemented (if the HMO desires) by additional
nominal payments for specific services, so long as these payments did
not serve as a barrier to the provision of health services.

Each federally qualified HMO was required to:

1. Produce satisfactory evidence of fiscal soundness;
2. Assume full financial risk on a prospective basis for basic
   health services. This means that HMOs must determine their
   fees based on expected as opposed to actual costs. Exceptions are that reinsurance may be obtained for annual costs in
   excess of $5,000 per member, out-of-area services, and up to
   90 percent of the amount by which its costs exceeded 115
   percent of its income for any fiscal year.
3. Enroll persons "broadly representative" of the demographic
   characteristics of the area it serves and not cancel or refuse
   to enroll high risk persons;
4. Have an annual open enrollment period;
5. Be organized in a way that assures that at least one-third of

the members of the policymaking body of the HMO are members of the organization, and that there is equitable representation on such bodies of members from medically underserved populations served by the organization;

6. Establish grievance procedures for members and for the HMO's providers;

7. Operate a quality assurance program acceptable to the Department of Health, Education and Welfare (HEW), stressing both procedures and outcomes;

8. Provide "medical social services" and health education to its members;

9. Provide or arrange for continuing education for its health professionals;

10. Operate a record system acceptable to HEW to enable HEW to monitor and evaluate the HMO's costs of operation; its utilization patterns; the availability, accessibility and acceptability of its services; developments in the health status of its members, and any other matters HEW requires.

BASIC AND SUPPLEMENTAL BENEFITS

To qualify as an HMO under the 1973 Act, a plan must offer a wide range of services. Basic benefits mandated under the act include:

1. Physician services;
2. In-patient and out-patient hospital services;
3. Emergency health services;
4. Short-term out-patient evaluative and crisis intervention mental health services (not to exceed 20 visits);
5. Medical treatment and referral to appropriate ancillary services for drug or alcohol abuse;
6. Diagnostic lab and diagnostic and therapeutic X ray services;
7. Home health services; and
8. Preventive health services, including voluntary family planning, infertility services, and preventive dental and eye care for children.

HMOs were also required to provide the following supplemental services:

1. Intermediate and long-term care;
2. Vision, dental, and mental health care not included in basic benefits;
3. Long-term physical medicine and rehabilitative care; and
4. Prescription drugs.

PROBLEM AREAS

The HMO Act encountered immediate problems. Although support for HMOs had come from an appreciation of the operational histories of several prepaid group practices, the prototype HMO designed by the act had never existed successfully. In fact, none of the then-operational plans could meet the standards set forth in the act without modifications in their benefit design, pricing policies, and organizational format. These existing plans complained that in order to qualify for assistance under the act, it would be necessary to make changes in their operation that were not required of the insurance industry and that would make financial success difficult, if not impossible.

As a compromise to win support necessary for passage of the act, two types of HMOs had been created: group practice and individual practice HMOs. Regulations concerning these types created another source of difficulty. According to the "principal professional activity" provision, to be considered a group practice, the physician component of the HMO not only had to be organized as a group, but also had to spend at least 51 percent of its professional activity time working for the HMO. This provision disqualified most of the existing fee-for-service group practice clinics in the country, despite the fact that some believed these were the logical places to develop HMOs because of the low initial capital needed to begin operation.

The provision was further considered to be unjust because it did not apply to both types of HMOs. Individual Practice Associations (IPAs) had been designated as the second type of HMO so that solo practitioners could become part of an HMO. Although IPAs were required to fulfill all of the other provisions of the law in the same manner as the group practice programs, the physicians who were to provide services to members of an IPA model HMO did not have to practice in groups, nor did they have to commit any minimum amount of their total practice to prepayment.

A third problem was that the act envisioned a growth in the number of HMO plans that could not be realized with the available resources. There were neither enough physicians interested in participating in an HMO nor enough experienced management personnel to fulfill the expectations of the act.

The act also stiffened resistance to HMO programs in the business community. The mandatory dual choice requirement only served to further polarize the business community which felt that it was being forced to offer HMO options because the HMOs had not been successful in getting anyone to buy their plans voluntarily. The long and complex regulation development process also served to alienate the business and labor communities, both of which found the emerging regulations objectionable and cumbersome. Amendments to the act were called for by virtually every interested party.

1976 Amendments

In response to the general discontent, the Health Maintenance Organization Amendments of 1976 made several significant changes in the operation of the act. Some of the most important changes were:

1. The provision of supplementary benefits by the HMO was made optional rather than compulsory;
2. The costly "open enrollment" provision was modified by exempting certain HMOs from this requirement and reducing the minimum number of enrollees in the open enrollment period. As further protection for the HMO organizations, the amendments allowed the plans to refuse enrollment to institutionalized individuals and permitted them to require a 90-day waiting period following enrollment;
3. The "principal professional activity" requirement was amended to provide a 36-month phase-in period;
4. Organizations that had previously provided comprehensive health services on a prepaid basis were given 48 months to comply with the community rating requirement. New organizations, however, were still required to be community rated from the beginning;
5. The dual choice requirement was amended to apply only to employers who had a minimum of 25 employees residing in the HMO service area, to make offering of the HMO option to union members subject to collective bargaining, and to reduce the penalty for noncompliance from criminal to civil; and
6. The life of the 1973 HMO Act was extended from three to five years.

1978 Amendments

Continued congressional support for the HMO program was evidenced by the passage of the Health Maintenance Organization Amendments of 1978. These amendments extended the program for another three years and appropriated additional funds for its operation. However, the most significant provisions of the amendments are those that provide for the establishment of a Health Maintenance Organization Intern Program to train individuals to become administrators and medical directors of health maintenance organizations. Other provisions further modified the "principal professional activity" provision by extending the phase-in period to 48 months and by reducing the percentage of the HMO group's physicians who must comply with this requirement.

Characteristics of HMOs

No definition of health maintenance organizations would encompass all of the organizations that call themselves HMOs. Nonetheless, certain characteristics are common to most HMOs. These characteristics can be best understood by comparing six facets of HMOs with similar facets of insurance plans.

BENEFIT STRUCTURE

Indemnity contracts offered by commercial insurers provide for the reimbursement of medical expenses incurred by an insured *after* those services have actually been provided. The insured is free to select any provider recognized by the state, including physicians, hospitals, pharmacies, and chiropractors. The only arrangement between the insurer and the providers prior to the delivery of the service may involve agreeing on the level of reimbursement for the service performed. Blue Cross and Blue Shield have been more active in obtaining this type of agreement than have commercial insurers, although the latter are increasing their activity in this field. Insurers usually involve themselves only with the buyers of health care and are concerned almost exclusively with the financing of health care expenses.

HMOs, on the other hand, negotiate with medical providers *before* services are delivered. These negotiations concern the most appropriate method of organizing the delivery of services so as to guarantee HMO members access to health care when needed, the level of reimbursement that the providers will receive, their degree of risk involvement, the monitoring of care rendered, and other aspects of health care delivery and financing. In effect, the HMO says to the provider, "We represent (or will represent) the purchasers of your services. We wish to negotiate on their behalf the relationship they will have with you. Then, in turn, we will negotiate on your behalf with them." Thus, the HMO organization serves as a middleman between the buyers and the sellers of health care services.

The disadvantage to the HMO members of this prearrangement is a limitation of their freedom in choice of physician and hospital. Even those HMOs with the broadest representation of physicians cannot realistically arrange for their members to use any doctor or hospital. It is up to the member to decide if this reduction in choice is offset by the advantages.

RATIONALE OF BENEFIT PLAN

By definition, insurance is an arrangement by which the individual is guaranteed compensation in the event that he or she sustains a loss. For this reason, health insurance policies contain a provision that the insured must actually have a diagnosed illness or have sustained an injury before the insurance company will pay the claim submitted. Expenses incurred by the individual that are intended to prevent loss are usually not reimbursed.

Health maintenance organizations on the other hand, agree to provide a set of health care services to their members, usually without any requirements that the individual prove "loss" before the services will be covered. In fact, most HMOs vigorously stress the coverage they provide for such routine and preventive medical care as physical exams, eye and ear exams, and well-baby care. In doing so, the HMOs hope to encourage their members to seek out medical care regularly so that diagnosis of disease can be detected early enough to either reduce the total care needed in treating that disease or to prevent the disease from occurring in the first place. While there is not yet much evidence that points to the probability of preventing disease from occurring, ample evidence exists to show that early detection and treatment of disease can prevent the need for more extensive and costly treatment at a later date. Long-range cost savings through early detection are made possible by actually encouraging the HMO members to seek medical services more often than they might otherwise be expected to seek them.

SCOPE OF COVERAGE

Health insurance plans have, from their initiation, emphasized coverage for the large potentially catastrophic expenses of hospitalization. This emphasis helped to shape the practice of many physicians and to encourage the hospitalization of many patients who could have otherwise been treated on an out-patient basis.

HMOs, on the other hand, stress care in the physician's offices by incorporating this concept into their benefit packages for members and by financially rewarding physicians for a reduction in hospitalization expenses. The economic advantages of emphasizing out-patient care are so great as to make this one of the HMOs' main competitive edges.

The result of the emphasis on out-patient care is that most HMOs experience hospital costs that are 10-50 percent lower than might be expected from an insured population. However, caution has to be exercised when comparing HMO and insurance company statistics to make certain that the figures have been adequately adjusted for differences in age, sex, and other factors that might influence morbidity. Some claimed savings by HMOs can be attributed to the differences in the population enrolled in the HMO. While out-patient utilization rates are usually much higher for HMOs (as much as 100 percent higher than insurance experience would normally indicate), the lower unit cost of out-patient care allows for a marked increase in out-patient utilization that does not threaten the cost savings achieved in reduced hospitalizations.

COST REDUCTION MEASURES

When an insurance company underwrites a health insurance program, it often tries to reduce the overall cost of the program by using coinsurance. With coinsurance, the insured remains a partner in the health care plan and retains some concern over the cost of the services needed. Coinsurance also provides a financial incentive to see that unnecessary care is avoided. The problem with this system, however, is that the health care industry is not organized so as to encourage price shopping or other attempts by the public to seek out the best buy for its health care dollar. Coinsurance, therefore, may cause the insured to delay or avoid receiving health care services rather than attempting to determine if those services could be purchased more economically elsewhere.

HMOs also try to reduce the total cost of the plan by using small co-payments (fixed charges made by the HMO in return for a service, for example, a $2 co-payment for each office call). These co-payments are intended to discourage frivolous use of medical facilities and to produce revenue for the HMO in order to keep the basic monthly fee as low as possible. Most HMOs are careful not to set these co-payments so high as to serve as a possible deterrent to seeking out care.

The HMOs often go a step further in their attempts to control health care costs by providing the medical practitioners with financial incentives. One common incentive is the "capitation compensation method." In this method a medical provider agrees to make available all necessary services to HMO members for a fixed fee, or "capitation," regardless of the number of visits a particular member may need. If the members need more services than envisioned when the capitation was developed, the medical provider stands to lose; the HMO and its members do not. Such loss may not actually require the paying out of cash. More often it means that the medical care provider will simply have to work more hours for the same compensation. Another common arrangement is a program whereby the physicians share in any surpluses or deficits in the pool of money the HMO sets aside to pay for hospital expenses.

The HMO incentives mean that both the patient and the doctor share in the overall cost of the plan. Each has a financial motive to see that medical care is provided as efficiently and effectively as possible. In an HMO, members can afford whatever care is truly needed, whereas previously economic reality may have forced many people into ignoring care they would otherwise have sought.

SELLING HMOs TO EMPLOYEES

The overwhelming bulk of health insurance coverage is written through group health insurance policies. These policies are designed with input from the employer or unions, but the individual employee is usually not included in any decisions about the types of coverage to be provided. The employer selects the insurer and pays part, or all, of the premium. The only decision left for the employees is whether or not they want the coverage that has been selected. Since most employees recognize the need for insurance coverage, they enroll in the plan without really investigating the various provisions of the policy. The real marketing of group health insurance, then, is with the employer, union, or the benefit consultant. Insurers do not greatly concern themselves with soliciting the individual employee.

The selling of an HMO is different. Though the need to convince the employer to offer the HMO remains, the arguments used by the HMO are quite different from those used by an insurance company. Because of administrative, philosophical, and legal constraints, HMOs have less flexibility in benefit design and often charge rates based on the HMO's experience rather than the experience of the group being solicited. The HMO, therefore, has to convince the employer that its program will not create an additional cost for the employee (the cost to the employer remains the same), and that an HMO may even help the employer to control long-range costs for health coverage.

If the HMO succeeds in selling the employer, it must then convince the individual employees to switch their coverage from the insurance plan to the HMO. To do so, the HMO must demonstrate that an HMO is not just another set of insurance benefits but is an entirely different concept—one that affects not only the financing of the employee's health care expenses but the delivery of those services. Many HMOs are careful to enroll those people who are at least partially sold on the HMO concept itself and not solely on the higher level of coverage. The problem in doing so is compounded because few employees understand their existing insurance coverage. Thus, making comparisons between the insurance plan and the HMO may require first explaining to the employees what the insurance plan entails.

Because HMOs are optional programs (taken in lieu of the insurance plan), and because HMOs encounter numerous difficulties in getting their message across to the employees, fewer than 10 percent of the employees typically elect to switch coverage. This penetration rate increases in subsequent years. Some HMOs, particularly those with physicians who have recognized reputations and fee-for-service practices in addition to their involvement with the prepayment plans, eventually reach an enrollment of 50 percent or more of the groups they solicit.

MANAGEMENT NEEDS

The management needs of insurance plans and HMO plans are different. Assuming the insurance plan is properly rated and underwritten, competency of insurer management may not have a major effect upon the financial success of that plan. Competent, professional claim reviews and a smoothly functioning administrative unit can assure good premium flow and low expenses. However, the claims will still be claims. While good management can assure that the insurance company does not take unwarranted risks, this management has not been utilized as a method to control the health care costs themselves.

On the other hand, an HMO with incompetent or inexperienced management has little chance to succeed. Whereas the insurance manager's job is largely done when he or she properly selects and underwrites a risk, the HMO manager's job only begins at that point. The manager must then organize and maintain a sound program of risk management and utilization control.

To date, the lack of a sufficient number of managers capable of underwriting and administering an HMO program has been the most pressing problem faced by HMOs. This gap in competent management between insurers and HMOs may be the insurance companies' biggest competitive advantage.

TYPES OF HEALTH MAINTENANCE ORGANIZATIONS

One approach to categorizing HMOs is to divide all HMOs into either "group practice plans" or "individual practice plans." If this approach is used, it would seem that a good definition of group practice would be that used by the American Group Practice Association: "Any group of three or more full-time physicians and/or dentists, organized in a legally recognized entity for the provision of health care services, who share space, equipment, personnel, and records for both patient care and business management and who have a predetermined arrangement for the distribution of income." Using this definition, if the physicians practice in a group or groups, the HMO is considered to be a group practice plan. If the physicians are not required to be a part of a group, the HMO is considered to be an individual practice plan. The federal government's definition, however, goes further by also requiring that to be considered a group practice, the physicians must not only practice in groups, but must also spend at least 51 percent of their professional activity in prepayment (though the two subsequent amendments to the HMO Act of 1973 have considerably modified this requirement). For those plans that have been in existence long enough that the "principal professional activity" provision applies, fee-for-service physicians whose group practice occupies less than the required 51 percent of their time are considered to be individual practice physicians despite the considerable potential inaccuracy in doing so.

The difficulty with describing all HMOs as either group practice or individual practice plans is that this may very well lump together significantly different plans. The relationship of each physician to the HMO entails more than the organizational manner in which the physicians practice. It entails the physicians' financial involvement with the HMO; that is, their compensation for services performed and the risk assumption for the cost of providing services. Since financial involvement by the physicians in the HMO is the major difference between prepayment plans and insurance contracts, the degree of this involvement must be included if the basic differences between HMO models are to be reflected accurately.

The terms "open panel" and "closed panel" as they relate to HMOs also require some clarification. These terms have been commonly used to describe two main "types" of HMOs. A closed panel HMO is one that arranges for medical services to be provided through only certain physicians and hospitals and does not offer to contract with any medical provider in the area who may wish to do so. Closed panel plans are usually group practice plans that, in essence, require a physician to become part of the group before he or she is eligible to participate in the HMO program. Open panel plans, by contrast, allow any physician or hospital in the community wishing to be included in the HMO to enter into an agreement to do so. Open panel plans are often sponsored by the local medical society and are usually comprised of solo practitioners and small group practices (although some open panel plans do have larger group practices participating as well). Many people believe that closed panel programs are more likely to succeed because they have greater control over their providers and can therefore operate more effectively. Open panel plans however, are often more attractive in the marketplace because the inclusion of a large number of community physicians allows individuals to enroll in the HMO without severing ties with their personal physicians.

Four HMO Models

When the characteristics mentioned above are taken into consideration, four major HMO models can be identified: the staff group practice plan, the capitated group practice plan, the capitated individual practice plan and the fee-for-service individual practice plan.

STAFF GROUP PRACTICE PLANS

Under this model, the physicians are employees of the HMO. The HMO has to create its own facilities; purchase needed equipment; hire nurses, technicians, and clinic management personnel; and otherwise prepare to actually deliver health care services (as opposed to contracting for the delivery of those services). Since the HMO's staff includes medical personnel, the total size of the staff for this model is much larger than that of the other HMO models. Management must not only be able to handle the function of risk bearing but also must be capable of clinic administration.

The physicians may or may not share in the overall risk of the cost of providing services. Some HMOs of this type provide certain financial rewards or penalties to their physicians. These may include sharing surpluses or deficits that accrue in the fund established to pay for hospital expenses or pharmacy expenses. Other HMOs, while providing no direct financial incentives or penalties, rely on peer review and other management controls to limit overutilization.

Several staff group practice managers claim to be able to rely on physician dedication to the program as a way of controlling costs. There seems, however, to be no actuarially sound utilization discount that can be applied as a result of this dedication. In any case, the characteristic that distinguishes the physicians' financial involvement in this model is that if the HMO does not succeed, its staff physicians will be out of work. The extent to which this type of involvement is significant depends on how difficult the physicians perceive it will be to find employment in the event of cessation of operation. However, since each physician will be at least inconvenienced by having to find a new source of income, they have an interest in the financial success of the HMO and are at risk in a manner different from both the insurance system and the other HMO plans.

Proponents of staff group practice plans contend that this direct financial interdependence between the HMO and its physicians provides the HMO with the greatest control over the actions of its physicians. The HMO can clearly identify what it expects from its physicians.

One disadvantage is the difficulty in finding persons with the skills required to effectively administer this type of HMO due to the lack of available training experiences. In recognition of this difficulty the 1978 HMO amendments established an HMO intern program.

Another major disadvantage is the tremendous capital needed to initiate, staff, and equip one of these programs. The debt service created by this capitalization may, in many cases, prevent the HMO from offering its plan at a competitive cost. Staff group practice plans also typically need a much larger number of enrollees before they reach a cash-flow break-even point (20,000 members or more is often considered the minimum enrollment needed).

The problem of the high level of enrollment necessary for break-even is compounded by the fact that these HMOs usually have the greatest difficulty in obtaining members. Since the HMO is not likely to be well known in the community when it starts operation, many employers and employees are hesitant to enroll. Most individuals who might consider the HMO would have to sever any ties they have with their current physicians. Many individuals will also be concerned that they do not know anything about the reputation of the HMO doctors, since many of them may not have had private practices prior to their involvement with the HMO.

Employers are reluctant to offer a program of unproven value to their employees. The HMO must overcome employer fears about the competency and adequacy of its care. These problems prevent the HMO from obtaining its needed enrollment as quickly as desired and can also raise the marketing costs. Certain HMOs organized and financed in this manner have encountered financial difficulties. One example of a plan that has successfully utilized this organizational and financial arrangement is the Group Health Cooperative of Puget Sound, Seattle, Washington. This plan, organized in 1947, currently serves over 249,000 members.[4]

CAPITATED GROUP PRACTICE PLANS

In this model the physicians are organized into a group practice and contract with the HMO to provide medical services on a capitation basis. The HMO may or may not have been instrumental in developing the physician group or in causing it to be developed. In some cases the physician group will be an already existing fee-for-service medical center that has decided to provide prepaid care alongside its other practice. The contract between the physician group and the HMO may be simply an oral agreement by the physicians to provide services or it may be a detailed delineation of what the two parties expect from each other. Under this model, the staff of the HMO is not concerned with managing a medical facility, but serves as the intermediary between the members and the physicians. The size of the administrative staff, therefore, can be quite small, particularly if there is an affiliation with an existing medical clinic that can assist by lending the HMO some of the management services it will need, for example, accounting, billing and personnel.

The main component of the physician risk assumption is the capitation the physicians agree to receive in return for providing all the medical care for members of the HMO. The physician has an incentive to eliminate unnecessary medical services and to find the most effective way of delivering care when it is needed by the prudent use of paramedical personnel, nurse practitioners, or physician assistants. Since it is the physician who controls hospital admissions and length of stay and decides which tests will be performed, giving the physician an incentive to eliminate unnecessary hospital expenses has proved one way to reduce the total cost of hospitalization.

Potentially, this HMO model has less control over the physicians than the staff group practice plan. Because the physicians are not employed by the HMO, directing the daily activity of the physicians is

[4]"Results of the 1978 HMO Survey," *Group Health News* (December 1978), p. 11.

outside the scope of the HMO. The HMO has to rely upon the group to run itself in a manner acceptable to the HMO management. Where the physician group is an existing fee-for-service clinic, the fact that the group will run itself is an advantage to the HMO because the HMO will be able to use the existing talents and management skills of the group. In addition, standards for quality, access to care, cost containment, and other factors can all be agreed to by both parties, and systems for monitoring progress in these areas can be implemented.

A major advantage of this plan is the relatively small capital needed to establish the HMO. While the development cost for a staff model can run into the millions of dollars, similar costs for the capitated group practice model can be $250,000 or less, especially if an existing medical group is used. The ability to begin operation with only minimal capital needs makes starting this type of HMO very simple. The disadvantage is the difficulty in convincing an existing fee-for-service clinic to risk some of its success on a prepayment plan.

Marketing capitated group practice plans is easier than marketing their staff counterparts. Nonetheless, consumer acceptance is by no means automatic. An existing clinic with an established reputation can overcome concerns about the competency and adequacy of care which the HMO will provide. However, though individuals already using the clinic will be a source of enrollment for the HMO, unless the clinic comprises most or all of the physicians in the community, the HMO still faces the problem of convincing most of its potential members to disassociate themselves from the physicians they are currently using. Many HMOs are careful about overtly encouraging people to break a satisfactory relationship with a non-HMO doctor. This is not done totally out of altruism; people who have reluctantly left their physicians to join the HMO are the most likely to find fault with the new medical group.

One example of a capitated group plan is the Nicollet/Eitel Health. Plan in Minneapolis, Minnesota. Organized in 1973 by the Nicollet Clinic and Eitel Hospital, the plan now serves a membership of 15,000.

CAPITATED INDIVIDUAL PRACTICE ASSOCIATION PLANS (IPAs)

Termed an "individual practice association" under P.L. 93-222, this plan attempts to combine the cost control advantages of capitation with the market appeal of an open panel plan. The IPA is an entirely separate entity from the HMO itself, although the separation may not be more than an arm's length since both the HMO and the IPA may be organized by the same party, often a local unit of the medical society. The HMO contracts with the IPA in the same manner as with a capitated group practice. The IPA then turns around and contracts with the individual physicians who agree to participate in the program. The IPA is run by, or at least takes its direction from, the physicians. While the IPA may include physicians who are practicing in groups, association with the IPA is predicated only on having a license to practice medicine. Therefore, IPAs are usually dominated by physicians who either practice alone or in small groups.

This type of HMO, in addition to the functions performed by HMO managers in the previous models, is often called upon to provide certain administrative functions for the IPA such as claim payment and financial accounting. The HMO may even be responsible for recruiting physicians to participate in the IPA. These tasks serve to increase the size of the staff of the HMO so that it typically is larger than one needed by a capitated group practice. Still, it is much smaller than needed for the staff model. Although HMO management under this model does not get involved with the actual delivery of care as occurs in the staff group practice plan, it definitely has a greater role in organizing the services than in the capitated group practice.

The IPA accepts a capitation from the HMO and is therefore at risk for the provision of services. Since it is difficult, if not impossible, for an individual physician to accept this full risk, the IPA agrees to pay its member physicians on a modified fee-for-service basis. Under a typical arrangement, the physician submits a bill to the IPA for a service performed for an HMO member. The IPA pays the physician a prearranged percentage of the fee charged by that doctor. The remainder of the fee (10–25 percent) is held in an account from which distributions can be made to the individual physicians at the end of the year if the IPA has money left over after paying all the bills submitted during the year. There may also be provisions for paying off any deficits for hospitalization before the physicians receive any of their held-back-money. Some HMOs may also agree to pay the IPA a portion of any hospital surpluses. In some cases, an IPA may not be able to pay its physicians their full initial percentage of fees because of overutilization of services. In this case, the physicians may have to agree to receive a smaller front-end fee. For example, the IPA may have intended to pay 80 percent of the physicians' fees but be forced by heavy losses to change to 70 percent or less. In effect, then, the physicians as a whole absorb the risk for providing medical services; each individual physician is involved only to the extent of the IPA hold-back.

A number of administrative complexities face a manager of this type of HMO. The fact that the physicians are so spread out, both physically and organizationally, makes the control of those physicians very difficult. The incentives for physicians to contain costs may be perceived so remotely that the hoped-for understanding of cause and effect that the IPA must rely on to encourage changes in physician practice patterns does not occur. In addition, getting the HMO members to understand the ramifications of their actions is also difficult, since the members may well perceive the HMO as just another insurance plan rather than an entirely different concept. IPAs that succeed, therefore, do so by implementing rigorous utilization and quality control programs.

Capitated individual practice plans are less expensive to get started than staff model plans, but they do require more capital than a capitated group practice. The time involved to educate and solicit area physicians can be expensive. Furthermore, while there is little need to spend money for facilities, the administrative needs of the IPA are such that significant sums can be consumed developing claim payment systems and other services. This problem, however, can be reduced by contracting with outside companies to provide some of these services.

The brightest aspect of an IPA plan is its marketing appeal. If the IPA is successful in enrolling a large percentage of the physicians currently practicing in the area, the need for a potential member to change doctors is almost eliminated. The resulting wide distribution of physician offices also means that care will be conveniently located for most people. This creates an ample, accessible market for the IPA and can reduce marketing costs accordingly. By offering the opportunity to join the HMO without the necessity of breaking an established tie with a physician, IPAs may attract older individuals who would not be interested in a group practice plan.

FEE-FOR-SERVICE INDIVIDUAL PRACTICE PLANS

This type of plan is similar to the capitated IPA plan in that the IPA is a separate entity from the HMO. The major difference between this model and the capitated IPA model is that the HMO itself bears the risk for the cost of medical services. The physicians are compensated on a fee-for-service basis and, while there may be a holdback provision similar to the IPA, the percentage is fixed so that the physician is guaranteed his or her money at that rate. Those fee-for-service individual practice model HMOs that do not include any holdback provision resemble insurance so closely that differentiating between the two is difficult. Indeed, some Blue Cross-Blue Shield plans claim they are actually HMOs under this plan. The primary differences, however, lie in access to care, prearrangements regarding fee schedules, and perhaps a peer review program.

Because the physicians' risk is so low when using this plan, the HMO management of this model has a monumental task in finding ways to control costs. Reliance on physicians' goodwill appears to be the largest component of the utilization control program, although ample use of computerized information systems that monitor the activity of the physicians (through physician profiles) can be of assistance. This HMO plan may be best suited for small towns or rural areas where existing peer pressure can create an environment in which the doctors feel a stronger obligation to see the HMO succeed than is likely in a large city where anonymity may effectively destroy this potential feeling of identity with the community and its projects. The capital needs and marketing advantages that characterize the capitated IPA plan are usually also present in this plan.

PRIVATE INSURERS AND HMOs

The development of HMOs has provided a new market for the services of the commercial insurers. In addition, these insurers perceive HMOs as having the potential to help curb the increases in medical care costs experienced over the past several years. Thus, many private insurers have participated in the development and/or operation of HMOs. By 1976, 22 commercial companies were involved in some 50 operational HMOs, 12 of which were federally qualified.[5] This involvement ranged from minimal to all-encompassing, and included the following types of activities:[6]

1. Offering consulting services in areas such as benefit design, actuarial assistance, and management;
2. Providing administrative services such as the monitoring of claims, collection of fees, accounting, and computer services;
3. Offering marketing assistance;
4. Giving financial support by providing loan capital and grants, purchasing stock, sharing in operating losses, and providing lines of credit;
5. Providing out-of-area emergency coverage;
6. Providing reinsurance;
7. Providing hospitalization coverage;
8. Guaranteeing acceptance of risk on failure to perform.

Perhaps the clearest indication of the commitment of private insurance companies to the HMO concept can be seen in those situations where private insurers have developed and continue to own and operate HMO plans. While the numbers of such plans remain small, those carriers that presently own such plans have expressed an intent to expand their activities in this area.

EVALUATING THE HMOS

Initial evaluation of HMOs indicates mixed success. Development and expansion of HMOs has been slower than expected. This

---

[5]"Private Insurance Company Involvement in HMOs," *Medical Economic Bulletin* Health Insurance Association of America, (July 14, 1976).
[6]*Ibid.*

development has been hampered by difficulties on the federal level, because Congress has been reluctant to appropriate adequate funding. In addition, HEW has been unable to coordinate the program effectively or to speed up the issue of the final regulations and guidelines needed to implement the HMO Act.[7]

The most comprehensive evaluation to date has been that conducted by the General Accounting Office (GAO), the conclusions of which were presented to the U.S. Congress in June, 1978. The GAO report summarized the results of their evaluation of 14 federally qualified HMOs, all of which had received grants or loans under the 1973 HMO Act. These HMOs were judged on the basis of their ability to comply with the act in several areas:

1. The provision of health services;
2. The organization and operation of the plans;
3. The inclusion of indigent and high-risk individuals in their membership;
4. The ability to achieve a fiscally sound basis in order to operate without continued federal financial assistance.[8]

The report indicated that the plans had successfully complied with the 1973 act in the provision of health services, and were, for the most part organized and operated in the prescribed manner. It faulted the organizations, however, on their general lack of enrollment of elderly or indigent persons, and their failure to conduct open enrollment periods and thus to enroll high-risk individuals.

The financial difficulties experienced by the HMOs were felt to be the result of several factors. To earn federal qualification, an HMO must offer more comprehensive benefits than its competitors. Yet, it must keep its prices comparable. In addition, HMOs that depend heavily on health care services in the fee-for-service sector lose control over a significant portion of their costs. Problems related to inadequacies in the individual HMOs were also cited. These included insufficient pricing strategies and ineffectual management.[9]

HMOs give evidence of reducing in-hospital utilization rates, sometimes achieving figures of less than half the number of hospital days per thousand as are experienced in the fee-for-service sector. Such figures must be viewed with caution, however. The large number of HMO members whose participation in the plans is an employee benefit and the small number of indigent, and high-risk individuals enrolled in the plans must be taken into account when analyzing these utilization rates.

---

[7]*Can Health Maintenance Organizations be Successful?—An Analysis of 14 Federally Qualified HMO's*, U.S. General Accounting Office, Report to the Congress (June 30, 1978), p. ii.

[8]*Ibid.*, p. 2.

[9]*Ibid.*, p. 46.

Though the federally qualified HMOs evaluated in the GAO report enjoyed only limited success, it is important not to generalize such findings to all HMOs. Many HMOs enjoy considerable success. According to a survey conducted by InterStudy Inc., of Minneapolis, Minnesota,[10] by August 1978, 26 HMOs could boast a membership of 20,000 or more members and an increase of at least 10 percent from June 1977 to August 1978. A total of 199 HMOs, 65 of which were federally qualified, were operational in 1978. This figure represents a 20.6 percent increase in the number of HMOs over the 1977 figure, an increase that was complemented by a 13.9 percent increase in national HMO enrollment during this period of time.

SUMMARY

This chapter began by outlining the historical development of prepaid health plans. The difficulties in the traditional health care system that led to the need for federal legislation were then analyzed. Following this analysis, the goals, provisions, and shortcomings of the Health Maintenance Organization Act of 1973 were examined, as were the 1976 and 1978 amendments to the act. This examination was followed by a description of the four types of HMOs currently in operation. The chapter concluded with a brief discussion of the role of private insurers in the development and operation of HMOs and a discussion of the recent GAO evaluation of federally qualified HMOs.

[10]"Results of the 1978 HMO Survey," *Group Health News* (December 1978), p. 11.

PART 4

ADMINISTRATION OF GROUP PLANS

CHAPTER 22

MARKETING OF GROUP INSURANCE

INTRODUCTION

The importance of group insurance, both life and health, is reflected in figures describing its size and growth. In life insurance, group policies are fast becoming the predominant type of coverage when measured in terms of coverage in force, as shown in Figure 22-1.

FIGURE 22-1

Life Insurance in Force
in the United States
by Type, 1977[1]

Type	% of Total
Ordinary	50
Group	43
Industrial	2
Credit	5

In the period from 1967 to 1977, the amount of group life insurance in force in the United States nearly tripled, compared to a doubling of ordinary insurance. If that trend continues, group will soon account for the majority of life insurance in the United States, as it already does in Canada. In Canada, group policies accounted for over 57 percent of life insurance in force at the end of 1977.[2]

[1]American Council of Life Insurance, *Life Insurance Fact Book, 1978* (Washington, D.C.), pp. 7, 27, and 29.
[2]*Ibid.*, p. 105.

by
BERNARD F. KALB, CLU, *formerly Group Vice President, Massachusetts Mutual Life Insurance Company, Springfield, Massachusetts.*

In health insurance, group coverage has, from the beginning, been the predominant form sold by insurance companies in the United States. Figure 22–2 shows the figures at the end of 1976.

FIGURE 22–2

Number of Persons Protected by Health Insurance Issued by U.S. Insurance Companies[3] (000s omitted)

Type of Coverage	Group Policies	Individual & Family Policies
Hospital Expense	86,824	26,996
Surgical Expense	88,327	16,072
Regular Medical Expense	88,886	11,384
Major Medical Expense	88,520	6,672

The success of group insurance is due to several factors that have already been discussed: lower premium rates, due to economies in underwriting and administration; favorable income tax treatment of premiums paid by employers; and availability of coverage to parts of the population who otherwise might not become covered. The success of group insurance shows that this type product is well-conceived, meeting a need of the market. However, as with any product in any industry, acceptance by the market is not automatic. Effort is required to locate prospects and to sell them.

Marketing may be defined broadly as the activities involved in moving products to markets through distribution channels. This definition holds for both group and individual insurance, as, indeed, it does for non-insurance products. But while the major functions apply to both group and individual insurance, the specific means of fulfilling those functions may be significantly different. A comparison of marketing group versus marketing individual insurance shows some similarities, but also some significant differences, between the two lines.

INDIVIDUAL VERSUS GROUP MARKETING

Several differences can be observed when comparing individual and group marketing. These include differences in the markets, the products offered, and the channels of distribution.

---

[3]Health Insurance Institute, *Source Book of Health Insurance Data, 1977–1978*, pp. 23, 25, 26, 27.

Markets

The market for individual insurance exists, quite simply, wherever there are individuals. Reaching that market and inducing a prospect to buy requires extensive selling efforts, usually by the agent, and often in the prospects' homes during evening or weekend hours.

Typically, the individual prospect has a limited knowledge of insurance and little or no motivation to buy. Most prospects would rather buy some material thing they can see and enjoy than an intangible. In addition, most people would rather buy something they view as a necessity or luxury, than buy insurance, which is associated with duty, obligation and sacrifice. Therefore, motivation to purchase insurance, particularly life insurance, must be generated by the agent. Generating such motivation is usually the major part of each selling situation.

In most cases, the individual prospect does not compare products among competing insurers. The buying decision is often based on personal qualities of the agent, whether, for example, the agent can establish a "trust" relationship with the prospect. Competition between companies for a specific prospect is the exception, rather than the rule. If a sale is not closed, the reason is likely to be that the prospect declined to make any purchase at all.

In the case of group insurance, the persons covered (the certificate holders) are not the true prospects for selling a group policy. Sales efforts are directed toward the head of each group (in most instances an employer). These prospects are found in more centralized locations, with national groups usually located in or near major cities. Thus, the market for group insurance is less dispersed than that for individual insurance.

In many situations, the group prospects are already motivated to purchase insurance, either through their own initiatives, through union requests for employee benefits, or because competitors already provide benefits to their employees. The sales challenge then is not one of building motivation, but of being selected from among competing insurers.

Many group prospects, particularly the larger ones, are very knowledgeable about the benefits they desire. Large employers and unions, for example, often have benefit specialists on their staffs; smaller ones may be equally knowledgeable by virtue of utilizing the services of brokers or consultants for advice. The group prospect, or a party acting for the prospect, may request proposals from several competing insurance companies. Selling is done during business hours, at the place of business. The final selection of the carrier is made primarily on the basis of such factors as cost, benefits, and service, rather than on personal qualities of the insurers' representatives.

These differences, however, tend to become blurred in certain circumstances. For example, the sale of a very large insurance policy to an individual has many of the features of the sale of group insurance. The prospect is already motivated to buy and is either knowledgeable about insurance or is being counseled by someone who is. Such a prospect may very well consider competitive proposals from two or more insurers.

Conversely, small-group prospects share many of the characteristics of the individual market. This group prospect is less knowledgeable about insurance. Because of the comparatively small amount of business involved, the sales effort may involve only the prospect and a single agent, excluding brokers and consultants. Part or all of the selling may be done outside normal business hours.

Products

The range of protection available to individuals—life insurance, health insurance, and pensions—is also available under group policies even though a given coverage may not be offered by every company. The preponderance of individual life insurance is ordinary insurance, while in group life and health coverages, one-year term insurance dominates. As a result, the premium rates for most individual life insurance policies are guaranteed for the life of the policy; premium rates for group life and health policies are usually guaranteed for only a single year. Premium rates of individual policies are not affected by individual experience, but rates for group policies, except for small groups, are influenced by the previous claim experience of the group through experience rating.

An individual purchaser of insurance selects one or a combination of plans from the portfolio of the insurer, with relatively little opportunity to modify specific plans. (However, considerable flexibility is usually available to the individual prospect through various options and riders.) Group prospects, particularly those representing larger groups, often negotiate with insurers over provisions of the group policy. In many cases, insurers respond to specifications requested by the group prospects or by their brokers. Thus, group policies, particularly for very large groups, can be tailor-made to suit the needs of the policy owner.

Channels of Distribution

The traditional method of marketing individual insurance has been through the use of soliciting agents, organized under either the branch office system or the general agency system. These agents also account for most sales involving small groups, with the policies being standard products of their companies.

With larger groups, the sales effort requires more specialized knowledge of group products. Policies for large groups are more complex, more flexible, and more subject to change than are individual policies. Relatively few soliciting agents specialize in group insurance. This specialization is usually supplied by brokers, who account for most group business as measured in premium dollars, by independent consultants, and by employees of insurance companies called group representatives.

THE GROUP INSURANCE MARKET

Entry into the group market offers potential increased profits for the insurer. Nonetheless, this entry is not without its difficulties. Successful entry into the group market depends upon the insurer's ability to resolve a number of complex problems. It also demands a clear understanding of the various segments of the group insurance market.

Entering The Group Market

The primary reason for a company's decision to enter the group market is increased profit. This increased profit can be achieved in several ways:

1. Additional profit or surplus resulting directly from the sale of group products;
2. Sales of other products and services resulting from contacts established through group business;
3. Increased sales of all lines through the establishment of a reputation of offering a full range of products and services;
4. Additional earnings for the company's agency force, resulting in reduced turnover and greater motivation; and
5. An increase in the company's asset base, resulting in more investment income and providing the means for supporting additional business.

A company entering the group market faces sizable costs. Both field and home office personnel must be recruited and/or trained in new products. Plans, rates and administrative procedures must be prepared. Decisions must be made as to the products to be marketed, the market segments to be prospected, and the territory to be served. Policy and certificate forms must be prepared and filed.

Company management must also consider the likely reaction of its agents to entering the group business. While the company may view group products as a potential source of additional income for the agents, many of the agents may view the group products as a threat to their individual line sales. The dominant position of brokers in large case business may also cause trepidation among agents. The ultimate success of the company in the group market will depend largely on how well it solves these problems.

Segments of the Market

The total market for group insurance is divided into segments based on the relationship between the policyowner and the persons insured.

INDIVIDUAL EMPLOYERS

By far the dominant segment of the group market is made up of individual employers providing coverage for their employees. In 1973, the latest year for which this information is available, this segment accounted for nearly 90 percent of all group life master policies, and for 86 percent of all group life insurance in force. The average coverage per employee was $11,645.[4] (So great is the dominance of this market segment that, in many writings, the terms "employer" and "employees" are used interchangeably with "policyowner" and "group members," respectively.) Although the employers are the policyowners and, hence, the buyers of the insurance, this market segment is strongly influenced by unions negotiating benefits for their members.

Because of its size, this market segment receives most of the marketing attention of insurance companies. Large cases involving over a hundred employees are usually sold through brokers. However, the employer-employee market segment also accounts for most of the group sales made by soliciting agents—sales to smaller employers.

MULTIPLE EMPLOYER TRUSTS

Small employers were long at a disadvantage in purchasing group insurance. Their premium rates were usually higher than for larger groups. One reason for this was that the sales and administrative expenses of the insurer were higher on a per-member basis because of the fewer group members. Another reason was that fluctuations in claim experience were often greater than with large groups, also because of the smaller numbers of people involved. In some states, legal restrictions prohibited sales to small groups altogether.

The potential small group market is significant to insurance companies; by one account, it may be as large as 20 million people.[5] One

---

[4]American Council of Life Insurance, *Life Insurance Fact Book, 1977* (Washington, D.C.), p. 29.

[5]Howard J. Bolnick, "The Regulation of Multiple Employer Trusts," *Best's Review—Life and Health Edition* (June 1978), p. 74.

means of reaching this market has been through the use of multiple employer trusts (METs). A multiple employer trust is a legal entity formed for the purpose of insuring participating small employers and their employees. It is not necessary that the participating small groups belong to the same industry. However, sales efforts are facilitated when the MET has the sponsorship or endorsement of a specific industry trade association or other similar organization.

In their early days, METs were considered to have a legal attraction: The insurer issued only a single policy to the trust, in the state of domicile of the trust. Eligible employers throughout the country could then join the trust and participate in the coverage, but the insurer was not required to file with the insurance authorities in each state from which business was drawn. This eased the administrative requirements of running such trusts, thus reducing premium rates. However, since the mid 1970s, there has been a trend toward state regulation of METs drawing business from within their jurisdictions, thus diminishing the earlier legal attraction.

Some METs are self-insured, but most are underwritten by insurance companies. An insurance company may participate in one of two basic ways: it may both underwrite and administer the trust, or it may only underwrite, with administration done by a third party, such as a trade association. In both cases, participating employees are assured of their benefits from the insurer. Sales efforts may be by the insurer or by the third-party administrator, or by both. When done by the insurer, selling is done by soliciting agents, since they are usually in the best position to reach the small employers.

UNION-EMPLOYER TRUSTS

Most states permit the sale of group policies to labor unions. However, federal law prohibits employers engaged in interstate commerce from making payments directly to a union for the purpose of providing group insurance. Joint union-employer trusts are, however, legal. A single trust may involve more than one union and more than one employer. The group insurance policy is issued to the trustees of the trust, who represent both the union(s) and the employer(s). Most sales to this market segment are made through brokers and insurance consultants.

DEBTOR-CREDITOR GROUPS

Credit life insurance is sold to lending institutions such as banks, credit unions, savings and loan associations, small loan companies, retail merchants, colleges, credit card companies and mutual funds. However, not every state accepts all these as eligible groups, and not all insurers pursue business from the full range of groups.

The marketing of credit life insurance involves three parties: the insurance company, the creditor, and the debtor. The "first sale" of the product is between the insurer and the creditor. This selling effort may involve soliciting agents, group representatives, or brokers. However, the role of the agent usually does not extend to preparing a formal proposal; that proposal is usually done by home office specialists.

The relationship between the creditor and the individual debtors comprises the "second sale," and poses a problem. In dealings with the insurance company, the representative of the creditor is typically a loan officer or credit manager, and is rarely a licensed insurance agent. Nonetheless, that person assumes part of the mantle of an agent. Indeed, to the debtor, the representative of the creditor may be an agent. This is a situation that places the insurance company in a potentially difficult spot.

Under the federal Truth-in-Lending regulations, the creditor is required to inform the debtor about the cost, type, and amount of coverage offered. Many insurers issue standard instructions to creditors, seeking to avoid anything representing solicitation or selling of insurance. The aim of this is to avoid misrepresentation and other selling abuses. (One study by the NAIC advocated the licensing of credit insurance policyowners as agents, but this approach has not gained much ground.)[6]

OTHER INTERMEDIARY GROUPS

Many states also permit the sale of group insurance to various groups of individuals through an intermediary. Examples of such groups include:

Professional associations (accountants, physicians),
Bank depositors,
Credit card holders,
Customer groups (utility or oil company customers), and
National Guard units.

The process of selling to this market segment is similar to that of employer-employee groups. The purchaser is usually an officer of the intermediary, often acting with approval of its board of directors. However, subsequent enrollment of group members differs because the individual members are usually dispersed. In these groups, the intermediary rarely has the centralized focus of an employer. Enrollment is generally performed by mail after solicitation by the intermediary.

---

[6]National Association of Insurance Commissioners, *A Background Study of the Regulation of Credit Life and Disability Insurance* (Milwaukee, 1970).

ORGANIZATION OF MARKETING FUNCTIONS

In the marketing of group insurance, as with the marketing of all other lines of business, there is no one "right" form of organization. While the basic functions of moving products to markets through distribution channels apply to all insurers, the organization and assignment of these functions vary from company to company.

Field Organization

In selling group insurance, an insurance company may use its soliciting agents, independent brokers and consultants, supported by its group representatives. One common method is to have the group representative work directly with agents, brokers, and consultants on new prospects, but work directly with the policyowner after the policy has been installed.

AGENTS

Agents selling group insurance have been most successful with small cases. A 1976 survey by Life Insurance Marketing and Research Association (LIMRA) showed that, in responding companies, 90 percent of small-case (2 to 49 members) business was written by career agents.[7] Policies for small groups are generally standard within a company, and typically contain fewer complexities than do policies designed for large cases. Agents here have the advantage of being close to prospects, whereas group representatives and specialized group brokers and consultants cannot always find enough business to justify their locating in sparsely settled areas.

In a typical sales situation, the agent locates the prospect and attempts to develop a degree of interest. If standard small group products are appropriate, the agent may proceed directly to a sales proposal. Otherwise, the agent may contact a group representative for advice and assistance in selling a plan. The agent's motivation comes not only from compensation from sale of the group product, but also from potential sales of individual insurance to the prospect.

GROUP OFFICES AND GROUP REPRESENTATIVES

Group offices are most insurance companies' basic organizational units for marketing group insurance. The offices are typically located

---

[7]From a paper presented by Donald O. Nelson for the panel on "Obtaining Realistic Persistency Objectives on Small Group Cases," 1st Group Marketing Conference of Life Insurance Marketing and Research Association at Hartford, Connecticut, September 9, 1976.

in large cities, and are staffed by one or more group representatives, with clerical personnel. Group offices are responsible for sales and service of group insurance within an assigned territory. If the company's group business is comparatively small, the manager of each office may report directly to the home office. More commonly, office managers report to regional group managers.

In marketing group insurance, group representatives work both individually and with agents, brokers and consultants. Major activities include developing prospects; preparing field group proposals; submitting case data to the home office for preparation there of proposals; presenting proposals to prospects or to their representatives; assisting in the enrollment of new group cases; and keeping the home office informed of local competitive developments. Group representatives usually specialize in one of two broad areas: group life and health insurance or group pension plans.

In servicing policies, group representatives work with new policyowners in establishing administrative procedures, make periodic calls upon policyowners, assist in installing premium rate increases, and work generally toward conserving the business. In some companies, group representatives are responsible for both sales and service functions; in others, the representatives specialize in one or the other.

BROKERS

Most new group business, as measured in terms of dollars, is sold through brokers, who may be divided into three categories. All-lines brokers typically do most of their business in property-liability insurance, using that customer base as a source of life business. These brokers usually do not specialize in life insurance; their motivation to sell life insurance may be at least partly to prevent other brokers from gaining access to their customers.

Brokerage firms that do specialize in various types of insurance, such as group life insurance, are often termed independent brokers. The independent broker in many cases is a former soliciting agent who was highly successful. These brokers usually work with clients whose operations are in the same territory as the broker.

Group buyers whose operations are widespread, such as national employers, usually are served by national brokers. These national brokers specialize primarily in employee benefit packages. They advise their clients on all types of coverages, and may deal with property-casualty products also.

Brokers of all types provide advice on plan design, costs, regulatory requirements, administration and claim procedures, periodic reviews of benefits, and communications with individual group members about the plan. During the sales process, the broker represents the client with competitive insurers. Working with the employer, the broker prepares a preliminary plan design and submits it to several insurers. The insurers then present their proposals to the broker for review and, often, revisions. Finally, the broker makes recommendations to the employer regarding selection of an insurer.

Brokers are also active during renewal of plans. In large cases, the plans are usually customized to the needs of the buyer. Initially, the competing proposals may be compared in terms of cost and benefits. However, after several years have elapsed, the policyowner may not be certain that the best combination of cost and benefits is being obtained. The broker can then be used again to put the coverage up for competitive bidding. Transfers from one carrier to another are common. By one estimate, 90 to 95 percent of the industry's new group business represents transfers from one carrier to another.[8] Obtaining lower premium rates is not the only reason why a policyowner changes carriers. Other reasons include dissatisfaction with service received and desire for a coverage not offered by the carrier.

CONSULTANTS

Group insurance consultants typically provide the same services to policyowners as do brokers. The distinction between consultants and brokers, such as it is, usually lies in the method of compensation. Brokers usually receive a commission from the insurance company, the amount of which is included as a factor in calculating premium rates. Consultants are most often paid by the purchaser of the insurance, generally on a fee basis. Often the services provided by the consultants include actuarial support as well.

Home Office Organization

If group business constitutes only a very small portion of a company's total business, group insurance functions may be established as subunits within such departments as marketing, underwriting and policyowner service. However, when group becomes a significant part of the total business, most companies find it desirable to organize a separate department for performing nearly all functions pertaining to that line.

There are other considerations that influence the form of organization. A company doing a large amount of business through brokers may well establish an organizational unit for those activities. A company specializing in a certain type of group insurance, such as pensions, or in a certain market segment, such as debtor-creditor, is likely to have corresponding specialization in its organization.

---

[8]From a paper presented by R. W. Stivers for the "Panel on Profitability," 1st Group Marketing Conference of Life Insurance Marketing and Research Association at Hartford, Connecticut, September 9, 1976.

A typical organization of a group insurance department is shown in Figure 22–3. A notable point is that in this organization, as in many companies, there is no single group marketing unit. Rather, the functions of group marketing are divided among various units in the department. Actual sales efforts, such as contacting prospects and preparing proposals, comes under field operations. The relative importance of the three subunits—group field offices, agents, and brokers—varies according to their importance as distributors of the company's products. The group insurance department in the home office exercises line authority only over the group field offices. Soliciting agents invariably are in a department called agency or individual sales. Brokers, of course, are independent business people not subject to direct control by insurance companies.

Whatever the method of developing the prospects, the actuarial and group underwriting departments are important to the sales negotiations. The actuarial area determines the manual rates for all benefits, the adequacy of policy reserves and the general profitability expected of the group line of business. The underwriting department then uses these guidelines to determine adequate premium rates for specific policies. In addition, the underwriting department must be satisfied that the terms of the proposed contract do not encourage antiselection or abuse before the carrier proceeds with the sale.

The sales promotion unit provides sales material, such as brochures and booklets, used as part of the sales effort. On a staff level, its activities include planning and budgeting, market research and measurement, and other functions related to management of the department. Noticeable by its absence from this organization chart is the essential function of advertising. This is because, in most companies, advertising of all product lines is centralized, sometimes within the marketing department, but often as a separate entity, possibly combined with public relations. There are several reasons for this separation of advertising from product line departments to a single unit: better coordination of advertising schedules and production; economies through larger purchases of media space and time; and coordination of product advertising with more general institutional advertising and with other public relations activities.

In its relations with other departments, the group department is in many respects similar to the individual insurance department. The group department has the same need for communication with the legal, medical, accounting and administrative services departments as does individual insurance. However, it differs from the individual insurance department in its interactions with such units as investments. More interaction is necessary because the company's investment performance may be very important in selling pensions (or other products) when done through separate accounts. Purchasers of group pensions are likely to compare the earnings performances of competing insurers as one part of the buying decision.

FIGURE 22-3
Organization of Group Insurance Department

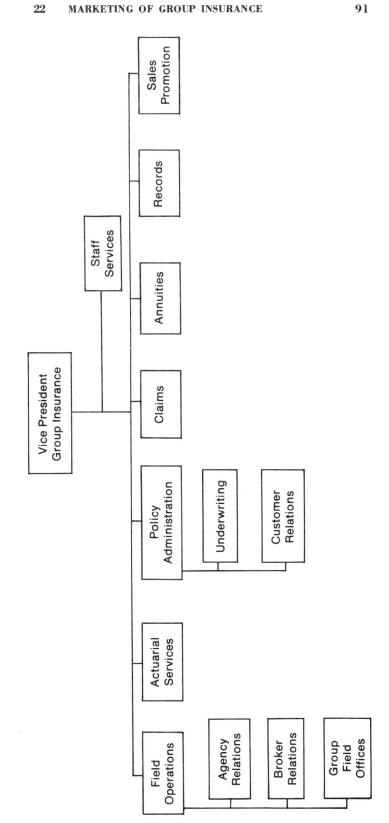

Data processing is another function important to group marketing. In order to respond quickly and efficiently to prospects' requests for proposals, many insurance companies have computerized the preparation of small case proposals. The company representative, usually a soliciting agent, codes a minimum amount of data. The computer produces one or more policy plans for consideration by the small group prospect. With larger cases, group representatives use the computer to analyze various combinations of costs and benefits that can be offered to the prospect. The advantages of computerized processing for at least part of this process lies in the speed of response plus, for small cases, the economy. For large cases, the advantage lies in the flexibility of plan design that is possible.

THE SALES PROCESS

The sales process is a continuing one. If this process is to be successful, attention must be paid not only to the initial encounters with the prospective policyowner, but also to the introduction of the plan to those individuals who will be insured by its provisions.

Presales Activities

A series of interrelated activities are involved in the presales process: prospecting for new clients, preparation and presentation of a proposal, and solicitation and enrollment of group members.

PROSPECTING

Group insurance business can be developed in several different ways: through referrals, by extension of benefits in insurance already being provided to a prospect, through social meetings, or simply through "cold calls." Agents and brokers may use any of these methods in an effort to generate new business. Group representatives usually prospect for new clients through agents and brokers.

Prospecting through agents and small brokers usually requires that the group representative take time to train them in group insurance, establish a continuing relationship, and motivate them to prospect for group insurance. The situation is different when prospecting through large brokers. These persons are likely to be well versed in group products. The task of the group representative then becomes one of demonstrating the advantages of the group products of his or her company. Establishing and maintaining a good relation with the broker is important, in order to obtain prospects from the broker.

PREPARING THE PROPOSAL

The first step in the process of preparing any group insurance proposal is obtaining data necessary for making an underwriting decision. This information includes data on group members, such as age, sex, salary, occupation, location, and additional information on dependents of each member. If there is already a group plan in force, a description of that plan, plus its claim experience is included.

Preparation of the proposal involves designing the plan of benefits, underwriting the prospect, and calculating the premium rates. With small cases, the proposals will be for standard products offered by the insurer. With larger cases, the plan of benefits is likely to be specified by the prospect or broker involved. Underwriting and rate calculation is usually done in the insurer's home office; computerized processing of proposal data is common.

Presentation of the proposal varies. Group representatives naturally prefer to make the presentation directly to the prospect, and this is frequently done, particularly when small cases are involved. However, when a broker or consultant is involved, the presentation must often be made to that representative of the buyer. In either case, there may be further negotiation on the plan design, with the insurance company revising its proposal several times.

Evaluation of the proposal and selection of a carrier are based on several factors: plan benefits; premium rates; facilities of the carrier for administration and claims processing; reputation and expertise of the carrier; and, for large policies, projected retention. Retention refers to the excess of premiums over claims plus dividends; in other words, the amount the insurer retains to cover all its administrative expenses on the policy. The retention figure is sometimes used by prospects as a basis for comparing alternative proposals. However, the retention is affected by a number of factors, such as the quality of service provided by the carrier or reserve evaluation methods. Evaluation of competing proposals, therefore, calls for careful attention to these underlying factors.

Post-Sale Activities

In one sense, the sale of a group policy is completed when the prospect selects an insurer, and agrees to the provisions of the proposed contract. However, the sale can fall through if enrollment of group members fails to come up to minimum participation established either by legal regulations or by the carrier's underwriters. So, while solicitation and enrollment of group members is customarily regarded as a post-sale activity, it nonetheless represents a selling effort in its own right, one aimed not at the policyowner, but at the eligible members.

SOLICITATION OF GROUP MEMBERS

The method of soliciting enrollments depends on the nature of the group, but always involves the policyowner. Normally, the insurance company prepares the solicitation materials: letters, plan booklets, and even audio-visual presentations. Where large numbers of eligible members are available in centralized locations, as with employee groups, the insurance company may hold meetings where group representatives explain the plan and answer questions.

If the group consists of widely dispersed subgroups, such as employers in a multiple employer trust, the company may use both group representatives and agents to contact individual employers. When the group consists of dispersed individuals, such as members of a professional association, personal contact is not feasible, since the low premium rates of group insurance preclude such costs. In such cases, solicitation of eligible members is done through the mail.

ENROLLMENT OF GROUP MEMBERS

The enrollment of members follows closely after the solicitation activities. If solicitation involves a meeting and presentation to eligible members, enrollment cards are usually available immediately for signing. When the group consists of employees, supervisory personnel are often used to follow up on enrollments. When solicitation is made by mail, enrollment forms are included at the same time.

Some cases, such as those written for certain associations or alumni groups, involve a certain amount of individual underwriting beyond the underwriting for the group as a whole to prevent antiselection. When this is the case, individual enrollments are accompanied by questionnaires, to be completed by the enrollees. The group underwriters then decide on each individual application for enrollment.

INSTALLATION OF THE CONTRACT

When the enrollment procedure is completed, the home office calculates final premium rates, based on enrollments, and issues the master contract and the certificates for the individuals insured. Installation of the contract involves training of the policyowner's staff in administrative, billing and claims procedures, and issuance of descriptive materials to enrolled persons. These activities usually involve all parties concerned: policyowner, group representative, and any agents, broker, or consultant who had been involved. Effective installation is an important factor to the ultimate success of the plan.

COMPENSATION FOR GROUP SALES

Most insurance companies serving the group market operate on the basis of group representatives working through producing sources, who consist of soliciting agents, brokers and consultants. Compensation of all these persons is a combination of commissions, bonuses and salaries.

Commissions

In the insurance industry, producers of all lines of business are commonly compensated by commissions. In group insurance, the major producers are brokers, followed by agents. Commission payments account for the largest part of payment for new group business. In the case of agents, commission terms may be included in the agent's contract with the company, or they may be set as each case arises. Commission terms with brokers are most often set for each case. The two components of commission terms are the *rate* and the *schedule* of the commissions.

Commission rates are nearly always lower for group insurance business than for individual sales. This is due to several characteristics of group business, as contrasted to individual:

1. The dollar amount of premiums per group policy is usually much higher than for an individual policy. While not suggesting that selling group business is easy, the amount of selling time required usually yields a much higher amount of premium income than would be the situation in selling individual insurance;
2. The producer of group business usually receives considerable assistance from a group representative and from home office personnel, more so than does an agent in an individual sales effort;
3. Competition for each group sale is usually high, with several insurers involved. While higher commission rates might be an added motivating factor to brokers and agents, they would likely be counterproductive in such a competitive environment;
4. Most buyers of group insurance are conscious of price, and are aware of the effect of the commission rate on the cost of insurance (The Federal Welfare and Pension Plans Disclosure Act (Public Law 85-836) requires insurers to disclose the identities of persons receiving commissions, and the amounts of those commissions); and
5. Group policies require more continuing service in such areas as membership changes and experience ratings than do individual policies. This adds to the cost of group policies during their in-force periods; more so than for individual policies on which premium rates remain unchanged.

COMMISSIONS FOR REGULAR GROUPS

Total commissions consist of *selling* commissions and *service* commissions. Selling commissions are intended to compensate for initial solicitation of the prospect; service commissions compensate

the producer for preparing and presenting the proposal, and for securing the application and the initial premium payment. The service
commission component of the total commission is discontinued if the
agent or broker loses involvement with the policyowner.

The purchaser of group insurance has considerable influence in
determining just who is to receive commissions from the business. In
some instances the purchaser provides a so-called "agent of record
letter" to an agent or broker, who may then request quotations from
several insurers. In other instances, the determination by the purchaser may be made later in the sales process. Lacking any other
indication, most insurers recognize whoever obtains the signed application as the producer entitled to commissions.

Commission schedules specify the formula by which commissions will be paid to the producer. There are two basic types of
commission schedules for group insurance: standard and level. Under
a standard commission schedule (such as shown in Figure 22–4), the
first-year commission rate is higher than that (or those) of subsequent
years. This approach is similar to that commonly used in compensating for the sale of individual insurance. On the other hand, a level
commission schedule (Figure 22–5) provides the same scale for both
the first year and renewal years. The two scales are designed to
provide the same amount of commissions over a ten-year period
(sometimes longer) for a given amount of premium. Hence, assuming
no change in the amount of annual premiums paid by the group
policyowner, there should be no difference in the total commissions
received by the producer, after allowance for interest.

FIGURE 22–4
Standard Group Commission Schedule

Annual Premium Volume	Commission Rate First Year	Commission Rate Renewals
$ 0–$ 1,000	20.0%	5.00%
1,001– 5,000	20.0	3.00
5,001– 10,000	15.0	1.50
10,001– 20,000	12.5	1.50
20,001– 30,000	10.0	1.50
30,001– 50,000	5.0	1.50
50,001– 250,000	2.5	1.00
250,001– 500,000	1.0	0.50
500,001– 2,500,000	0.5	0.25
Over $2,500,000	0.1	0.10

Since the producer usually has the option of choosing either
commission schedule (exceptions are cited shortly), the choice usually
depends on personal factors. A new producer, who has not yet built up

FIGURE 22–5
Level Group Commission Schedule

Annual Premium Volume	Annual Commission Rate
$ 0–$ 1,000	6.50%
1,001– 5,000	4.70
5,001– 10,000	2.85
10,001– 20,000	2.60
20,001– 30,000	2.35
30,001– 50,000	1.85
50,001– 250,000	1.15
250,001– 500,000	0.55
500,001– 2,500,000	0.25
Over $2,500,000	0.10

a book of renewal commissions, may well prefer the standard schedule, which provides higher first-year commissions. On the other hand, a producer with a large amount of renewal commissions may prefer the level schedule, to avoid higher income tax rates in the current year.

Choice of a commission schedule is also influenced by expectations about future group premium volume. As noted above, if the annual premium volume is constant, there is no eventual difference (after allowing for interest) between the two types of schedules. However, it is not common for annual premium volume to remain constant over the life of the policy. More often than not, premium volume increases. Such increases result from any of three factors: increases in the size of the group; increases in plan benefits; and increases in premium rates as a result of inflation or other reasons. Because of this, it is often advantageous to the producer to choose commissions under the level schedule. This schedule provides for higher commission rates during renewal years, which will translate into additional commission income because of increased annual premiums.

In contrast, if declining premium volume is anticipated, the producer would benefit from selecting payment of commissions under the standard commission schedule. That schedule would apply the higher first-year commission rate to the first-year premium income, which would be expected to be the largest annual income. However, as a safeguard, insurance companies normally require the level commission schedule in cases where a higher than normal probability of lapse is anticipated. Such cases include: (1) business transferred from another carrier; (2) reinstated cases; and (3) associations in which individual participants pay all the premiums.

The two commission schedules in Figures 22–4 and 22–5 show typical commission rates for group term life insurance and group health insurance. Commission rates for group permanent life insurance are usually calculated differently, in recognition of the fact that such policies compete in a market where protection is sold on an individual basis. Insurance companies have felt that, in order to successfully market group permanent life insurance, they must provide producers with greater incentive than is offered by the comparatively low group commission rates.

COMMISSIONS FOR SMALL GROUPS

Commission rates on small-group business (typically, groups of fewer than twenty-five members) are higher than those for regular groups. This reflects several characteristics of small group business: plans are usually simpler and involve less negotiating than regular group plans; soliciting agents require less assistance from group representatives during the sales process; the lower premium volume calls for higher commission rates if producers are to be motivated to sell small group business.

As with regular group commissions, small-group commission rates are generally graded downward as premium volume increases. The grading often consists of only a few steps, due to the smaller amount of premium volume expected from small groups. Most companies provide for both standard and level commission schedules, as in regular group. From the point of view of the producer, there is little likelihood of significant increase in the size of a small case; therefore, there is less incentive to select a level commission schedule. Again, however, the companies often require payment under the level schedule when the probability of lapse is higher than normal.

OTHER FORMS OF COMPENSATION

Most group representatives are paid a basic salary, plus bonuses based on production and on servicing of existing business. In some companies, group representatives also are paid a nominal override on agents' group production, in recognition of the training and assistance they provide the agents. The amount of compensation paid to group representatives does not directly affect commission rates paid to agents and brokers.

As noted earlier, group insurance consultants are compensated by the purchaser of insurance, not by the insurance company. This compensation is generally in the form of fees, although some consultants receive a commission as well from the purchaser.

SELF-INSURANCE

The purchase of insurance protection of any sort is a transaction involving both a benefit and a cost to the buyer. The benefit is the transfer of a stated risk to the insurer, which may or may not eventually result in payments from the insurer to the policyowner or beneficiary. The cost to the buyer is the premium, the calculation of which includes provision to cover administrative expenses of the insurer. In every instance, an alternative to the purchase of insurance is acceptance of the risk of loss. In business, this is known as "self-insurance."

Reasons for Self-Insurance

The term "self-insurance" is often a misnomer since there is not necessarily any provision for insurance protection. Rather, self-insurance implies the acceptance of risk, rather than its transfer to another party. Large businesses have long engaged in self-insuring of some property-liability risks. For example, a company owning many dispersed retail outlets might self-insure against fire losses. Risk managers in such companies would carefully analyze the potential losses, just as would actuaries in an insurance company.

In recent years, the growth of employee benefits, and their attendant costs, have led many employers to consider a degree of self-insurance of employee benefits. The impetus for this came from two factors included in the cost of purchasing insurance protection: state premium taxes and insurer reserves.

The taxes levied by states on premium receipts of insurance companies have ranged as high as 4 percent. Such taxes represent an operating expense of the insurers, one that is reflected in the calculation of premium rates. An employer who, in one way or another, self-insures employee benefits incurs no such expense. Even though the employer might assume the same risk as the insurer, insofar as the benefits are concerned, the cost is somewhat less. (The gain is not equal to the amount of the premium taxes paid because the employer treats total premiums as a taxable deduction.)

Though this premium advantage still exists to some companies following self-insurance, several states have begun to develop methods of acquiring equivalent income, such as special taxes imposed on self-insurers, based on benefit payments made to employees. Today, then, avoidance of the cost of premium taxes remains an important advantage of self-insuring. However, its future is uncertain.

The second major advantage of self-insuring was the avoidance of the insurer's cost of establishing policy reserve liabilities. Many employers had chosen the route of "pay as you go" on employee benefit plans. That is, as claims came due, they were paid out of current earnings. There was no policy reserve, such as would be maintained by an insurance company. Some self-insurers did establish reserves to cover benefit liabilities; these firms benefited by the investment income earned by the amount in the reserve but the rate of return might well have been less than could have been earned through reinvestment in the business.

The advantages of self-insurance have been considerably lessened in recent years. ERISA legislation now requires employers to fund their benefit liabilities, and insurance companies now usually allow interest earnings to the policyowner on reserves held by the insurer. Nonetheless, large employers are looking more closely at the feasibility of self-insuring parts of their benefit plans.

For self-insurance to be economically feasible to an employer, two conditions must be present. First, there must be a large number of employees in the group. Large numbers are necessary in order to effectively spread the risk, and also to reduce the average expense per person for various administrative costs. Second, the risks assumed should have a high claim frequency coupled with a low claim amount. This would preclude self-insuring such risks as death and accidental death and dismemberment, because they involve a liability that is substantial when compared to the relatively low premium rates charged by insurers. By contrast, basic medical and hospital benefits and short-term disability benefits would be appropriate for self-insurance. It is, in fact, in these areas that most examples of employer self-insuring of benefits have occurred.

The reaction of private insurance companies to self-insurance of benefits has taken several forms. So-called *minimum premium* or excess risk plans provide that the employer self-insures most of the benefits; the insurance company's obligation is limited to major fluctuations in benefit costs. *Delayed premium* payment plans permit the employer to retain cash for longer periods of time before premium payments become due. Lastly, insurance companies have responded to self-insurance with administrative services only (ASO) contracts.

ASO Contracts

Under Administrative Service Only contracts, an insurance company provides the employer with specified administrative services, usually including claim processing. There is no underwriting of the plan by the insurer; the employer is liable for benefits due employees. If reserves are established by the employer, such as for pensions, they are usually under the control of a trustee.

The services to be performed by the insurer are specified in the contract between the plan sponsor and the insurance company. Among the services that may be purchased are: plan design, actuarial calculations, claim processing, statistical reports, plan booklets and other communications to employees, conversion to insurance coverage upon employee termination of employment, investment advice, and preparation of governmental reports. While the definition of the services to be performed is the most important part of an ASO contract, that agreement also specifies the authority and responsibility of the administrator, the procedures to be employed in the relationship between the parties, the duration of the contract, and provisions for contract termination and, in case of dispute, for arbitration.

The charters of some insurance companies prohibit their engaging in ASO services. Those companies that do provide ASO services have minimum conditions that the group must meet for such a contract. Minimum group criteria are expressed in various ways. Three examples of minimum requirements are: $500,000 annual premiums; $200,000 annual claims; 500 group members. Most insurance companies will not provide ASO services for health benefits unless they underwrite the employer's group life plan.

BENEFITS AND DRAWBACKS FOR SELF-INSURERS

ASO contracts have benefits and drawbacks for both the employer and the insurance company. Some of these benefits and drawbacks are outlined below.

Benefits to the self-insured employer include:

1. State premium taxes are avoided, thereby reducing one cost of insurance;
2. The employer has greater control over cash, because there is no obligation for payment of regular insurance premiums;
3. The employer may be able to earn a return on funds allocated to a reserve that is higher than would be returned by an insurer who invested the same funds;
4. Sales commissions of insured plans are avoided, further reducing the cost of coverage; and
5. The employer may have greater control of plan design, being able to provide coverages that may not be available from an insurer.

The decision to self-insure also entails certain risks and drawbacks. These include:

1. The employer assumes a liability for benefits that is uncertain and, in the absence of a stop-loss provision in the contract, that is also open-ended;
2. Cash flow requirements are uncertain and irregular, complicating the process of financial planning;
3. Payments to reserves are not deductible expenses unless the reserves are trusteed;
4. The employer incurs a legal liability for payment of benefits, a liability that would otherwise be borne by the insurer; and
5. Unions may resist a situation whereby the employer is solely responsible for ensuring ultimate payment of benefits gained through collective bargaining, preferring instead an insurance

company whose operations are regulated and whose benefit payments are guaranteed.

BENEFITS AND DRAWBACKS TO INSURANCE COMPANIES

Advantages of the ASO contract to the insurance carrier include:

1. The company is able to respond to a competitive situation, in which an employer who wants ASO services could turn to other sources;
2. The insurer is able to profitably market its administrative and data processing capabilities, possibly enjoying the economies of scale of large computer systems;
3. The company presents itself to both the industry and to its own sales force as offering a wider range of services to the market;
4. The insurer is able to retain group life business with the self-insurer, business that would otherwise move to the competitor providing ASO services; and
5. The insurer maintains a presence in the employer's company, which may lead to additional business.

ASO contracts are, however, not without their disadvantages to carriers. These drawbacks include:

1. Plan members may not understand the limited role of the insurer in the plan, and may impute to the insurer responsibilities that actually are those of the self-insurer;
2. The insurer usually faces start-up costs, in terms of new systems, procedures, forms and training;
3. Acting as "agent" of the self-insurer generates a new legal relationship, with few legal precedents to guide the actions of the insurer in case of disputes with the employer;
4. The insurer's public image may suffer from inability of the self-insurer to meet benefit obligations; and
5. Fostering self-insurance is intrinsically at odds with the company's primary product lines.

CHARGING FOR ASO SERVICES

Insurance companies charge for ASO services in a variety of ways, including:

1. A percentage of the amount of claims paid;
2. Cost-plus-profit charge for use of personnel time and materials;
3. A fixed charge per claim check processed;
4. A flat charge per member plus a percentage of the amount of claims paid;

5. A fixed charge for the employer; and
6. A fixed charge per group member.

In general, insurance companies regard income from ASO contracts as being fees for services rendered, on which neither premium taxes nor commissions are paid. In lieu of commissions, service fees or finder's fees are paid to sales personnel. However, most ASO contracts specify that if states retroactively levy premium taxes against the insurance companies' ASO income, the expense must be borne by the plan sponsor.

SERVICING ASO CONTRACTS

Four major functional areas are involved in servicing typical ASO contracts: field sales, underwriting, administration, and claims.

Field sales is involved in:

1. Consulting with employers over installation of the ASO contract;
2. Negotiating charges, both initially and at time of renewal;
3. Periodically reviewing claim experience with the employer;
4. Installing new and revised plans; and
5. Resolving administrative problems that arise.

Underwriting is involved in:

1. Establishing the charge for the ASO services;
2. Analyzing the effects of plan changes;
3. Advising on the cost effects to the plan of changes in the cost and utilization of health care; and
4. Informing the plan sponsor of the amount of incomplete and unreported claims at the end of the year.

Administration is responsible for:

1. Preparing and issuing ASO contracts and amendments;
2. Issuing employee booklets and subsequent communications; and
3. Providing accounting instructions to the plan sponsor.

Claims is involved in:

1. Preparing claim forms and instructions for claimants and for claim personnel;
2. Evaluating claims and either paying or denying them;
3. Arranging for investigation of selected claims;

4. Auditing the claim process;
5. Maintaining claim records;
6. Reporting claim payments to the Internal Revenue Service as required for tax collection purposes.

Insurance companies are divided in their approach to legal suits brought by claimants because of rejected claims or disputed amounts of claims. Some insurers undertake the defense of such suits, as one of the services available to the plan sponsor. Other insurers refuse to do that, on the basis that the sponsor is responsible for legal suits based on questionable and disputed claims.

SUMMARY

This chapter has discussed the marketing of group insurance. After outlining the markets, products, and distribution channels of group insurance, the chapter detailed the various ways in which marketing functions are organized. An explanation of the sales process and of the methods of compensating group sales personnel followed. Finally, the reasons for and nature of Administrative Services Only contracts were analyzed.

CHAPTER 23

INSTALLATION OF GROUP PLANS

INTRODUCTION

Once the sale of a group insurance plan has been made, the master group application completed and signed, a binder check (usually for the first month's premium) obtained, and the effective date of the new plan established, it is necessary to proceed with the installation of the group plan.

This chapter examines the process of installing group plans. It begins by outlining the essential components of the installation process, then goes on to describe the enrollment process itself. The role of the group representative and the insurer's home office involvement are considered. The chapter concludes with a brief discussion of the special procedures needed if the contract involves the dual option or an ASO arrangement.

THE INSTALLATION PROCESS

Installation of the plan requires that both the insurer and the policyowner carry out specific responsibilities as described below:

1. The group insurance carrier prints booklet-certificates describing details of the plan for the employees. If the booklet-certificates are not to be used for the initial installation activities of the plan, then a summary description of the plan's benefits will be printed instead.
2. The group policyowner arranges to obtain completed and signed application/enrollment cards from all eligible employees. If any part of the cost of the plan is to be paid by the employee, then a waiver card will usually be obtained from any employee not wishing to participate in the contributory

by
GEORGE M. HIDER, *Vice President, Pilot Life Insurance Company, Greensboro, North Carolina*

    coverages of the plan. If there are noncontributory coverages, an enrollment card will also be obtained from eligible employees.

3. The group field representative delivers administrative supplies and claim forms to the person designated by the employer to act as the employer-policyowner contact in the organization. An administration and claim guide is also delivered to that person. At that time the group field representative goes over all of the administrative details of the plan that involve action by the employer's representative. If the case is to be administered by the home office of the insurance carrier, the initial premium statement and the list of insureds prepared by the carrier are also delivered to the employer's representative.

4. The group field representative sends the completed enrollment cards to the home office of the carrier. There they are checked for completeness and, in the case of contributory coverages, for assurance that necessary minimum enrollment participation has been obtained from eligible employees of the group. The enrollment cards and the other documentation of details of the plan and the original proposal rates quoted are then referred to the group underwriting department at the carrier's home office, or to the appropriate department within the group department responsible for such matters. Age, sex, earnings, and amounts of group life insurance are taken into account by the group underwriting department in recalculating the premium rates for the case.

5. The underwriting department passes the enrollment cards to the new business unit or its equivalent if the case is to be administered and billed by the home office of the carrier. This occurs after the group underwriting department has made final determination of premium rates.

Enrollment

    The actual enrollment procedures encompass the preparation and printing of various explanatory materials and the canvass of employees. Since most newly sold group insurance plans represent the transfer of business from one insurance carrier to another, this chapter discusses the various procedures in that light.

EXPLANATORY MATERIALS

    In recent years, insurance companies have almost universally adopted a combined booklet-certificate. This document serves a dual purpose. It acts as an explanatory document for the group plan when distributed to employees prior to the enrollment procedure. Once the insurance has become effective on the individual employee, the booklet-certificate then becomes the legal and formal evidence of the employee's insurance in its role as a certificate.

The availability of a booklet-certificate for information purposes prior to the general enrollment depends on when the master application is signed in relation to the effective date of the plan, since the information contained in it should accurately reflect the benefits and other details of the final plan mutually agreed upon by the employer and the new insurance carrier. Not infrequently there is insufficient time for the booklet-certificate to be available for the general enrollment. In those circumstances, a brief summary of benefits is printed for distribution to employees at or prior to the general enrollment process. Whenever the complex and detailed language of an insurance document is summarized, extreme care must be taken to make sure that the summary does not mislead the employee.

THE PURPOSE OF NEW ENROLLMENT CARDS

The completion of new enrollment/application cards on the new carrier's forms is customary when a change of carriers takes place. Exceptions are sometimes made to this practice, but there are many reasons why it is advisable to have new cards prepared. These include:

1. An enrollment/application card contains reference to payroll deduction authorization by the employee with regard to the employee's share, if any, of the cost of the benefits furnished under a plan underwritten by a specific carrier. Unless the policyowner retains a separate payroll deduction authorization card as evidence of the employee's authorization for payroll deduction, it is certainly questionable whether continuing use of the enrollment card secured by the previous carrier represents a proper authorization for payroll deductions under the new plan.

2. If the case is to be administered by the home office of the new carrier, the format of the card may not be suitable as a data processing entry source document for the new carrier. The only alternative in such circumstances is for someone, most likely a person in the new carrier's field office or home office, to copy the data from the old cards onto the new carrier's cards.

3. It gives the employee an opportunity to consider updating his or her beneficiary designation if life insurance or accidental death and dismemberment insurance is involved in the plan.

4. It serves as an additional reminder to the employees of what the employer is doing for them in providing group insurance benefits.

5. It gives employees who were late applicants for dependent coverage under the previous plan and who were unable to

secure this coverage, or who may have overlooked adding
dependent coverage, the opportunity to review their needs and
wishes with regard to coverage on their dependents.

6. It furnishes the new carrier with up-to-date data on which to
establish correct records, in a format suitable to the carrier's
data entry source document needs.

7. It has the potential of securing a higher percentage participation of eligible employees in coverages where the employee
contributes a portion of the cost.

However, if the employer is unwilling or unable to make the
opportunity available for the new insurance carrier to obtain new
enrollment cards on its forms from eligible employees in the group, the
insurer should suggest to the employer that a notice be posted or
circulated to employees stating that a change of insurance carriers is
pending, and reminding them that they should review their current
beneficiary designations for their life and accidental death and dismemberment insurance. If they wish to make a change, the notice
should give them the name of the person in the employer's organization from whom they can secure a proper form for that purpose by a
given deadline date. If there are contributory coverages in the new
plan, employees who had not enrolled in the previous plan should be
reminded of the deadline for enrolling in the new plan.

USES OF ENROLLMENT CARDS

The enrollment/application card clearly serves a number of necessary purposes for the employer, the carrier, and the employee.

In noncontributory plans, the enrollment card becomes a record
card rather than an application. Because the eligible employee in such
cases, provided the employee is actively at work, is automatically
insured, securing a new enrollment card in such circumstances may
seem unnecessary. However, the designation of a beneficiary on the
enrollment card signed by the employee has an obvious legal significance. Where there is a mixture of noncontributory and contributory coverages in a plan, it is still necessary for the employee to take a
positive step to enroll for the contributory coverages if the employee
wishes to participate under the new plan. An example of this mixture
could be where the employer pays the entire cost of the employee's
personal coverages and contributes only a part or none of the cost of
coverage on dependents. Another example is where an employer may
pay all of the cost of the life insurance on the employee, but only a part
of the cost of the health coverages. In the latter instance, since it is
usually the practice of carriers to require that the employee coverages
be available as a package to the employee, positive application by the
employee is necessary.

In the case of contributory coverages, the carrier often suggests
that the employer have employees who are not interested in obtaining

coverage sign a "waiver" card. Typically, the employee certifies that he or she has been given the opportunity to participate in the plan and has declined to do so. The card also states that should the employee later decide to participate in the plan, he or she must furnish satisfactory evidence of insurability.

In addition to giving evidence to both the employer and the carrier that the employee has been given an opportunity to enroll for contributory coverages in the plan on a timely basis, the waiver card tends to act as a stimulant to securing a higher enrollment of eligible employees. Employees realize that, should they change their minds at a later date and make application to enroll beyond the end of the eligibility period, they will have to furnish evidence of insurability satisfactory to the carrier before their application can be accepted.

THE ENROLLMENT CANVASS

The arrangements for the enrollment of the eligible employees of a group are customarily discussed with the employer at the time the master application is completed and signed. The enrollment procedure is necessary whether the case is administered by the home office of the insurer, by the policyowner, or by a third party organization.

The purpose of the enrollment procedure, called by some in the business a "canvass" or "solicitation," is to acquaint the employees of the details of the plan with the new carrier and to give everyone a proper opportunity to enroll.

It is preferable and, strictly speaking, legally necessary in the case of contributory coverages, for the enrollment to be concluded before the effective date of the group plan with the new carrier. The insurance on an employee usually cannot become effective until the employee has made application by signing an enrollment card and is actively at work. Therefore, if application is made by the employee in an enrollment conducted after the effective date of the new policy, there might be a question of the employee's contributory insurance being effective coincident with the initial effective date of the new group plan.

The ideal way to conduct enrollment under a plan with a new carrier is on an individual employee basis. However, in the interests of conserving the employer's working time, certain streamlining methods may be necessary. On the assumption that new enrollment cards will be obtained from all employees, the carrier usually suggests to the employer that as much information as possible on the enrollment card be prepared by the employer in advance. Then there are several alternatives in presenting the plan to the employee and securing the employee's enrollment. The method selected will be dictated primarily, if not exclusively, by the employer's preferences.

Where the employer wishes the new carrier's group personnel to be primarily responsible, possibly with the assistance of the agent or broker, one time-saving method, assuming the cards have been partially prepared by the employer, is to hold meetings of groups of employees to explain the plan and to answer questions and then immediately thereafter to have them complete the remainder of the cards and sign them at tables or desks manned by the insurance carrier's representatives.

A second method is to hold meetings of the employer's supervisory staff at which they are briefed on the details of the plan and on the enrollment procedure. The supervisors of each department then secure the completion of, and signature on, the cards.

In other instances, the employer will only want the insurance carrier's representatives to brief the personnel department or personnel director, with the personnel department being responsible for the conduct of the enrollment purely on an internal basis.

THE ROLE OF THE GROUP REPRESENTATIVE

At the conclusion of the general enrollment period, the insurance carrier's group representative usually collects all of the completed enrollment cards, and based on the number of eligible employees, determines whether the minimum percentage enrollment for contributory coverages has been met. If waiver cards are used for those who decline to enroll for the contributory coverages, these are also initially collected by the group representative as a basis for determining whether minimum percentage enrollment has been attained.

The success of a plan with contributory coverages depends directly upon securing the enrollment of the highest possible percentage of eligible employees. Most carriers require a minimum of 75 percent enrollment of eligible employees for contributory coverages before the insurance can become effective. In smaller groups this minimum percentage is typically 85 percent.

Most plans provide for all full-time employees to be eligible for the insurance, unless there is a separate plan for union or hourly paid employees. For a nonunion related plan, it is usual to waive the employment probationary period for the initial group of employees who are on the payroll as of the effective date of the new plan. However, if the probationary period is not waived for the initial group of employees, care must be taken in arranging for the general enrollment so that employees who are not eligible are not included. Depending on the length of the probationary period in such circumstances, enrollment cards may, nevertheless, be secured from such employees with the clear understanding that their insurance will become effective only upon completion of the probationary period. In such circumstances the enrollment cards completed by employees who will not be eligible on the effective date of the plan are held by the employer and sent to the insurance carrier when, or just before, the employee completes the probationary period.

The group representative reviews the enrollment cards for completeness. Also, the group representative typically secures from the employer a list of those employees absent during the general enrollment period and makes arrangements for them to enroll upon their return to work.

At that point many group health insurance carriers compile a report of the results of the general enrollments showing the total number of eligible employees, the total who enroll during the general enrollment period, the number who decline to enroll for contributory coverages, and the number who were absent from work during the general enrollment period.

REVISIONS OF PLAN BENEFITS

Whenever new coverages are added to a plan, or when the benefits of existing coverages are substantially increased for contributory insurance, it is not unusual to conduct a general canvass or enrollment of employees. Such a general enrollment would be somewhat different from the procedure for a new plan since employees already insured under the plan would be involved.

To save loss of working time such an enrollment is sometimes made on a so-called waiver basis. This means that information with regard to the proposed changes in the plan is circulated to the employees, and they are given the opportunity to inform their supervisor or the personnel office that they do *not* wish to be insured for the additional or increased benefits. However, this approach usually includes the provision that the employee will not be eligible for any contributory benefits under the plan if he or she does not elect to participate for the increased or new benefits, since the benefits of the plan are usually treated as a package. In such circumstances the employee would be required to sign a form that requests the discontinuance of all payroll deductions under the group plan. This form would be accompanied by a warning that should the employee elect to reverse this decision beyond 31 days following the effective date of the revised plan, the employee would be required to furnish evidence of insurability for those coverages satisfactory to the insurance carrier for the employee and for any eligible dependents if dependent coverage existed.

Depending on the nature and magnitude of the changes in the plan, some carriers and employers might, when adding new coverages in the plan, allow the employee, at the time of revision, to retain the existing coverages held at that time. Such exceptions to the "package" approach complicate the administration of the plan and call for even greater scrutiny and care at the time of a claim. Thus, insurance carriers ordinarily discourage this practice.

When a plan undergoes a substantial revision, eligible employees who had not previously enrolled for the contributory coverages under the plan are customarily permitted to enroll at the time of the general canvass for the revised plan without furnishing evidence of insurability. Exceptions to this privilege may occur for some employees, who with respect to themselves or their dependents or both, were late applicants for insurance under the plan *prior* to the revision, and had been declined based on medical evidence furnished at that time, as these employees represent an extra risk.

A waiver method can be used for a revision of benefits because the payroll deduction authorization on the original enrollment card is worded so as to make the authorization of additional deductions unnecessary. Although the same reasons given earlier in this chapter for the desirability of new enrollment cards hold good for securing new cards at the time of a major revision of the group plan, these cards are rarely obtained by most carriers at the time such revisions take place as most employers are reluctant to relinquish the time needed to explain the new benefits. Usually, in the cases of substantial revisions in benefits or coverages (or both) under the plan, the insurance company issues a revised booklet-certificate. In this way employees are reminded of their new coverages.

Setting Up the Home Office Records

Once the enrollment procedures have been completed and the group representative has screened the enrollment cards for completeness and minimum percentage requirements, the completed cards and the report of the general enrollment results are transmitted to the carrier's home office for further screening. The waiver cards are returned to the employer for retention as evidence of the employees' having had the opportunity to enroll for any contributory coverages. After the enrollment cards and the general enrollment report are matched with the master application, they are reviewed and approved by the underwriting department at the carrier's home office.

Depending on the functional organization and practices of the insurance carrier, the approved file is sent to the group administration department, where an abstract of the file is made for preparation of the master group policy and also for the booklet-certificate (if the latter had not been prepared and made available at the time of the general enrollment.)

The file and the enrollment cards are reviewed by the new business section of the group administration department, and the enrollment cards are coded according to the particular carrier's needs for data entry in establishing the insurance records on the case if the plan is to be administered by the home office of the carrier. If a case is to be administered by either the policyowner and/or third party, many carriers typically prepare the initial premium report for the self-administrator and send the cards, the initial report and an administrative procedures guide to the appropriate group field office for delivery.

If the case is to be administered by the home office, the new business section proceeds with the establishment of the insurance records and usually produces an initial computer-printed list of insureds and the premium statement.

A similar procedure to that followed for the establishment of records for a new plan is used by the group insurance carrier for a major revision of benefits.

Installing the Plan

The installation of the group plan provides an opportunity to establish an atmosphere of cooperation and open communication between the insurance carriers and the policyowner. The group representative's ability to communicate the importance of certain activities on the part of the employer and his or her willingness to clarify the terms of the contact are essential to the successful implementation and administration of the plan.

DELIVERY OF ADMINISTRATIVE SUPPLIES

Once the appropriate action as described briefly above has been taken by the home office of the insurance carrier, it is usual to send the administrative supplies and claims forms together with an administration and claims guide to the appropriate group field office. Many carriers do not wait for the preparation of the master group policy to be complete before taking this action. If booklet-certificates are prepared after the general enrollment of the case, these are usually sent with the forms to the group field office.

The group representative then arranges to deliver these supplies and review the administrative and claims procedures with the person in the employer's organization responsible for securing and forwarding the necessary documentation and information to the carrier for the ongoing administration of the plan. At this time, it is important that the employer's representative be impressed with the need to see that the plan is presented to future new employees and that they have an opportunity to enroll. In plans with contributory coverages, this is particularly necessary to maintain a high percentage of participation in the plan by eligible employees.

REVIEW OF CONTRACT PROVISIONS

If the master policy is included in the initial material delivered in the installation of the plan, the group representative usually reviews this document with the appropriate executive in the policyowner's organization. The group representative should be certain that both the administrative and executive correspondents of the policyowner properly understand the benefits and contractual provisions contained in the master policy by reiterating the coverages provided under the policy, the benefits payable, and the circumstances under which these benefits are payable for each type of coverage. This approach enables the employer's organization to give informal guidance to employees about necessary administrative transactions resulting from changes in status. An example would be a single employee who marries and becomes eligible for dependent coverage for the first time.

The installation of the plan, when the provisions of the master policy are discussed and clarified with the employer's representative, provides an excellent opportunity to confirm the employer's wishes regarding the period of time an employee's insurance will be continued during an absence due to disability, layoff, or leave of absence. Most carriers provide in the master policy for a maximum period of continuance of insurance. Typically, this is 12 months during absence from work because of disability and 3 months during leave of absence or lay off. However, many carriers permit the employer to specify a longer period. It is not unusual for provisions to be made for insurance to be continued throughout the duration of an absence due to disability, unless the individual becomes eligible for Medicare as a disabled person or as a result of attaining age 65.

At this time, the employer may also indicate if the employer's contribution will continue at the same level (or at all) during the period of continuance of insurance, as well as specify if a returning employee who had terminated employment will be required to satisfy the probationary period as would a new employee.

One problem with regard to the continuance period caused by lay off occurred during the recession in 1974–1975 when the number of employees laid off was exceptionally high. Congress attempted to pass legislation that would have provided for the continuance of health insurance on laid-off persons for a longer period than that provided under the insurance carriers' contracts. In addition, the insurance commissioners in North Carolina and Florida asked the insurance industry to cooperate in encouraging employers to allow a longer period of coverage in circumstances where their employees were unemployed as a result of extensive layoffs. Commercial health insurance carriers and Blue Cross in North Carolina agreed to offer continuance for as long as six months for those who were laid off, subject to the employer's willingness to make arrangements with laid-off employees to continue their insurance coverage. This could be on the basis of the employer's continuing to make the same contribution toward the premium as for active employees or the laid-off employee's paying a larger share or all of the premium cost while the insurance was being continued. The practices of employers varied, depending on their financial ability and willingness to continue to pay part of the premium for laid-off employees during a period of serious downturn in business activity.

Securing decisions and elections by the employer in these

specific policy matters at an early stage in the relationship between the employer and the insurance carrier facilitates mutual understanding of how the plan will be administered and avoids the danger of discrimination by the employer in favor of particular employees.

Equally important is a clear understanding by the policyowner's representatives of the exclusions from coverage or the limitations on coverage in certain circumstances. Since the group representatives are usually salespersons, they are often reluctant to dwell on the negative side of the contract provisions (such as limitations or exclusions). Nevertheless, if the plan is to run smoothly, with a minimum of misunderstanding, a well-balanced understanding of the group plan by the employer is essential.

When a plan of benefits is substantially revised, it is as important to familiarize the employer's designated representative with the changes in benefits as it is when a plan is installed for the first time. The visit by the group field office representative to deliver the new material and to explain the impact of the changes in benefit is essential for the success and smooth operation of the plan.

SPECIAL CONTRACTS

Special contracts are those that contain significant differences from the customary group plan. Because of these differences, the installation of plans containing special contracts becomes more complex. Two special contracts in particular, those involving the "dual choice" option, and administrative-services-only contracts have become increasingly common. The special procedures involved in the installation of these contracts are discussed below.

Dual Choice Option

The Health Maintenance Organization Act of 1973, and the resulting regulations from the federal Department of Health, Education, and Welfare (HEW) introduced new elements into the general enrollment process, whether the enrollment results from a change in group insurance carriers or from a situation where an employer is offering a plan of group health insurance benefits to employees for the first time. Regulations published by the secretary of HEW state that where one or more qualified HMOs had made timely application for inclusion as an alternative means of providing medical expense coverage for the employees residing in the service area of the HMO, and the employer has elected the inclusion of the specific HMO or HMOs in its health benefit plan, the employees must be given the opportunity to consider joining the HMO at the time of the general enrollment.[1]

---

[1]*Federal Register, Rules and Regulations,* Secretary of Department of Health, Education, and Welfare, Subpart H, Section 110.805 (October 28, 1975).

This option must be made known to the employees at the time of the general canvass. If this is the first time they are being offered this option, they must make a positive choice about whether they wish to be covered under the conventional group health insurance benefit plan or by an HMO.[2] Only those employees who reside in the service area(s) of the qualified HMO(s) included in the employer's health benefit plan are eligible to elect the HMO option. Any employees electing the HMO option are, of course, also eligible for coverage for the other benefits of the employer's plan, such as life insurance, accidental death and dismemberment insurance, weekly disability benefit insurance, and any other supplemental health coverages for expenses that are not part of the HMO's array of benefits. In a contributory plan these additional coverages are customarily offered to all employees, regardless of whether or not they elect the HMO option at the time of enrollment.

The requirement that the employee make a positive choice the first time the HMO is offered necessitates that an additional enrollment document be included along with the employee group certificate and the master group policy. It also necessitates that special provisions for this option be made in the employee group certificate and in the master group policy, particularly since the HMO Act provides that the employee may transfer back and forth between the regular group health insurance medical expense plan and the HMO at annual intervals if he or she so desires.[3] The availability of this privilege presents the need for a clear understanding and statement in the provisions of the group certificate and master policy of how continuity of coverage will be maintained.

The HMO option further complicates the insurance carrier's establishment of insurance records, since it represents an additional class of employee benefit coverage for both premium and claims purposes.

Because of the limited number of HMOs that have qualified in the initial years under the terms of the HMO act, this factor is not present in many general enrollments. However, the number of qualified HMOs is expected to increase steadily in the next few years. Thus, this feature will be present in more and more enrollments.

Administrative Services Only Plans

Within the last few years a growing number of employer benefit plans have not included the medical expense benefits for employees and their dependents in the insured portion of the plan. This medical expense benefit portion of the plan has been self-insured by the employer, or more properly stated, uninsured. Ordinarily, only employers

[2]*Ibid.*, Section 110.803(f).
[3]*Ibid.*, Section 110.803(e).

who have a large number of employees, usually a thousand or more, elect to self-insure, or not insure. (These employers do so in hopes of improving their cash flow position and avoiding the payment of premium taxes.)

In such situations the employer usually continues to insure the life insurance and disability income coverages with the insurance carrier and to pay the insurance carrier a fee for the processing and payment of medical expense claims with checks or drafts drawn against a bank account established for that purpose by the employer.

The mechanics and procedures used during the enrollment and installation of a plan with a combination of insured and uninsured coverages are quite similar to those used when the coverages are fully insured. A group enrollment card, which serves the dual purpose of providing evidence of enrollment for the insured and uninsured coverages under the plan, is distributed to the employees. Since no premium is paid to the insurance company for the uninsured benefits, the insurance carrier has no responsibility for keeping up with the coverage status of the employees and their families under the uninsured plan. The administration of both the insured and uninsured coverages is performed by the employer.

It is therefore almost exclusively from a claims processing standpoint for the medical expense coverages that there is any day-to-day relationship between the employer and the insurance carrier since, in this respect, the function performed by the insurance carrier is that of an administrator and claims processor rather than as an insurer. Of course, with respect to the insured coverages, the normal group policyowner-insurance carrier relationship continues to exist.

Although it is not entirely appropriate in this chapter to develop great detail about this type of arrangement, it should be stated that there may be an insurance involvement by the insurance carrier on the medical expense coverages in the form of a stop-loss agreement with the employer. Simply stated, this arrangement limits the liability of the employer to a stated figure in the aggregate amount of medical claims for which the employee will be responsible during a given period, or limits the employer's liability during a stated period to a stated maximum amount per employee or eligible dependents, or a combination of both approaches.

In the development of such a plan of benefits there usually has been a much greater involvement of persons in the employer's organization than is typical with a conventional insured plan of benefits. Therefore, the need for providing instruction to attain a thorough understanding of the provisions of the plan at the time of installation may be somewhat less. Of course, just because a portion of the plan is uninsured is no reason for the carrier/administrator to neglect making every effort to see that the provisions and the benefits of the plan for both insured and uninsured coverages are clearly understood by the persons in the employer's organization responsible for advising employees about benefits and claim-filing procedures.

SUMMARY

This chapter has considered the procedures for the installation of group plans. The chapter began with a discussion of the basic responsibilities of the insurer and the policyowner when a plan is installed. Following this, the provision and nature of explanatory materials issued by the insurer, the use of new enrollment cards, and the arrangements needed for the enrollment of employees were described in detail. The role of the group representative in assuring the successful installation of the plan was described, as was the procedure for setting up the home office records. The chapter concluded with a discussion of the installation of special contracts such as dual option contracts and administrative services only plans.

CHAPTER 24

ADMINISTRATION OF GROUP PLANS

INTRODUCTION

This chapter discusses the administrative systems used for group insurance. First, setting up records of insurance is described. Each of the items customarily found on the enrollment card is listed and analyzed. Then the two basic types of group plan administration, home office or insurer administration and policyowner or third party administration, are differentiated and described in detail.

The administrative systems used for group insurance reflect the mass-marketing nature of this kind of insurance. One group insurance characteristic that results in cost savings is that, generally speaking, a single invoice or premium statement is used to cover the whole premium due, sometimes on several thousand insured persons. It is not necessary to bill individually and to collect and record premiums for each of the insured persons. Whether the plan is administered by the home office of the carrier or is self-administered, these substantial administrative cost savings can be reflected in reduced premium rates.

Another characteristic of the group insurance administrative process is that the carrier places a great deal of trust on both the accuracy and honesty of the group policyowner's reporting. The only other type of insurance in the private sector where this type of relationship exists is in workers' compensation. Of course, in government-related insurance, such as social security and unemployment insurance, similar characteristics are present, but the employer faces legal penalties for any gross negligence or dishonesty in reporting and remitting funds for those programs.

SETTING UP RECORDS OF INSURANCE

Proper administration of a group insurance plan requires that accurate, up-to-date information be available for each individual in-

by
GEORGE M. HIDER, *Vice President, Pilot Life Insurance Company, Greensboro, North Carolina*

sured under the plan. To facilitate the acquisition of this information, an enrollment card is filed for each of the insureds. It may be helpful to analyze the data that are generally provided for on the enrollment card and the use of these data in the administrative process.

Date employed. This applies to those individuals subject to the probationary period under the group policy. They are usually employees whose effective date of employment occurs after the effective date of the group policy. This information is needed to determine their eligibility date under the group plan.

Marital status. This is used to determine eligibility for dependent coverage if it is offered under the plan.

Whether hourly or salaried. This can determine the class or classes of benefits for which the employer is eligible if a distinction is made between hourly and salaried employees.

Sex. This distinction may no longer be used to determine eligibility for benefits or to differentiate for amount of insurance. Remaining valid uses of this information include:

(1) The calculation of the life insurance rates, where the calculation process gives credit for the proportion of life insurance on females in the form of a discount reflecting the longer life expectancy of females as a whole compared with males. In the case of group permanent, or group ordinary life insurance, many carriers have a lower table of rates for females for the same reason, and

(2) The determination of the percentage of benefits on females for purposes of loading the health insurance premium (because of the demonstrated higher morbidity rate of females compared with males).

Date of birth. This information serves several purposes. First, it is used to calculate the life insurance premium. Second, it is needed where there is a reduction in the amount of life insurance upon an attained age such as 60 or 65. Third, it reminds the administrator of attainment of eligibility age for Medicare, which usually results in a change of coverage under the health insurance benefits of the policy. The latter reason also accounts for the presence on the enrollment cards used by many carriers of the date of birth of the spouse.

Basic earnings amount. This is usually required only if the schedule of insurance is based on the employee's earnings. An example is a schedule that relates the amount of life insurance to the employee's monthly or annual earnings.

Name and relationship of beneficiary. This is the employee's designation and authorization of the persons to whom the proceeds of life insurance or accidental death insurance are to be payable upon the employee's death.

Group permanent life insurance. Where group permanent life insurance is an option in the plan, the employee must indicate whether he or she wishes to elect the permanent form of life insurance, and in most cases, which particular plan of permanent insurance and in what amount within the total amount of life insurance for which the employee is eligible.

Date on which enrollment card is signed. This is essential where contributory coverages are involved as evidence that the employee applied within 31 days of the date on which he or she became eligible under the plan.

Social Security number. Enrollment cards used by many carriers request this information. Some carriers use this as the individual's identification number under the plan, sometimes in lieu of a certificate number and sometimes in addition to the certificate number, because it is the single identifying number that can accurately distinguish two or more insured employees, particularly those with the same given names. However, the Privacy Act of 1974 states that the social security number may not be used for any other purpose except directly in conjunction with the person's identity under the Social Security Program itself without the consent of that individual.

Regardless of the method of administration used on a particular case, the data provided by the enrollment cards form the basis for the premium billing or reporting.

TYPES OF ADMINISTRATION

Two basic types of administration are used in group insurance plans: home office administration and self-administration. (The old-fashioned terms for each type are long-form accounting and short-form accounting, respectively.)

In turn, there are two forms of self-administration. The most common involves delegating the administrative function to the policyowner. The insurance carrier usually does this where the group plan insures 100 or more lives, and the policyowner has the facilities to meet the demands of this administrative responsibility.

The second form of self-administration is, in fact, third party administration and is found most often in union welfare fund, association, and multiple-employer groups. In third party cases the administrator is usually appointed by the policyowner and may be a broker, an insurance consultant, or an independent specialist in this type of administration. It is most often used in union health and welfare plans involving multiple employers, particularly where the eligibility of the union-member employee is based on the number of hours worked within a given period such as a calendar quarter. Trades subject to employment fluctuations often maintain "banks" of hours worked to determine eligibility. Experience has shown it is much easier for a third party administrator to keep track of such information than it is for the insurer to do so.

Home Office Administration

Under this system all of the records needed to determine insurance status and to calculate the premium are maintained by the insurer. The new business section or unit, usually part of the group administration department, processes the case to the point of setting up insurance records within the department's administrative system for the initial group, and produces a list of insureds and an initial premium statement for the case.

Not all carriers, however, produce a list of insureds on an ongoing basis for home office administered cases. Some produce such a list when the case is initially issued and as monthly changes take place. These changes may be adding new insured employees, deleting terminating employees, reflecting changes in insurance class or changes in dependent coverage that affect premium. These are reflected on change lists issued monthly, showing only the transactions involved for that period.

Many carriers, on the other hand, produce a complete list of insureds every month for the group policyowner reflecting the changes that have been reported by the policyowner.

In a conventional employee group of a single employer, a premium statement for billing purposes is issued separately from the list of insureds. This is helpful for those carriers that provide a copy of the previous month's list of insureds for the policyowner to annotate by indicating the changes that are to be recorded by the carrier and reflected in the next premium billing. The use of a separate premium statement enables the carrier to use that document purely for premium accounting purposes.

Figure 24-1 shows part of a typical list of changes. A copy of one form of premium statement used by a carrier is shown in Figure 24-2.

The design and content of the forms for the list of insureds and the premium statement vary among carriers. However, since these documents are intended to communicate information to the policyowner, sufficient information should appear, regardless of the variations in format and content, so that the policyowner can verify the accuracy with which the carrier has reflected the transactions reported by the policyowner. Where the list of insureds is used as the basis for communicating transactions to the carrier, it is necessary that various supplementary forms, most of which are completed and signed by the insured person, be sent to the carrier as evidence of the employee's decisions and intention.

FIGURE 24-1
List of Changes*

Policy No	In account with			Pilot Life	Pilot Life Insurance Company Group Administration Dept P O Box 20727 Greensboro, NC 27420	PAGE 1		Termination Codes (Show effective date)
1023 1	XYZ COMPANY P O BOX 123 ANYWHERE	US 00000			List of Insureds From 11-01-78 To 12-01-78			1 Voluntary Cancellation by employee - still eligible (applies only to coverages for which insured contributes) 2 Resignation or Discharge (show date last worked) 3 Deceased (show date of death of insured) 4 Retired (use only if coverages are not continued during retirement) 5 Leave of Absence or Temporary Lay Off (show date coverage ceased) 6 Transferred (indicate to where transferred and date) 7 Disabled (show date coverage ceased) 8 Change in type of Life Insurance

579-10

Certificate No	Name	Class	Dep	Amt Life Ins		Permanent Life Premium Employee	Employer	LTD Prem	Total Prem All Coverages	Certificate Date Termination Date	Remarks
	LATEST CHANGE DATE IS THE 31ST * SEE REVERSE SIDE FOR EXPLANATION										
2	DOE JANE	2	HW	25,000					14.50	11-01-78	
3	DOE JOSEPH W JR	2		25,000					41.43	11-01-78	
1	DOE JOSEPH W SR	1	HW 3	50,000					88.43	11-01-78	
7	JONES ROBERT T	3	MC	5,000					16.37	11-01-78	
8	JONES SAMATHA	3		10,000					32.73	11-01-78	
6	SMITH JAMES	3	3	10,000					65.23	11-01-78	
5	SMITH LORETTA	3	3	10,000					65.23	11-01-78	
4	WILLIAMS FRANK	3		10,000					32.73	11-01-78	

INSUREDS	DEPENDENTS		LIFE VOLUME				PREMIUMS			
8	SINGLE	0	TERM	145,000		TERM LIFE	75.40	HEALTH	281.25
	MULTIPLE	3	PERMANENT	0		EE PERMANENT	.00	L T D	.00
						EMPR PERMANENT	.00	TOTAL	356.65

EMPLOYER'S COPY - RETAIN FOR YOUR FILE   See reverse side for code explanations and how to report changes.

*Reprinted with permission of the Pilot Life Insurance Company. This form may not be reproduced without prior written consent of Pilot Life.

FIGURE 24-2
Premium Statement*

Pilot Life Insurance Company
Group Administration Dept.
PO Box 20727
Greensboro, NC 27420

Statement of Premium

Due and Payable on   Group Policy No   Branch

11-01-78   1023   1

EMPLOYEE TERM LIFE INSURANCE $75.40
ALL OTHER GROUP INSURANCE $281.25

TOTAL PREMIUM DUE $356.65

MS JANE DOE
XYZ COMPANY
P O BOX 123
ANYWHERE   US   00000

RETAIN FOR YOUR FILE

G3663

Please remit payment for amount shown. Any necessary adjustments will be reflected on a subsequent billing.

111478-10-809-579

*Reprinted with permission of the Pilot Life Insurance Company. This form may not be reproduced without prior written consent of Pilot Life.

The effective date of additions and terminations depends upon the provisions of the policy about the effective and termination dates of individual insurance. In some plans additions are automatic and take effect on the date of eligibility or, for contributory coverages, on the date the enrollment card is signed by the employee, whichever is the later, provided the employee is actively at work on that date. For automatic terminations, termination of insurance takes place on the last day of employment.

In policies with the automatic date provision, premiums commence to be charged for additions with the next following premium due date, unless the effective date is a premium due date. In terminations, no premium credit is given if termination occurs during the premium month.

In policies where the provision for individual effective dates of insurance is on the basis of the next following premium due date, then the effective date of coverage is deferred until the later date, unless it coincides with a premium due date. Terminations of insurance under such a policy provision are also deferred until the end of the premium month.

In the event that the transactions affecting the amount of premium due are not promptly reported by the policyowner to the carrier, it is necessary for the carrier to reflect these retroactively to the earliest effective date of premium due, either as a debit or credit, depending on the transaction. Many carriers do not make the retroactive adjustment for transactions that date back more than 12 months because dividends or experience-rated refunds would be affected. Depending on the use of a list of insureds by the carrier, identification of such retroactive charges or credits is shown at the end of the list of insureds and, of course, carried forward into the premium statement.

PREMIUM BILLING

The premium bill received by the policyowner reflects the number of individuals of each age and sex insured for the various classes of available benefits.

Typical transactions affecting premiums due. As mentioned above, many factors affect the amount of premium due from the group policyowner for a given month. The most important factors are:

1. The addition of a new eligible employee for insurance under the policy. In this instance, a completed and signed enrollment card is necessary.
2. The termination of insurance of an individual employee under the policy. This can occur as a result of the employee's ceasing to be a member of the eligible classes under the policy or terminating employment with the group policyowner. Such

termination can also occur in a plan where the employee is required to contribute toward the cost of the insurance and chooses no longer to do so, despite the fact that the employee remains eligible for the insurance. In this instance a waiver form such as the one shown in Figure 24-3 is necessary.

3. The addition of dependent coverage with respect to an employee. This usually occurs when an unmarried employee marries and, therefore, acquires an eligible dependent for the first time, or when a child is born to or adopted by an employee.

4. Termination of dependent insurance. This can occur as a result of divorce of a married employee, or, in some cases, as a result of legal separation if there are no eligible dependent children involved. It can also occur if the insured employee's spouse becomes employed by the same company, especially if the cost of the coverage available is paid by that spouse's employer, or if a child of the employee reaches the limiting age. When dependent coverage is added or terminated, a form of the type shown in Figure 24-4 is typically used.

5. The change in class of an employee. This usually results in the employee's becoming eligible for a higher amount of life insurance under the plan as a result of increased earnings or a change in job title resulting from a promotion, or, where the

FIGURE 24-3
Notice of Cancellation or Waiver of Group Insurance*

NOTICE OF CANCELLATION OR WAIVER OF GROUP INSURANCE

☐ CANCELLATION OF INSURANCE (Attach Group Certificate(s)	Certificate No.	Group Policy No.	Date of Cancellation (Home Office Only)

I hereby surrender the above certificate(s) for cancellation. I will make no further contributions to apply toward the cost of the insurance and hereby revoke my authorization to make deductions from my pay for the purpose of the insurance. Date to which contributions made_____

☐ WAIVER OF INSURANCE

I hereby certify that I have been given the opportunity to participate in the contributory Group Insurance Plan underwritten by PILOT LIFE INSURANCE COMPANY, Greensboro, N. C., and hereby decline to apply.

It is understood and agreed that by the completion of this form I forfeit my rights to coverage under the Group Policy, and should I elect at a later date to participate in the plan, I must furnish at my own expense, evidence of insurability satisfactory to Pilot Life Insurance Company.

_____ (Witness)   _____ (Signed)

_____ (Date)   _____ (Name of Group Policyholder)

G-988   PILOT LIFE INSURANCE COMPANY, Group Administration Dept., Greensboro, N. C.

*Reprinted with permission of the Pilot Life Insurance Company. This form may not be reproduced without prior written consent of Pilot Life.

FIGURE 24-4
Addition or Termination of Dependent Coverage*

Application for Change, Addition or Exclusion of Dependent Coverage	Policy No.	Certificate No.	HOME OFFICE USE	
			Premium	Effective Date of Change
Name of Employee (First) (Middle Initial) (Last)			S ____ M ____ C ____	Evidence of Insurability Approved By____ Date

I request a change in insurance benefits to plan checked below:

☐ No Dependent Coverage   ☐ Coverage for Eligible Spouse. I have no Eligible Children.   ☐ Coverage for Eligible Spouse and Eligible Children.   ☐ Coverage for Eligible Children. I have no eligible spouse.   Spouse's Date of Birth   Mo.   Day   Yr.

Reason for change _____ (I.E.: MARRIAGE, DIVORCE, BIRTH, DEATH, AGE LIMIT, ETC.)

Date eligible dependents acquired _____

Date dependents became ineligible _____

{ Please complete applicable sections.

I agree to any change in contribution necessitated by the requested change in coverage.

WITNESS _____   SIGNATURE OF EMPLOYEE _____

DATE _____   EMPLOYED BY _____

G-456D   PILOT LIFE INSURANCE COMPANY   GROUP ADMINISTRATION DEPARTMENT   GREENSBORO, N C

*Reprinted with permission of the Pilot Life Insurance Company. This form may not be reproduced without prior written consent of Pilot Life.

schedule of insurance is based on length of service, completing a certain period of service that entitles the employee to a larger amount of insurance. Customarily, no additional form is needed in this instance.

6. The death of the employee. Although the carrier will at some point receive notice of the death of the employee through submission of a claim, for administrative purposes it is important that the employer inform the carrier of this fact separately. Some carriers allow the continuation of medical expense coverages on the remaining eligible dependents of the deceased employee. In plans that follow this practice, the employer usually indicates on the list of insureds (assuming it is used for reporting transactions) that continuance of the dependent coverage is desired for the period permitted by the contract or for the period permitted by administrative agreement.

7. The attainment of eligibility for Medicare. Under the Social Security Act eligibility for Medicare occurs on meeting any one of three criteria—attaining age 65, reaching the 25th month of receipt of social security disability benefits, or suffering from chronic kidney disease. The employer usually has the responsibility to report these changes. These changes

can also affect the dependent spouse if covered under the plan.

Billing for dependents. The premium for dependents can be calculated for a given plan on one of three bases. The first and the most common is the "composite rate," a flat premium charged regardless of the number of dependents. On this basis the same rate is charged for an employee with only a spouse as is charged for an employee with a spouse and numerous eligible children. The second basis is known as the "two-way split," and provides for one rate for a spouse *or* children only and another rate for spouse *and* children. The third basis is known as the "three-way split," and provides one rate for spouse only, another rate for children only, and yet another rate for spouse and children. It is relatively rare that a carrier will bill other than on a composite basis. If dependent coverage is contributory and the employer wishes to differentiate in the amount of contributions, then the split is handled on that basis for payroll deduction purposes only, and the composite rate charged approximates the mix of employees with dependents for whom the employer is making a differential in contributions for dependent coverage.

MODE OF PREMIUM PAYMENT

The group insurance system is geared to a monthly cycle. Most plans of group insurance provide for the monthly payment of premiums. However, some policyowners elect to pay their premiums in advance, quarterly, semi-annually, or annually. Because of this monthly cycle, it is customary to furnish such policyholders with an accounting for earned premium each month based on monthly reporting of transactions to the carrier. At the end of the premium period, either a credit or debit balance is applied to the next period's premium. One of the exceptions to the use of a separate premium statement is for association groups. In such cases it is not unusual to also use the list of insureds premium total as the premium billing.

PREMIUM COLLECTION

All premiums are payable in advance. Technically, payment is due on the first day of the period covered by the statement. The group master policy provides a grace period of 31 days, however, during which the policyowner may pay the premium. Technically, if the premium is not paid within the grace period, the policy lapses for nonpayment of premium. Practices with regard to the strict application of this provision tend to vary among carriers, but there has been a distinct trend in recent years for carriers to apply this provision more strictly.

The carrier usually sends a delinquent premium notice to the policyowner at the end of the grace period, or within a few days thereafter. Insurance carriers with somewhat more liberal practices with regard to delinquent premiums provide in this delinquent notice a period of 15 days during which the premium may be remitted with what is technically an automatic reinstatement of the policy. This requirement is usually coupled with the additional requirement that when the delinquent premium is paid it must be accompanied also by the current premium due.

Many carriers issue a second delinquent premium notice at the end of the 15-day period following the grace period, informing the policyowner that the policy has lapsed but that, if the delinquent premium and the current premium are paid when due, the carrier will consider reinstatement of the policy. For those carriers who follow this more liberal practice, the question of optional reinstatement on their part is determined by the previous history of premium delinquency of that policyowner and various other aspects of the financial experience of the case, especially whether the plan is contributory and what proportion of employees is currently insured.

The insurance commissioners of New Jersey, Wisconsin, Arizona and Florida have adopted regulations, however, providing that, if any action by the carrier indicates to the policyowner that the policy has not automatically lapsed for nonpayment of premium within the grace period, then the policy shall be considered as remaining in force until three days following the date on which the employer furnishes notice of termination of the policy to the employees on forms provided by the insurance carrier. Because of the financial implications of this requirement should the insurer be unable to collect all of the premium due, including that for the extended period, most carriers operating in states with such regulations have adopted procedures that give notice of lapse to the policyowner no later than the last day of the grace period.

Because of the grace period provision in the policy, the nonpayment of premium by the policyowner during the grace period does not absolve the carrier from liability for claims incurred during that period. The collection of the grace period premium then becomes a separate matter. Some carriers have adopted the practice of charging interest on premiums that are paid beyond the end of the grace period. In instances where it is apparent that the policyowner has no intention of paying the delinquent premium and requesting reinstatement of the policy, some carriers use the services of collection agencies to try to obtain the grace period premium.

The lapsing of the policy because of failure of the group policyowner to pay the premium on a timely basis and the termination of insurance at the end of the grace period has given the legislatures in some states, such as Connecticut, Wisconsin and New Jersey, concern about the lack of notice of termination of insurance being given to the actual persons insured. All three states passed statutes requiring employers to give proper notice to their insured employees of such events. It appears likely that other states will take similar actions.

LOCK BOX PAYMENTS

Some carriers with widespread operations throughout the United States or with concentrations of group business at considerable distances from their home offices have adopted a lock box premium collection system. A carrier whose home office is located on the East Coast but which has a large portfolio of group business in force on the West Coast and chooses this collection method makes arrangements with a West Coast bank to receive premium payments from policyowners located on the West Coast. Usually these are mailed to a post office box established by the bank for such purposes. The bank then deposits the premium to the carrier's account at the bank, makes a daily reporting to the carrier of such deposits, and mails the accompanying premium statements to the carrier's home office. Such a system has two possible advantages to the carrier. First, the premium funds are banked earlier to the carrier's account than if they had been mailed to the East Coast home office. Second, if the carrier has local field claims offices on the West Coast, time is saved by drawing claim checks against the West Coast bank account rather than transferring funds or having checks or drafts drawn against the bank at which the carrier has the corporate bank account. However, the main advantage is the first mentioned, because the funds become available to the carrier earlier than they otherwise would, so the carrier is in a position to earn the investment interest on such funds sooner. Usually in such an arrangement the bank makes no charge for its services if a certain minimum balance is maintained in the bank account that receives the post office lock box deposits of the carrier.

SETTLEMENT OPTIONS

The group life insurance portion of a group insurance policy usually provides for the election by the insured employee, or by the employee's beneficiary after the insured's death, of a settlement option under which the proceeds of the policy may be paid at the time of the employee's death in lieu of payment of the proceeds in a lump sum. It is also customary for the carrier to allow any proceeds payable under the accidental death coverage portion to be included in such arrangements. If the insured employee wishes to elect such an option during his or her lifetime, then a settlement option agreement is drawn up for the employee's signature by the carrier and filed as part of the home office records.

EVIDENCE OF INSURABILITY

If an employee in a contributory plan applies for coverage after passing the deadline for this action, either with respect to the employee or eligible dependents, or both, the employee is required to complete what some carriers call a "health certificate." The reverse side of this form is completed by a medical examiner and is used only at the request of the insurer after receiving the completed front page, or for late applicants who have attained a certain age, such as 60.

Evidence of insurability is also required where the employee is a member of a class that is eligible under the policy for life insurance benefits in an amount that exceeds the guaranteed issue amount under the policy.

In both these circumstances the evidence of insurability is subject to the approval by the insurance carrier at its home office. The insurance, if the evidence is found satisfactory, may become effective on the date of approval by the home office. The basis for the effective date of insurance in such circumstances varies among carriers and also depends on the provisions of the policy about the effective dates of insurance coverage.

DUAL-CHOICE OPTION

The dual choice option and its effect on group insurance plans were discussed in Chapter 21. Under those group insurance policies where the employer also has included a qualified HMO as an option in the health benefit plan, the premium under the group policy of any employee electing the HMO option obviously will be affected. Employees transferring back into the group plan for their medical expense benefits or transferring from the group plan into an HMO will require premium adjustments. Thus, it will be necessary for carriers to develop special reporting forms for use in conjunction with this dual-choice option privilege. Since HMO situations are relatively new to all group insurance carriers, there has not yet been time to determine if there will be any uniformity in how the carriers will handle these matters administratively.

There are many potential combinations of circumstances that require careful and clear instructions to be given to group policyowners about such transactions, regardless of whether their plan is home office-administered or self-administered. Most of these transactions will be concentrated into the period that is set aside each year for open enrollment, thus facilitating their administration.

OTHER TRANSACTIONS

In addition to changes affecting the employee's status that have an impact on the premium, there are others that require changes in administrative records.

1. **Change of name.** This occurs most frequently in the event of marriage, remarriage, or divorce of a female employee.
2. **Change of beneficiary designation.** This requires a signed

request by the employee and typically occurs in the event of marriage, or divorce, or because of the death of the original beneficiary.

These two changes may require the reissue of the face page of a certificate or of the validation label that identifies the insured's name, amount of insurance, and class of insureds for benefit purposes if used in conjunction with the booklet-certificate.

3. Issue of a new certificate or booklet-certificate. Unless the latter is on a "no name" basis, it has become common to furnish the policyowner with a supply of the certificates or booklet-certificates and to mail only a face page or a validation label when new employees are being insured.

4. Extended insurance coverage for handicapped children. The majority of states have passed legislation requiring insurers to cover handicapped children past the normal maximum age of eligibility for coverage as dependent children. Such policy provisions usually call for the insured parent to notify the insurer that the parent has a handicapped child, to do so before the child attains age 19, and to furnish medical evidence substantiating the handicap that continues to make the child dependent upon the parent and renders the child incapable of earning his or her own living. This requirement poses administrative problems because insured employees sometimes fail to give employers the necessary notice and evidence.

Policyowner and Third Party Administration

An alternative to home office or insurer administration is administration by the policyowner or by a third party organization. Under such arrangements, the policyowner or third party maintains the same records as would the insurer in the case of home office administration.

DELEGATION OF ADMINISTRATIVE FUNCTIONS

To protect the interests of the carrier, the policyowner or third party administrator, and the insured persons, some carriers have adopted the practice of requiring a signed contract that spells out the functions delegated to the administrator, specifies liability in case of clerical errors and omissions, and defines the ownership of records maintained by the administrator.

PREMIUM PAYMENT

A monthly premium report furnished by the administering party accompanies the premium remittance to the insurance carrier.

In such premium reporting, the report form usually shows the previous month's insurance totals for premium purposes, with adjustments for debits and credits resulting from transactions that have occurred in the subsequent month. The identity of employees being

FIGURE 24-5
Report Form for Policyowner or Third Party Administration*
(front)

PREMIUM STATEMENT AND REPORT
Prepare this report monthly in duplicate.
Send original to address shown in the
Administration and Claims Guide.

Pilot Life
Insurance Company
Group Administration Dept.
PO Box 20727
Greensboro, NC 27420
Telephone 919 299 4720

Name of Policyholder: XYZ Company	Policy Number: F-8000	Division	Period Covered From 11-1-78 To 12-1-78

See reverse side for instructions.

1. Group Coverages	2. Total In Force Last Report (Lives)	(Volume)	3. Additions and Increases (Lives)	(Volume)	4. Terminations and Decreases (Lives)	(Volume)	5. (2+3-4) Total In Force This Report (Lives)	(Volume)	6. Premium Rates	7. (5 x 6) Premium
Employee Life	87	2,277,000	5	111,000	0		92	2,388,000	$ .56	$ 1,337.28
AD&D	87	2,277,000	5	111,000	0		92	2,388,000	.06	143.28
Employee Medical	87		5		0		92		13.35	1,228.20
Dependent	82		3		0		85		34.41	2,924.85
8. Long Term Disability	86	(Covered Payroll) 123,730	5	(Covered Payroll) 6,450	0	(Covered Payroll) *	91	(Covered Payroll) 130,180	.68	885.22

10. Net Adjustments
11. Total Premium Due $ 6,518.83

*9. Indicate here the number of employees included in your "Total In Force This Report" lives for whom no salaries are included For Long Term Disability. (Ex: One (1) insured employee absent due to disability and off payroll. The number "1" would be entered in this blank.)

I declare to the best of my knowledge and belief that the information furnished on this report is correct.

12.   Jane Doe   11/1/78
Authorized Signature   Date

Pilot Life

G-3623A

FIGURE 24-5
Report Form for Policyowner or Third Party Administration*
(back)

INSTRUCTIONS FOR FIGURING NET ADJUSTMENTS

*NET ADJUSTMENTS

If the insurance on an employee and/or dependent became effective, increased, terminated or decreased prior to the period covered by this report, and through error, or for other reasons it was not listed on the proper report, it must be recorded in this report.

For coverages where the rate basis is per $1,000 per $100 of Covered Payroll or per $10, multiply the Applicable amount for each employee for whom an adjustment is necessary, by the premium rate. The resulting figure should then be multiplied by the number of periods for which either a back premium charge or premium refund is due.

For coverages where the rate basis is on a per employee and per dependent unit basis, multiply the appropriate rate for each employee and/or dependent, by coverage, for whom an adjustment is necessary. The resulting figure should then be multiplied by the number of periods for which either a back premium charge or premium refund is due.

If the amount of back premium charges exceeds the amount of premium refunds, record the difference opposite "NET ADJUSTMENT" and add the amount to this period's premium in arriving at the total premium due.

If the amount of premium refunds exceeds the amount of back premium charges, record the difference opposite "NET ADJUSTMENT" and subtract the amount from this period's premium in arriving at the total premium due.

Complete this summary.

BACK PREMIUM CHARGES $ _____

BACK PREMIUM REFUNDS _____

*NET ADJUSTMENT $ _____ (CHARGE OR REFUND)

FOR LONG TERM DISABILITY ONLY USE THE SPACES AND INFORMATION BELOW FOR DETERMINING YOUR COVERED PAYROLL.

Additions and Covered Salary Increases

Cert. No.	Name	Effective Date	*	Covered Payroll*
			Total	

Terminations and Covered Salary Decreases

Cert. No.	Name	Effective Date	*	Covered Payroll*
			Total	

*Enter:
A – For Addition
I – For Increase
T – For Termination
D – For Decrease

* Enter total covered payroll for each addition or termination.
Enter only the amount of increase or decrease in covered payroll for such changes.

added or terminated is not usually shown on such reports, but the number of such employees is always indicated. There is flexibility in the basis on which the carrier agrees for the premium calculation to be shown on the premium report by the administrator. A typical form using one such base is reproduced in Figure 24-5.

As noted in Chapter 23, some carriers prepare the initial premium report for the policyowner. It is not unusual for the carrier to prepare a list of insureds for the initial insured group and furnish it to the policyowner at the time the case is processed by the new business unit for issue.

CERTIFICATES

If personalized certificates or booklet-certificates are to be used on the case, the responsibility for the issue of the initial certificates varies. In some cases the policyowner, or third party administrator, will perform that task; in other cases the insurance carrier will do so. In any circumstance the policyowner or administrator will be responsible for the preparation and issue of subsequent certificates or certificate booklets from supplies furnished in bulk by the insurance carrier.

ADMINISTRATIVE COMPLEXITIES

Under self-administration, it is still necessary for the administrator to submit evidence of insurability for late applicants or for amounts of insurance above guaranteed issue limits on individuals for approval. Settlement options and more complex beneficiary designations are also submitted to the carrier, who prepares and issues appropriate papers. Any questions about the interpretation of the provisions of the group contract as they affect individual insureds or their dependents are also referred to the insurance carrier's home office for guidance and decision.

Exceptions to self-administration are group plans that include group permanent life insurance. Because of the more complex nature of this type of coverage and the need to establish individual certificate reserves for permanent life insurance, it is necessary for the carrier to retain the responsibility for the administration of these plans.

Delinquent premium procedures for self-administered cases are similar to those used on cases administered by the home office of the carrier.

LONG-TERM DISABILITY INCOME INSURANCE

Because of the direct relationship of premium to covered payroll (the gross amount on which the employee's benefits are based) in long-term disability insurance, this coverage is often self-administered by the policyowner, even though other coverages under the plan may be home-office administered. This is particularly true where the long-term disability insurance is covered under a separate master group policy. However, there is a trend toward the home office administration of this coverage also. Where this coverage is self-administered, a different type of premium report form may be used, but some carriers have adapted the regular self-administered report form to provide for long-term disability insurance.

ADMINISTRATIVE SERVICES ONLY (ASO) PLANS

In ASO plans, the employer is self-insuring the medical expense coverages, and the claims are being administered for the employer by the insurance carrier. Any remaining coverages in the plan, such as life insurance and disability income insurance, are insured on a conventional basis. Because the coverage status records of employees for the ASO portion of the plan are usually located with the employer, the insured coverages are automatically self-administered.

It is customary for the employer to include the fees, with proper identification, for claim administration service rendered by the insurance carrier on the uninsured portion of the plan in its monthly premium report to the insurance carrier, and to include the amount due with its premium remittance.

CREDITOR INSURANCE

There are basically two types of creditor insurance: the single premium type, used when an individual policy is issued, and the outstanding balance type, usually known as group creditor insurance. Both types insure the outstanding balance of covered installment loans. Both are self-administered by the creditor organization and employ a very simple report form for premium remittance purposes.

For single premium creditor insurance, a quantity of forms is given to the creditor lending institution, which is responsible for issuing them to the insured borrowers. Organizational responsibility for this type of insurance varies considerably from one insurance company to another.

In group creditor insurance, usually included in the responsibilities of the carrier's group division, a master policy is drawn up and certificates are issued by the creditor institution to insured borrowers, as is done with other forms of group insurance. The premium reporting form usually provides for showing the outstanding covered balance at the beginning and the end of the month and then taking the average of these two as the amount of covered loans on which premium is remitted.

AUDIT OF ADMINISTRATOR'S INSURANCE RECORDS

Many carriers follow the practice of a periodic, usually annual, audit of the policyowner's or third party administrator's records. In some companies this is performed by auditors from the controller's department, rather than group division auditors. In other instances the audit is performed by the carrier's group field personnel because of their greater in-depth knowledge of group insurance and their ability to answer technical questions about the administration and interpretation of the contract.

EFFECT OF COMPUTERIZATION

With the increasing sophistication of computerized systems used by the home offices of group insurance carriers, including systems developed for the administration and premium billing of group insurance, there may be a discernible trend toward a greater proportion of group policies being administered by home offices. Since computer systems can allow remote access to the insurance status of individual insureds, the existence of such data in home office computer files enables the field claims offices of carriers to check on insurance status at the time of claims. One major group insurance carrier who has established this type of facility uses it for the benefit of the policyowner by not requiring that the policyowner complete insurance status information on the claim form. This capability of a computerized system may become more widely used by commercial carriers that have significant volumes of group insurance in force in order to combat the advantage that Blue Cross-Blue Shield plans have in this respect, since the latter do not require the employer to furnish such information as part of the claims process.

SUMMARY

The chapter opened by discussing setting up records of insurance. Specifically, each item usually found on the enrollment card was analyzed. Then the two principal types of group plan administration were defined. The discussion of home office or insurer administration included typical transactions affecting premiums due; the dual-choice option (HMOs); such transactions as change of name and beneficiary; issue of a new certificate or booklet-certificate; extended insurance coverage for handicapped children; settlement options, evidence of insurability; premium billing; and lock box payments.

The discussion of group plan administration by the policyowner or third party described special contracts for delegation of administrative functions, long-term disability insurance arrangements, administrative services only plans, creditor insurance, and audits of administrators' insurance records. The chapter concluded with a brief note about possible effects of computerization on administrative practices.

CHAPTER 25

THE PROCESSING OF GROUP CLAIMS

INTRODUCTION

The purpose of processing claims for benefits is self-evident. It is the way the insurance carrier, as a result of receiving the necessary information and evidence, fulfills its contractual obligation under the policy. In order to do so, the carrier must secure the facts about the death, injury, or sickness for which a claim has been filed, relate these facts to the terms of the contract, and determine the amount of benefits payable to the insured or the beneficiary.

The term "claims processing" encompasses all the above. In addition, claims processing reflects each insurance company's claims philosophy, which determines how claims under its policies are handled. Every company's claims philosophy should have as its objective the prompt, fair, courteous and accurate processing of applications for benefits under its policies.

The performance of the claims department is vital because this performance strongly influences the company's reputation and directly affects customer satisfaction. Dissatisfaction with the claim service of an insurer can become dissatisfaction with the concept of insurance or with the coverage provided by the particular company.[1]

This chapter begins by briefly considering the general characteristics of claims. It then describes in detail the processing and payment of benefits under group life insurance and under group health insurance. The discussion of claims payable under group life insurance includes death claims on dependents, death claims payable under accidental death and dismemberment insurance, credit life insurance, and other benefits. The discussion of claims payable under group health insurance includes a detailed discussion of medical ex-

---

[1]George D. Stengel, *Claim Administration—Life and Health Insurance* (International Claim Association, 1969), p. 1.

by
GEORGE M. HIDER, *Vice President, Pilot Life Insurance Company, Greensboro, North Carolina*

pense claims and a briefer discussion of short-term and long-term disability claims. Three methods of payment for medical expense claims are considered: payment by the home office, payment and processing in company field claim offices, and payment by the policyowner or third party. Processing aspects of medical expense claims are described in detail.

BASIC CONSIDERATIONS

Some basic questions must be answered as part of the process of settling all claims, under any coverage afforded by group policies:

1. Was the group policy in force at the time the claim was incurred?
2. Was the person a member of one of the eligible classes?
3. Was the person currently insured at the time the claim was incurred? (If the answer to 1 or 3 is "no," then the remaining question is—was the person with respect to whom claim is now made covered under the extended benefit provision of the policy?)
4. Has the proof of claim, or notice of claim, been submitted within the time limitations specified by the provision of the policy?
5. Has sufficient information been furnished so that the carrier can determine (a) whether it has any liability, and (b) if so, can the nature and amount of the carrier's liability be properly and accurately identified?
6. If a benefit is payable, to whom is it payable?
7. Does the carrier have the necessary authorization to make payment of benefits to the person or organization making the claim?

GROUP LIFE CLAIMS

Group life claims encompass claims under group life insurance with respect to an employee or a dependent, accidental death claims payable under the accidental death and dismemberment coverage in group policies, and claims in conjunction with credit life insurance.

Organization of Claim Department

In group life insurance, almost without exception, only the home office or, in the case of very large companies, the regional home office of the carrier has the authority to process and pay life claims. Some carriers may make rare exceptions to this practice by allowing claims for smaller amounts to be processed and paid by their own field claims offices or by certain larger brokerage houses who administer claims.

Processing Death Claims

The payment of group death claims is ordinarily a systematic process in which the claim processor answers a series of well-defined questions while remaining alert for unusual circumstances that might indicate the need for additional information. The factors with which the claim processor is concerned and the forms used to facilitate the gathering of necessary information are presented below.

FACTORS CONSIDERED

Three particular considerations apply to death claims and not to health claims. The first is whether the proceeds are to be paid in a lump sum, or under a settlement option selected by the insured employee during his or her lifetime, or by the beneficiary at time of claim. The second is the age of the beneficiary or beneficiaries. If the beneficiary has attained legal age there is no problem. However, if the beneficiary, or one or more of the beneficiaries, is a minor according to the law of the state of residence, documentary proof must be submitted to the insurer of the appointment of a legal guardian for that minor so that the insurer can properly and legally discharge its obligation.

A third consideration applying to death claims specifically is whether the beneficiary designated by the insured person is living at the time of the death of the insured. If the named beneficiary is not alive, unless the insured person has provided for contingent beneficiaries, that is, has named another person to become the beneficiary in the event of the beneficiary's predeceasing the insured, the proceeds normally become payable to the insured's estate. In such circumstances or where the insured has designated the estate as beneficiary, the carrier must be provided with evidence of the legal appointment, usually by a probate court, of a person or other entity as administrator of the estate.

Another provision found in some group policies, called a facility of payment clause, permits the insurance company to pay part of the death benefit for final illness and funeral expenses. Payments may be made even though a designated beneficiary is alive and competent. Usually an amount not exceeding $500 may be paid on this basis to any person appearing to the insurer to be equitably entitled to the money by reason of having incurred funeral or other expenses incident to the last illness or death of the insured.[2]

Where settlement options have been elected, the carrier issues a supplementary contract that reflects the elected type of settlement option upon receipt of the proper proof of death and in lieu of paying a lump sum benefit. Whether that settlement option is administered by the group division of the carrier after it has been executed varies. Some carriers have their ordinary (individual life insurance) claims

---

[2]Robert D. Eilers and Robert M. Crowe, *Group Insurance Handbook* (Homewood, Ill.: Richard D. Irwin, Inc., 1965), p. 492.

department assume responsibility for the fulfillment and administration of the terms of the supplementary contract. Other carriers, especially the very large ones, administer supplementary contracts arising from group business within their own group claims department.

Some states have enacted legislation requiring the carrier to pay accrued interest on the proceeds, payable from the date of death until the actual payment is made. Some carriers have adopted this as a company practice regardless of whether it is required by state statute.

Some jurisdictions, such as Puerto Rico, allow only a certain maximum amount of death benefits otherwise payable to be paid to the beneficiary prior to estate tax clearance being released by that jurisdiction. Other states, such as South Carolina, require that a form be completed by the carrier at the time of payment of benefits above a certain amount and sent directly to the estate tax division of the state in conjunction with estate or inheritance taxes.

CLAIM FORMS

It is usual to require that a claim under a group life insurance policy be submitted on a form specified by the carrier and furnished to the policyowner. A specimen of a typical form is reproduced in Figure 25-1.

Provision is made on the claim form for a statement to be completed by the group policyowner. As proof of death, a portion of the form may be completed by the attending physician who can certify that death occurred, with date and cause of death. In lieu of such a statement, a certified copy of the official death certificate is acceptable. Some carriers do not require that the copy be certified if it is a photocopy of a certified copy. Usually the same form can be used with respect to a claim for benefits on a deceased employee or on a covered dependent.

Variations in Group Life Claims

When a death claim under a group policy involves an individual insured under a dependent life policy or one insured through a lending institution, or when the policy includes certain riders, the claim processor must take these factors into consideration.

DEATH CLAIMS ON DEPENDENTS

Under dependent life insurance, the insured employee is usually the beneficiary. In fact, most such coverage automatically designates the employee as the beneficiary to receive the proceeds payable upon the death of the spouse or any of the covered dependent children.

In addition, the amounts of life insurance on dependents are relatively low compared with the amounts in force on the insured employee's life. Therefore, the proceeds are almost invariably paid in a lump sum to the beneficiary.

FIGURE 25-1
Life Claim Form

PILOT LIFE INSURANCE COMPANY
GREENSBORO, NC 27420

DEATH PROOF OF   ☐ INSURED   ☐ DEPENDENT

ATTACH GROUP LIFE CERTIFICATE IF THIS IS NOT FOR A DEPENDENT CLAIM

ATTENDING PHYSICIAN'S STATEMENT (An official certified death certificate may be attached in lieu of this physician's statement)

FULL NAME OF DECEASED		AGE	SEX	INSURED'S NAME (IF THIS IS A DEPENDENT CLAIM)
1.		2.	3.	4.

DECEASED'S ADDRESS	(Street)	(City)	(State)
5.			

INSURED'S EMPLOYER	IF DEPENDENT CLAIM, GIVE RELATIONSHIP TO INSURED	IF DEPENDENT, WITH WHOM WAS HE LIVING?
6.	7.	8.

DID YOU PERSONALLY EXAMINE THE DECEASED?	DATE AND TIME OF DEATH	A.M	PLACE OF DEATH
9.	10. Mo. Day Yr.	P.M.	11.

HOW LONG HAD DECEASED BEEN TOTALLY DISABLE TO WORK PRIOR TO DATE OF DEATH?	WAS DEATH DUE TO
12.	13. ☐ SUICIDE? ☐ HOMICIDE? ☐ ACCIDENT?

WHAT WAS THE IMMEDIATE CAUSE OF DEATH?	WHAT WERE THE CONTRIBUTING CAUSES OF DEATH?
14.	15.

IF DEATH DUE TO INJURY, PLEASE EXPLAIN ACCIDENT IN DETAIL.

16.

WAS THERE AN OFFICIAL INQUIRY AS TO THE CAUSE OF DEATH OR A POST MORTEM EXAMINATION ON THE BODY OF THE DECEASED?

17.   ☐ YES   ☐ NO

IF SO, WHICH, BY WHOM, AND WITH WHAT RESULTS?

18.

TYPE PHYSICIAN'S NAME	ATTENDING PHYSICIAN'S SIGNATURE
PHYSICIAN'S ADDRESS	DATE

EMPLOYEE'S CERTIFICATE (Complete only if this is a dependent claim)

HOW LONG HAS DECEASED LIVED IN YOUR HOME?	HOW LONG ENTIRELY DEPENDENT ON YOU?	WHERE DID DECEASED LAST WORK?
19.	20.	21.

DECEASED'S DATE OF BIRTH	DATE	SIGNED
22.		

EMPLOYER'S CERTIFICATE

FULL NAME OF DECEASED		AGE	INSURED'S NAME (IF THIS IS A DEPENDENT CLAIM)	GROUP POLICY NUMBER
23.		24.	25.	26.

CLASS	OCCUPATION, IF CLASS IS BASED ON OCC	SALARY IF CLASS IS BASED ON SALARY
27.	28.	28A.

INSURED'S CERTIFICATE NO.	DATE INSURED (EMP. COVERAGE) (DEP. COVERAGE)	DATE EMPLOYEE LAST WORKED	REASON FOR LEAVING WORK
29.	30.	31.	32.

IF DEPENDENT CLAIM, GIVE RELATIONSHIP TO INSURED	IF DEPENDENT CLAIM, WAS DECEASED ENTIRELY DEPENDENT ON INSURED?	IF YES, HOW LONG?
33.	34.	35.

CAUSE OF DEATH	DATE AND TIME OF DEATH	A.M	WAS PREM. PAID & CERT. IN FORCE AT TIME OF DEATH?
36.	37. Mo. Day Yr.	P.M	38. ☐ YES ☐ NO

IF DEATH WAS DUE TO INJURY, PLEASE EXPLAIN DETAILS OF ACCIDENT FULLY

39.

DID INJURY OCCUR ON OR OFF DUTY?	WORKMEN'S COMPENSATION	BENEFICIARY (IF INSURED CLAIM)	RELATIONSHIP	AGE
40.	41. ☐ YES ☐ NO	42.	43.	44.

IF THE BENEFICIARY IS A MINOR, PLEASE FURNISH THE GUARDIANSHIP PAPERS	IF THE BENEFICIARY IS THE INSURED'S ESTATE, PLEASE FURNISH THE CERT. OF ADMINISTRATIVE APPOINTMENT TO HIS ESTATE	BENEFICIARIES SOCIAL SECURITY NO.
45.	46.	47.

IN CASE OF HOMICIDE, DID BENEFICIARY CONTRIBUTE TO DEATH OF INSURED?

48.

THE POLICYHOLDER'S AUTHORIZED REPRESENTATIVE MUST SIGN THIS FORM.

| Date | this | day of | 19 | Name of Company _____ |

Company Phone No. _____   Signature _____   Official Position _____

G—4F

CREDIT LIFE INSURANCE

Under credit life insurance coverage the policyowner is usually the lending institution. In the event of the death of an insured debtor, the claim and the necessary forms and evidence are submitted by the lending institution.

In group credit life insurance the amount payable is usually the outstanding balance of the loan at time of death. The creditor policyowner furnishes this information on the claim form at the time of submitting claim, in addition to the proof of death. Figure 25-2 shows a typical claim form for this purpose.

For credit life insurance on the members of credit unions, the amount that the deceased member had accumulated in a savings (or share) account with the credit union is frequently covered for death benefit purposes up to a certain maximum or according to a formula. This insurance is purchased by the credit union for its members as an additional incentive to join the credit union. Thus, in the event of the

---

FIGURE 25-2
Death Claim Form for Credit Life
(Front)

PILOT LIFE INSURANCE COMPANY

CREDIT LIFE INSURANCE

I. PHYSICIAN'S STATEMENT

FULL NAME OF DECEASED	ADDRESS
1.	2.

DATE OF BIRTH	DATE OF DEATH	PLACE OF DEATH	CAUSE OF DEATH
3.	4.	5.	6.

DURATION OF ILLNESS OR INJURY CAUSING DEATH	WHEN DID YOU FIRST TREAT DECEASED FOR LAST ILLNESS?
7.	8.

CONTRIBUTORY CAUSE OF DEATH	DURATION OF CONTRIBUTORY CAUSE OF DEATH
9.	10.

These statements are true and correct to the best of my knowledge and belief:

_____, 19____   _____ M.D.

      Date   *Signature*

                                        _____

                                            Address

A Certified Copy Of The Death Certificate May Be Submitted For The Above

STATEMENT OF FINANCIAL INSTITUTION

INSURED'S FULL NAME	POLICY NO.
1.	2.

STREET ADDRESS	CITY AND STATE
3.	4.

COMPLETE THE FOLLOWING FOR LOANS

PURPOSE OF LOAN		OCCUPATION	
5.		6.	

DATE OF LOAN	TERM OF LOAN	AMOUNT OF MONTHLY INSTALLMENT	
7.	8.	9.	

DUE DATE FIRST INSTALLMENT	DATE LAST INSTALLMENT PAID	NO. OF DELINQUENT PAYMENTS, IF ANY
10.	11.	12.

INSURANCE WITH RESPECT TO THIS LOAN IS

13. ☐ REDUCING   ☐ LEVEL TERM   17. ORIGINAL AMOUNT COVERED BY INSURANCE $_____

                                         18. ORIGINAL AMOUNT OF LOAN $_____

14. PLAN NUMBER

                                         19. AMOUNT PAID $_____

15. BALANCE CLAIMED BY SECOND BENEFICIARY $_____   20. BALANCE DUE $_____

16. NAME OF SECOND BENEFICIARY _____

COMPLETE THE FOLLOWING FOR SAVINGS INSURANCE

INSURED JOINED CREDIT UNION ON _____

HAS MEMBERSHIP IN CREDIT UNION BEEN CONTINUOUS? _____

IF NOT WHEN DID INSURED LAST JOIN? _____

THE INSURED'S TOTAL INSURED SAVINGS ON DATE OF DEATH $_____

IF INSURED IS 55 OR OVER ATTACH A LISTING BY DATE OF HIS DEPOSITS AND WITHDRAWALS _____

The above is a true, correct and accurate statement:

     FINANCIAL INSTITUTION _____

     ADDRESS _____

     BY _____ DATE _____

     WITNESS _____

GROUP DIVERSIFIED RISKS AND SCHOLASTIC CLAIMS — 578

G—4061A   SEE REVERSE SIDE FOR LISTING DEPOSITS AND WITHDRAWALS

FIGURE 25-2
Death Claim Form for Credit Life
(Back)

LIFE SAVINGS INSURANCE

Share balance on date last performed usual duties: $_____
Lowest balance between date last worked and death: $_____
(Complete when applicable)

	Date	Amount
Share balance on 55th birthday:	_____	$_____
Lowest share balance between 55—59 years inclusive:	_____	$_____
Share balance on 60th birthday:	_____	$_____
Lowest share balance between 60—64 years inclusive:	_____	$_____
Share balance on 65th birthday:	_____	$_____
Lowest share balance between 65—69 years inclusive:	_____	$_____
Share balance on 70th birthday:	_____	$_____
Lowest share balance between age 70 and death:	_____	$_____

SHARE ACCOUNT TRANSACTIONS

(6 or 12 Months Prior to Death)

Date	Amount Received	Amount of Withdrawal	Balance
_____	$_____	$_____	$_____
_____	$_____	$_____	$_____
_____	$_____	$_____	$_____
_____	$_____	$_____	$_____
_____	$_____	$_____	$_____
_____	$_____	$_____	$_____
_____	$_____	$_____	$_____
_____	$_____	$_____	$_____
_____	$_____	$_____	$_____
_____	$_____	$_____	$_____

I certify the above figures and dates to be correctly extracted from the credit union's records. If as a result of audit on overpayment is discovered due to inaccuracy in the above information, the credit union will reimburse Pilot Life Insurance Companies.

_____ _____
Signature of Treasurer or Manager   Name of Credit Union

_____ _____
Title   City and State

death of an insured debtor who is a member of the credit union, the carrier would not only pay the outstanding balance of the loan to the creditor-lender, but would also pay an amount equal to the amount which the member had in the share account up to the stated maximum, or according to the stated formula, to the credit union member's beneficiary. There is, of course, no true insurance factor present in paying death benefits on share account balances as there is nothing at risk.

ACCIDENTAL DEATH AND DISMEMBERMENT INSURANCE

Where accidental death and dismemberment coverage is included in the group plan along with group life insurance, it is not usual to require the submission of a separate claim for the accidental death benefit. Rather, the death claim, if accidental death is involved, is regarded as being for *any* and *all* death benefits under that particular group policy.

However, because of the exclusions and limitations typically present in the accidental death and dismemberment insurance portion of the group coverage, the claims examiner must have more complete information with respect to the circumstances of the death if it is accidental. Since most states permit exclusions for suicide and death resulting from certain other circumstances, it is not unusual for the carrier to investigate the circumstances of death before paying the accidental death benefit.

An additional consideration beyond those applicable to group life insurance in death claims involving accidental death benefits is whether that coverage is for death occurring from nonoccupational accident only or whether the coverage is for both occupational and nonoccupational causes of death.

From the standpoint of settlement options, the carrier customarily allows the additional proceeds for accidental death to be included with the proceeds under the group life insurance for the purpose of setting up settlement options.

OTHER BENEFITS

Some group term life insurance policies include a provision for the payment of the face amount of the life insurance upon submission to the carrier of satisfactory proof of total and permanent disablement of the insured person. Such provisions may state that the face amount is payable as a lump sum to the insured person in such circumstances, or may give the insured person the option of receiving those proceeds under a settlement option. Other forms of the total and permanent disability benefit provision do not permit the payment of the face amount in a lump sum, but specify payment of either an amount of monthly benefits until the proceeds plus interest are exhausted, or the payment of the proceeds in monthly installments over a given maximum period of time.

This benefit on either of the bases described is relatively rare in current group life insurance policies.

Other circumstances under which the proceeds of the policy are payable during the insured's lifetime occur in group permanent life insurance coverage. Usually the certificates issued under this coverage permit the insured person to elect a settlement option for payment of the cash value upon termination of insurance or upon the insured's retirement at age 60 or 65.

HEALTH CLAIMS

The payment of group health claims is more complex than the payment of group death claims. The processing of death claims may involve some complex considerations. However, such complexities are more likely to be present with ordinary, or individual, life insurance policy claims than with group life insurance claims.

A major factor in distinguishing these two general types of claims is the volume of claims relative to the type of coverage. There are far more health claims incurred among an insured group than there are death claims.

The complexities created by the greater volume of health claims are compounded by rapid technological advances and double-digit inflation in the health care industry. The attendant need to restrain cost increases is frustrated by competitive pressures that encourage the liberal interpretation of claims. Since no group health policy can anticipate all of the questions that arise during claim administration, the claim processor must often make decisions without the benefit of detailed instructions. In making these decisions, the processor must be cognizant of all applicable insurance department rulings and state statutes. He or she must also be aware of current trends in the insurance industry.[3]

There are three basic kinds of claims for health insurance benefits. The first is a medical expense claim under a group policy, either on an employee or a covered dependent. These include hospital stays, surgery, and physicians' visits. The second is a disability income claim under the group policy, either under a weekly benefit short-term coverage or under a long-term disability income insurance coverage. The third is a claim payable under creditor accident and health coverage.

Methods of Health Claim Processing

There are basically three methods of payment of medical expense claims under policies issued by commercial insurers:

1. Claims are mailed to and processed by the home office of the insurer;
2. Claims are mailed to and processed by a field claims office of the insurer; or
3. Claims are processed and paid by the policyowner or by a third party.

The choice as to whether medical expense claims will be paid directly by the carrier, policyowner, or through a third party lies

---

[3]Health Insurance Association of America, *Principles of Group Health Insurance I*, (1972), p. 183.

largely with the policyowner. Many times the claim payment method is specified by the broker or consultant involved in the sale of the case. However, when the carrier retains responsibility for the claim payment function, the carrier's organization determines whether claims will be processed centrally at the home office or by a regional field claims office.

Where a third party is responsible for claim payment, arrangements are made by the carrier with the third party. The type of organizations serving as third party payors are large brokerage houses with their own claim payment facilities or administrative organizations specializing in the processing and payment of medical expense claims. In some instances third party payment may be performed by a smaller brokerage firm or by the agent who originated the case.

There has been a trend among the larger writers of group medical expense insurance toward the establishment of regional field claims offices. This has occurred in some cases in conjunction with the spreading of active group-writing territories of the carrier further and further away from the home office. Where the home office is far removed from the case, many employers demand local company regional office claims processing facilities before they will consider placing business with the carrier. The opening and location of company field claims offices, therefore, has become an integral part of the marketing and sales process.

The following discussion outlines some of the characteristics of these three basic methods of payment.

HOME OFFICE PAYMENT

The home office group claims department is usually an integral part of the carrier's group department. The manager of the group claims department typically reports to the senior executive in charge of group operations. However, in some companies, including both large and small group writing companies, the group claims are processed by a unit that is part of the central home office claims department for the company. This unit is responsible for processing claims on all lines of insurance written by the company.

Because of the centralization of authority and the volume of claims, home office claim operations are potentially more economical than their field office counterparts. Fewer supervisory personnel are needed. In addition, mechanization of routine processing and the initiation of electronic programming are facilitated. Centralization also expedites communication between supervisory personnel and the working force and between claim administrators and the company's legal and medical officers.[4]

---

[4]Eilers and Crowe, *op. cit.*, p. 559.

FIELD CLAIM OFFICE PAYMENT

The organizational pattern referred to for home office processing of claims applies also in many respects to the field claims office. The integration of the group claims payment responsibility into a general regional claims office operation is common, especially among multiple line carriers who write property, liability, and workers' compensation insurance in addition to group insurance.

Other carriers that are strictly life and health insurance companies usually have a separate and independent field claims office for the processing of medical expense claims if they have the field payment facility available.

It is customary for the supervisor or manager of the field claims office to have some dollar limit placed on the authority of the field office to issue checks or drafts in payment of claims processed. Claims that would result in payment in excess of that maximum amount are referred to the home office for payment approval.

Even when the payment function is decentralized through field claims offices, the data about claims payments are transmitted to and retained by the home office of the carrier.

Along with increasing automation of functions in the home offices of carriers, most companies with a significant field claims office operation have taken steps toward greater automation of the functions of the field claims offices. Such automation aims at increased efficiency in the claims process in the local field office and the ready availability and faster transmission of transaction data to the central files of the carrier at the home office.

Local claim payment facilities are potentially able to communicate more closely and personally with policyowners than are their home office counterparts. They have the additional advantage of being able to concentrate their attention on the fee levels and the individuals and institutions providing health care in their local area. Their ability to attract high quality personnel is enhanced by the existence of more than one employment market from which to recruit claim administrators.

POLICYOWNER OR THIRD PARTY PAYMENT

When payment is made by the policyowner or a third party administrator, a procedures manual is usually furnished along with a supply of claims worksheets and data sheets. The claims function is not delegated until the insurance carrier has determined that proper facilities and trained personnel are available to perform this function efficiently and accurately. Some carriers formalize the delegation of this function by means of a written contract or agreement similar to the

---

[5]*Ibid.*, p. 560.

agreements made when the administrative function is delegated to the policyowner or a third party. Figure 25-3 shows the wording of a typical form used in claims payment agreements. Note that a maximum draft or claim authorization is specified. This is similar to the procedure described under payment processing by field claims offices.

FIGURE 25-3

OWNERSHIP OF RECORDS*

All records maintained by the Agency in accordance with this Agreement are the property of Pilot Life. While such records are in the custody of the Agency, they may be examined by Pilot Life at any reasonable time.

PAYMENT OF CLAIMS

The Agency shall pay, by drafts on the account of Pilot Life drawn on forms furnished by Pilot Life, claims for Weekly Disability Benefits, Basic and Major Medical Expense Benefits, in accordance with all the terms and provisions of the Group Policy in effect when such claims are incurred. However, if proofs of loss received at any one time on account of any one person are such that they would generate a total payment in excess of $_____, the Agency shall make no payment on account of such proofs unless or until such proofs have been reviewed by Pilot Life and Pilot Life has authorized payment. The Agency shall maintain complete records of proofs of loss upon which claim payments are based, including verification of coverage of the claimants at the times such claims are incurred and computation of the amounts payable.

ERRORS AND OMISSIONS

Clerical errors or omissions made by the Agency shall not create any liability on the part of the Agency, in the absence of fraud or gross negligence, but the Agency and Pilot Life shall take whatever action may be necessary to correct the effects of such errors or omissions.

*Reprinted with permission of the Pilot Life Insurance Company. This form may not be reproduced without prior written consent of Pilot Life.

This function is usually delegated only when the group policy covers a relatively large number of employees. The policyowner or third party is expected to send copies of drafts, and sometimes copies of the claim file itself to the home office of the carrier. Some carriers with a strong network of field claims offices supervise and assist the payment process by the policyowner or third party from their local offices. Annual audits by the carrier are customary when the claim payment function is delegated.

Processing Medical Expense Claims

The payment of medical expense claims is a complex process. Adequate documentation must be available to determine the types of expenses incurred, the date on which they were incurred, and the provider of services. In addition, the claims reviewer must determine whether the claimant had insured status at the time the expense was incurred and whether the policy provides coverage for the specific services received. If a coordination of benefits clause is incorporated into the contract, the existence of other coverage must be examined as well. Having determined that the claimant and the services provided are covered under the policy, the reviewer evaluates the reasonableness of the provider's charges.

In order to assure that both the claims reviewer and the providers of care are adequately informed, various forms have been developed. These include forms that verify the benefits available to the patient at the time of admission to the hospital, those that provide for the assignment of benefits to the providers of care, and those that authorize the release of information.

Once the eligibility for and amount of benefit have been determined, the benefit payment, along with explanatory materials, is issued. Information about the transaction is used by the insurer in developing a data bank.

DOCUMENTATION

The carrier requires documentary evidence about the type of expense incurred, who provided the service, and when it was provided to properly determine whether its group policy covers the expenses incurred by the insured person or the insured's dependent. If medical supplies, particularly prescription drugs, are furnished to insureds or dependents who are not hospital confined, satisfactory descriptions of the supplies and indications that they were prescribed by a physician are needed.

Commercial insurance companies writing the bulk of group medical expense coverage are members of the Health Insurance Association of America (HIAA). There has been a consistent effort over many years by the former Health Insurance Council, now the Consumer and Professional Relations Division of HIAA, to work with the major providers of health care to develop standard claim forms acceptable to the provider that also contain sufficient information to be acceptable to the insurance carrier. The two largest groups of health care providers are hospitals and medical doctors. Therefore, the design of acceptable forms was negotiated on behalf of the industry by the Health Insurance Council with the American Hospital Association and the American Medical Association. An example of this form is shown in Figure 25-4.

For a number of years the standard forms were widely used by both providers and carriers. However, within the last ten years there has been a trend among the individual states, usually on state insurance department initiatives, to mandate the use of forms of a specific design for medical services (especially hospital services) for submission of claims to insurance carriers. These states also require the insurance carrier, where appropriate, to make supplies of these forms available to their group policyowners. The first states to institute this special requirement were North Carolina and South Carolina. For

FIGURE 25-4

Hospital Insurance Form

GROUP HOSPITAL INSURANCE FORM *TO BE PRESENTED TO THE HOSPITAL IN DUPLICATE*
Spaced for Typewriter — Marks for Tabulator Appear on this Line

To_____Hospital. This certifies that_____is insured for the following

Group Hospital Benefits (in behalf of his dependent_____) By

KENNESAW LIFE AND ACCIDENT INSURANCE COMPANY   *(Name)*   *(Relationship)*
(Name of Insurer)

BENEFITS FOR OTHER THAN MATERNITY CASES	BENEFITS FOR MATERNITY CASES
A. HOSPITAL ROOM AND BOARD (INCLUDING GENERAL NURSING SERVICES) ACTUAL HOSPITAL CHARGES UP TO $_____FOR EACH DAY OF HOSPITALIZATION UP TO_____DAYS.	HOSPITAL ROOM AND BOARD (INCLUDING GENERAL NURSING SERVICE) AND OTHER HOSPITAL SERVICES . . ACTUAL CHARGES UP TO $_____ OR 1. HOSPITAL ROOM AND BOARD (INCLUDING GENERAL NURSING SERVICES) $_____ FOR EACH DAY OF HOSPITALIZATION UP TO_____DAYS
B. OTHER HOSPITAL CHARGES FOR HOSPITAL CARE AND TREATMENT (EXCLUDING CHARGES FOR NURSES' AND PHYSICIANS' SERVICES AND TAKE HOME DRUGS) $_____	2. OTHER HOSPITAL CHARGES FOR HOSPITAL CARE AND TREATMENT (EXCLUDING CHARGES FOR NURSES' AND PHYSICIANS' SERVICES AND TAKE HOME DRUGS) $_____

THE MINIMUM HOUR HOSPITALIZATION REQUIREMENT WILL BE MET IF _____

GROUP POLICYHOLDER	ADDRESS		PHONE
BY *(Name and Title)*		ABOVE CERTIFICATION VALID FOR ONLY SEVEN DAYS FROM THIS DATE *(Exception — Maternity Cases)*	DATE

HOSPITAL COMPLETE FOLLOWING AND FURNISH COPY TO	ADDRESS		
NAME OF PATIENT	AGE	DATE ADMITTED	TIME ADMITTED AM PM	DATE DISCHARGED	TIME DISCHARGED AM PM
IF PATIENT HAD OTHER THAN SEMI-PRIVATE ROOM, INDICATE SEMI-PRIVATE DAILY RATE	$	OTHER INSURANCE INDICATED BY HOSPITAL RECORDS. IF YES, NAME OF COMPANY ☐ NO ☐ YES

DIAGNOSIS FROM RECORDS *(If Injury, Give Date and Place of Accident)*

OPERATIONS OR OBSTETRICAL PROCEDURES PERFORMED *(Nature and Date)*

HOSPITAL CHARGES (Complete This Section or Attach Copy of Itemized Bill Showing Information Below).

ROOM AND BOARD						
	☐ WARD	DAYS AT $	TOTAL	$		
	☐ SEMI-PRIVATE	DAYS AT $	TOTAL	$	TOTAL CHARGES	$
	☐ PRIVATE	DAYS AT $	TOTAL	$		$
	☐ OTHERS			$		$
OTHER CHARGES	OPERATING OR DELIVERY ROOM					$
	ANESTHESIA					
	X-RAY					
	LABORATORY					
	EKG BMR					
	PHYSICAL THERAPY				THIS FORM APPROVED BY THE HEALTH INSURANCE COUNCIL AND ACCEPTED BY THE AMERICAN HOSPITAL ASSOCIATION FOR USE BY HOSPITALS (see explanatory instructions).	
	AMBULANCE					
	MEDICAL AND SURGICAL SUPPLIES					
	PHARMACY *(Except Take Home Drugs)*					
	INHALATION THERAPY					
	INTRAVENOUS SOLUTIONS					
	TOTAL			$	TAX IDENTIFICATION NUMBER	

HOSPITAL   ADDRESS

TAKEN FROM RECORDS ON _____ 19_____   SIGNED BY

AUTHORIZATION TO RELEASE INFORMATION: I hereby authorize the above named hospital to release the information requested on this form.
Date_____, 19____Signed_____

AUTHORIZATION TO PAY INSURANCE BENEFITS: I hereby authorize payment directly to the above named hospital of the Group Hospital *Patient (Parent if a Minor)*
Benefits herein specified and otherwise payable to me but not to exceed the hospital's regular charges for this period of hospitalization. I understand I am financially responsible to the hospital for charges not covered by this authorization.

Date_____, 19____Signed_____
                                        (Insured)

161—21   PLEASE RETURN THIS FORM TO THE EMPLOYER AND NOT TO THE INSURANCE COMPANY.

1 - 1383

carriers with a concentration of group medical expense insurance in states with these special requirements, particularly carriers with local group claims offices located in those states, the mandated use of special claim forms does not present a problem. However, for carriers who have central home office claims processing arrangements and who operate in all or many states, the use of a wide variety of claims forms is an additional operating complication in their claim departments.

A recently adopted hospital billing form, which has been agreed upon between the American Hospital Association and the Health Insurance Association of America, is known as "UB-16." A specimen of the form is reproduced in Figure 25-5. It is anticipated that UB-16 will gradually replace the former standard form developed jointly by the American Hospital Association and the Health Insurance Association of America. Form UB-16 is now being used or is expected to be used in the near future in the following states: Arizona, California, Connecticut, Florida, Georgia, Massachusetts, Minnesota, New Hampshire, North Dakota, Oregon, and Washington. The procedure followed in the use of this form is similar to that referred to in the special forms that are required for use in North and South Carolina.

Special claims forms are needed for dental insurance, vision care, and prescription drug insurance plans where these are provided by separate benefit inserts within the group policy or under a separate policy.

Especially for claims under major medical expense insurance, once an initial claim has been established, rather than requiring the completion of a claim form by the provider, many carriers accept the actual bills from the provider of services or supplies, provided the bills clearly identify the person who received the services or supplies, the condition or diagnosis for which the services were necessary, and the physician who furnished or prescribed the services.

For out-patient prescription drugs, usually covered only under major medical expense insurance or under a separate benefit insert in the group policy, the requirements of the carriers vary. In general it is necessary that the name of the person for whom the drug was prescribed, the name of the physician who prescribed it, the prescription number, and the pharmacy's bill with the charge for the prescription be shown on the pharmacy bill submitted with the claim.

INSURANCE STATUS AT TIME OF CLAIM

The carrier usually requires that a statement be completed by the group policyowner showing the information provided in the example, Figure 25-6. This is customarily a part of the claim form.

Many carriers rely on the information furnished by the group policyowner as the sole means of determining the insurance status, at the time the claim was incurred, of the person for whom a claim is submitted. The information furnished on the employer's statement can

FIGURE 25-5
UB-16 Hospital Billing Form
(Front)

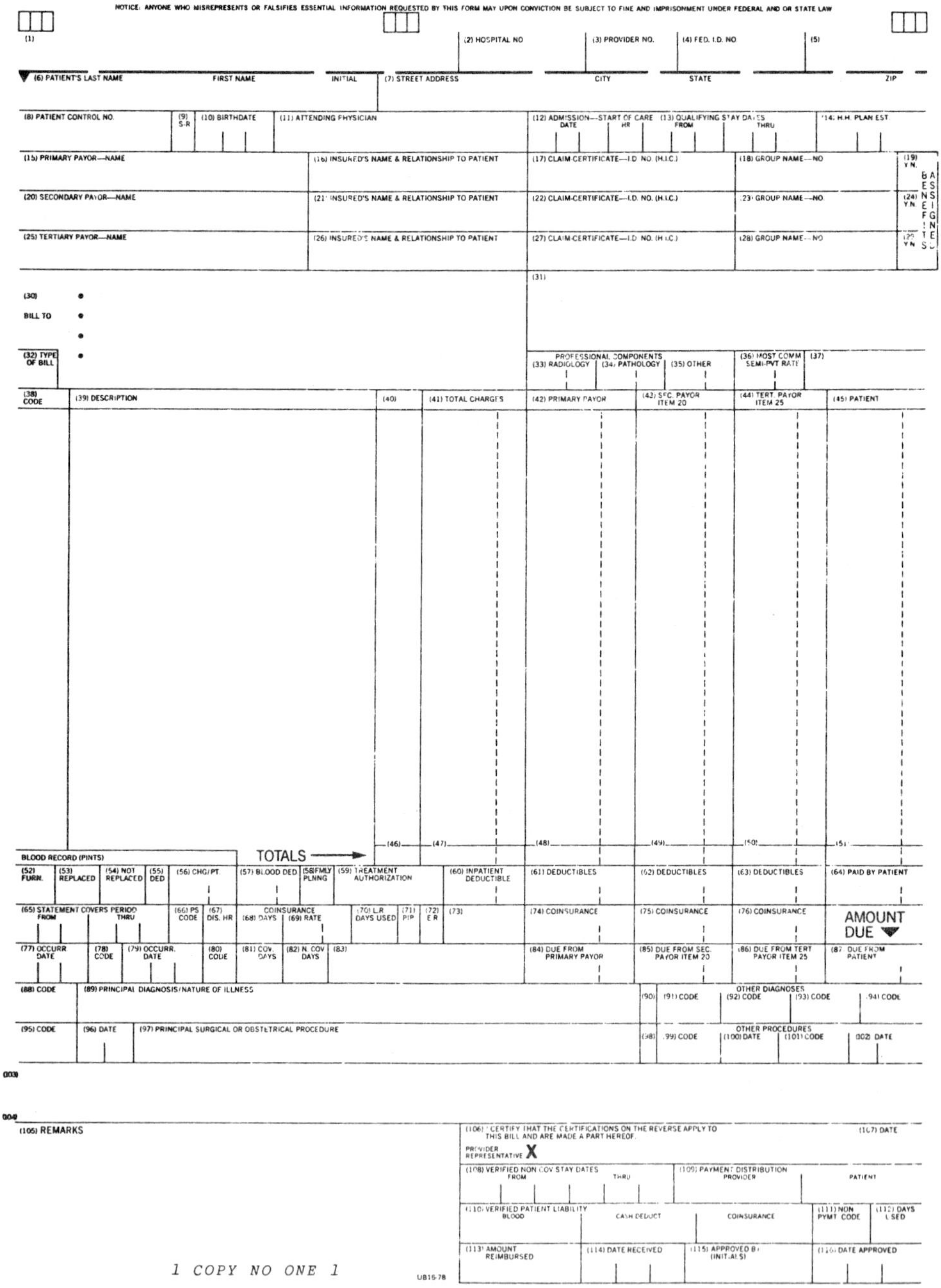

alert the claims processor to check provisions of the policy relating to
the maximum period of time provided for continuance of insurance
after cessation of active work and also furnish needed information for

FIGURE 25-5
UB-16
(Back)

SPACE FOR ADDITIONAL BILLING REQUIREMENTS AS NEEDED

Certifications Relevant to the Bill and Information Shown on the Face Hereof: Signatures on the face hereof incorporate the following certifications or verifications where pertinent to this bill:

1. If third party sponsor benefits are indicated as being assigned, on the face hereof; appropriate assignments by the insured and signature of patient or parent or legal guardian covering authorization to release information are on file. The hospital agrees to save harmless, indemnify and defend any insurer who makes payment in reliance upon this certification, from and against any claim to the insurance proceeds based in whole or in part upon an assertion that no valid assignment of the benefits to the hospital was made.

2. If patient occupied a private room for medical necessity, any required certifications are on file.

3. Physician's certifications and recertifications, if required by contract regulations, are on file.

4. For Christian Science Sanitoriums, verifications and if necessary, reverification of the patient's need for sanitorium services are on file.

5. Signature of patient or his representative on certifications, authorization to release information, and payment request, as required by Federal regulations and, if required by other contract regulations, is on file.

6. This claim, to the best of my knowledge, is correct and complete and is in conformance with the Civil Rights Act of 1964 as amended. Records adequately disclosing services will be maintained, and necessary information will be furnished to a governmental agency upon request.

7. For Medicare purposes: If the patient has indicated that other Health Insurance or State Medical Assistance Agencies will pay part of his medical expenses, and he wants information about this claim released to them upon their request, necessary authorization is on file.

8. For Medicaid purposes: This is to certify that the foregoing information is true, accurate, and complete.

   I understand that payment and satisfaction of this claim will be from Federal and State funds, and that any false claims, statements, or documents, or concealment of a material fact, may be prosecuted under applicable Federal or State laws.

ESTIMATED CONTRACT BENEFITS

short-term disability income benefits, especially if it is indicated that the employee has resumed work in the meantime.

There are also direct claims processing arrangements where the insured submits the claim directly to the carrier, rather than submitting it through the employer. In such circumstances, the employee's statement on the claim form is expanded to include information that

FIGURE 25-6
Employer's Statement of Insurance Status*

EMPLOYER'S STATEMENT: MEDICAL INFORMATION ON THIS CLAIM SHOULD BE TREATED AS **CONFIDENTIAL**				
NAME OF EMPLOYEE, AS IT APPEARS ON GROUP INSURANCE RECORDS 1		CERTIFICATE NUMBER 2	POLICY NUMBER 3	BRANCH 4
INSURANCE CLASS 5	BASIC WEEKLY EARNINGS 6.	DATE EMPLOYEE INSURED	DATE DEPENDENT INSURED 7	
IS THIS CLAIM COVERED BY WORKMEN'S COMPENSATION? 8. ☐ YES ☐ NO		IS THIS DISABILITY DUE IN ANY WAY TO THE INSURED'S OR DEPENDENT'S OCCUPATION? 9. ☐ YES ☐ NO		
DATE EMPLOYEE WAS LAST ACTIVELY AT WORK (Complete on Every Claim) 10. DATE EMPLOYEE RESUMED WORK 11	WHY DID EMPLOYEE CEASE WORK? ☐ ILLNESS ☐ QUIT ☐ INJURY ☐ DISMISSED ☐ VACATION ☐ TEMPORARY LAY OFF 12 ☐ LEAVE OF ABSENCE		HAS EMPLOYMENT TERMINATED? ☐ YES ☐ NO DATE _____ 13.	TO WHAT DATE HAVE EMPLOYEE'S PREMIUMS BEEN PAID? 14
IMPORTANT: EVERY ITEM MUST BE CHECKED OR ANSWERED BEFORE CLAIM CAN BE PROCESSED		ADMINISTRATOR'S SIGNATURE _____ DATE _____ TITLE _____ EMPLOYER _____		

*Reprinted with permission of the Pilot Life Insurance Company. This form may not be reproduced without prior written consent of Pilot Life.

otherwise would have been furnished on the employer's statement portion of the form.

In these situations the group policyowner does not act as the intermediary between the insured person and the carrier in the submission of the claim. The carrier has the responsibility, using the statement made by the employee on a special claim form, to verify insurance status from the carrier's own records prior to the processing of the claim for payment.

Some carriers who permit the use of the direct claims system have computerized facilities that allow the claims examiner to access, either from a field claims office or from the home office claims department, the necessary status information from computer records usually maintained at the home office.

In dealing directly with the insured, the carrier loses some of the benefits of having the employer screen the claim for completeness when it is submitted. Therefore, under direct claims submission arrangements, there tends to be a greater need for correspondence by the carrier to complete the information necessary for processing the claim, and a consequent additional expense. It is not unusual for the carrier to reflect this additional expense by increasing the expense portion of the dividend or premium refund formula used in experience rating a group policy with this arrangement.

These situations and the preliminary requirements in the claims payment process described in this section apply whether the claim is for the insured person or for an eligible dependent.

ELIGIBILITY FOR COVERAGE

The next step for the claims examiner is to relate the types of expenses incurred that are documented on the claim to the coverage under the policy for that specific insured. This means that if there are different classes of insureds under a policy, some of whom are not covered for certain elements of the medical expense plan or not covered for any of them, eligibility must be determined before further consideration is given to the claim. This information can be determined from insurance status at the time of the claim.

In assessing eligibility for coverage, the age of the patient is important. If the insured is eligible for coverage under Medicare, by virtue of attaining age 65 or having received a minimum of 24 months of disability benefits under Medicare, or because of chronic kidney disease, the claims processor's consideration of benefit payment will be affected, depending on the provisions of the group policy in such situations. The same consideration applies for the insured's dependent spouse. For unmarried dependent children, age is an important consideration in connection with the maximum eligibility age, usually attainment of the child's nineteenth birthday. Unless the child is enrolled in an accredited school or college as a full-time student beyond the nineteenth birthday, coverage on that child may cease. In most group policies a child who is enrolled and remains enrolled as a full-time student in an accredited school or college until the twenty-fifth birthday remains an eligible dependent throughout that period. There is also the possibility that a child may qualify for continuing coverage by virtue of being handicapped as defined in the policy.

COORDINATION OF BENEFITS

The details of the coordination of benefits provision are described in Chapter 13. In processing a claim, checking COB is the next step after determining eligibility. It is usual to obtain information on duplicate coverage from the employee at the time of submission of the claim. Questions seeking this information are usually provided on the claim form in the portion that the insured employee is required to complete.

Carriers obtain this information from other sources rather than relying solely on the employee to furnish it at the time of submission of a current claim. If there have been previous claims, there will be an annotation about the existence of other coverage on the carrier's claims records. Sometimes the hospital bill will indicate that there is another carrier, and sometimes a specific question is asked of the hospital or attending physician on the claim form itself.

If there appears to be a plan under which benefits are payable for the same expenses submitted in the claim being processed and the processing carrier's benefits should or could be coordinated with this plan, a duplicate coverage inquiry form (DCI) standardized for use in the health insurance industry is completed in the processing carrier's claims office and sent to the second carrier. An example of this form is reproduced in Figure 25-7.

FIGURE 25-7
Duplicate Coverage Inquiry

PILOT LIFE INSURANCE COMPANY • GREENSBORO, NORTH CAROLINA   Initial ☐   Subsequent ☐

MEDICAL EXPENSE INSURANCE DUPLICATE COVERAGE INQUIRY

THIS IDENTIFICATION SECTION MUST BE FULLY COMPLETED

PLEASE READ INSTRUCTIONS ON REVERSE SIDE BEFORE COMPLETING THIS FORM

TO:

NAME OF PATIENT	AGE RELATION TO INSURED

NAME AND ADDRESS OF INQUIRER'S INSURED

NAME AND ADDRESS OF INQUIRER'S GROUP POLICYHOLDER – OR INDIVIDUAL POLICY NUMBER

NAME OF RESPONDER'S INSURED	RELATION TO PATIENT

NAME AND ADDRESS OF RESPONDER'S GROUP POLICYHOLDER – OR – INDIVIDUAL POLICY NUMBER

NOTE TO RESPONDING COMPANY: Complete this form for (1) Group Only ☐ (2) Group or Individual ☐   RETURN WITHIN ONE WEEK

INQUIRER	PLAN	RESPONDER
Basic ☐ Supplemental Major Medical ☐ Comprehensive Major Medical ☐ None ☐ Group ☐ Individual ☐ Other ☐ _____ Effective_____ 19___	Coverage Identification	Basic ☐ Supplemental Major Medical ☐ Comprehensive Major Medical ☐ None ☐ Group ☐ Individual ☐ Other ☐ _____ Effective_____ 19___
Basic ☐ Supplemental Major Medical ☐ Comprehensive Major Medical ☐ Calendar Year ☐ Other (dates) ☐ _____	Date of Patient's Coverage	
	Coordination of Benefits Provision is in:	Basic ☐ Supplemental Major Medical ☐ Comprehensive Major Medical ☐ None ☐ Calendar Year ☐ Other (dates) ☐ _____
	Claim Determination Period	
Order of Benefit Determination ☐ Proration ☐ As secondary carrier, retain deductible & coinsurance ☐	Administer Coordination of Benefits By:	Order of Benefit Determination ☐ Proration ☐ As secondary carrier, retain deductible & coinsurance ☐

NOTE TO RESPONDING COMPANY: If you are secondary, complete the following only for that part of your coverage (1) which has no Coordination of Benefits, or (2) under which Coordination of Benefits is administered by proration (See Instructions No. 3 on reverse side)

(Show for all bills received)		(In absence of C.O.B.)		TYPE OF SERVICE	(Indicate by "x" if applicable)			(In absence of C.O.B.)	
Inclusive Dates	Amount Charged	Basic Benefits	Covered under Major Medical		Add'l Bills	No Bills Received	Not Covered	Basic Benefits	Covered under Major Medical
	$	$	$	Hospital R & B				$	$
				Hospital Misc.					
				Surgeon					
				Ass't Surgeon					
				Anesthesiologist					
				Physician - Home					
				Office					
				Hospital					
				Radiology					
				Pathology					
				Nursing					
				Drugs					

CERTIFICATION Were benefits certified to Hospital? Yes ☐ No ☐	TOTAL	TOTAL		CERTIFICATION Were benefits certified to Hospital? Yes ☐ No ☐	TOTAL	TOTAL
ASSIGNMENTS—Indicate with * in benefits column above and show amount paid. Amount Paid Type Service	$ LESS: Deductible	$ _____		ASSIGNMENTS—Indicate with * in benefits column above and show amount paid. Amount Paid Type Service	$ LESS: Deductible	$ _____
$_____ _____ $_____ _____ $_____ _____	Coinsurance MAJOR MEDICAL PAYABLE	_____ % _____ % $ _____		$_____ _____ $_____ _____ $_____ _____	Coinsurance MAJOR MEDICAL PAYABLE	_____ % _____ % $ _____

INQUIRING COMPANY (please print)	Basic Benefits Paid $	**RESPONDING COMPANY** (please print)	Basic Benefits Paid $
By_____	Major Medical Paid $	By_____ Address (if different from that given at top left):	Major Medical Paid $
Group Claims, Department 579 Pilot Life Insurance Company Box 20727 Greensboro, N. C. 27420 Area Code 919 Date Tel. No. 299-4720		Date_____ Tel._____	If prorate, payment based on Inquirer's expenses is $

G-3511

On claims for larger amounts, especially if the reply to the duplicate coverage inquiry indicates no other coverage and the carrier still suspects that other coverage may exist elsewhere, the carrier may institute an investigation. This would usually be done through a commercial reporting service, such as Equifax, that has services specifically geared for this type of investigation.

If such a form is initiated by the processing carrier, the claim is placed in a suspense file until a response is received from the second carrier. The follow-up procedures used by various carriers vary in the length of time between when the initial DCI has been sent and the time that the file is reactivated from the suspense file. Because the determination of whether a carrier is the primary or secondary carrier has been a major source of delays in payment of claims, most carriers attempt to expedite the securing and furnishing of this information. After the initial DCI has been sent to the second carrier, some carriers follow up by telephone. However, since all carriers realize that a prompt response is important, procedures are maintained by carriers for prompt response to the DCI. The operation of this system between commercial carriers usually means that the responding carrier makes an immediate search of its claims records on receipt of the DCI. If that carrier's records indicate no claim has been received at that time, the DCI from the other carrier is placed in suspense and responded to as soon as a claim is received.

REASONABLENESS OF CHARGES

Consideration of whether a charge is reasonable and customary applies mainly to physicians' charges under major medical expense insurance. However, an increasing number of plans are being written by commercial carriers that include a "reasonable and customary" provision for basic benefits as well.

When a claim concerns a type of expense or coverage that has the reasonable and customary provision, the claims examiner makes a determination about whether the charges submitted in the claim fall within reasonable and customary limits. If they do, then the full amount of the physician's fee is included in the figures that comprise the basis for calculating the benefits payable under the claim. If a fee, according to the guidelines used by the carrier, is above reasonable and customary limits, then only that portion within such limits is used as a covered expense in the calculation of the claim benefit to be paid.

In such circumstances, some carriers write a diplomatic letter to the physician asking whether any services of either greater complexity or duration were rendered other than the description of services furnished with the initial claim.

It is not customary for the charges made by hospitals to be subject to reasonable and customary standards. However, hospital charges and increases made in such charges are becoming subject to review through legislation passed by a growing number of states. From the claims examiner's standpoint, the decision to be made about hospital charges is primarily whether the charges billed were all, in fact, incurred by the specific patient. A question usually arises only if the types and amounts of expenses incurred by the patient as shown on the hospital bill appear inconsistent with the diagnosis shown or with the extent and nature of care usually provided for that condition.

VERIFICATION OF BENEFITS AVAILABLE

Hospitals in a number of states require a statement of the benefits for which the patient is covered at the time of admission to the hospital, or, if the admission is on an emergency basis or on a weekend, as soon after admission as possible. This certification is frequently obtained by the completion of a section on the hospital claim form, an example of which is reproduced in Figure 25-8. Certification may also be provided by the employer prior to admission. Alternatively, a phone call may be made to the employer or to the carrier's local claim office if one exists.

This section of the standard hospital claim form was incorporated as part of a procedure developed by HIAA in conjunction with the American Hospital Association to give the admitting office of the hospital more precise information about what benefits would be payable to the hospital under the group policy.

Some hospitals view this certification as similar to a purchase order. Although the certification may in some instances be incorrect, the hospital expects benefits to be paid in accordance with those that were certified. Certification is usually used by the hospital in conjunction with an assignment of benefits to the hospital from the insured person. The amount of benefits indicated in the certification is used by the hospital at the time of admission of the patient to determine whether a cash deposit is also required. This is done if the benefits

FIGURE 25-8
Certification of Hospital Coverage

TO _____ HOSPITAL. THIS CERTIFIES THAT _____ IS INSURED FOR THE FOLLOWING GROUP HOSPITAL BENEFITS (IN BEHALF OF HIS DEPENDENT _____) BY	
_____ (Name) (Relationship)	
_____ (Name of Insurer)	
BENEFITS FOR OTHER THAN MATERNITY CASES	**BENEFITS FOR MATERNITY CASES**
A. HOSPITAL ROOM AND BOARD (INCLUDING GENERAL NURSING SERVICES)—ACTUAL HOSPITAL CHARGES UP TO $_____ FOR EACH DAY OF HOSPITALIZATION UP TO _____ DAYS. B. OTHER HOSPITAL CHARGES FOR HOSPITAL CARE AND TREATMENT (EXCLUDING CHARGES FOR NURSES' AND PHYSICIANS' SERVICES AND TAKE-HOME DRUGS)—$_____.	HOSPITAL ROOM AND BOARD (INCLUDING GENERAL NURSING SERVICES AND OTHER HOSPITAL SERVICES)—ACTUAL CHARGES UP TO $_____ OR 1. HOSPITAL ROOM AND BOARD (INCLUDING GENERAL NURSING SERVICES)–$_____ FOR EACH DAY OF HOSPITALIZATION UP TO _____ DAYS. 2. OTHER HOSPITAL CHARGES FOR HOSPITAL CARE AND TREATMENT (EXCLUDING CHARGES FOR NURSES' AND PHYSICIANS' SERVICES AND TAKE-HOME DRUGS)–$_____.

shown in the certification are low compared with the hospital's actual charges.

ASSIGNMENT OF BENEFITS

A provision for the insured to assign benefits to the provider of medical service is included on the standard claim form. The completion and signature of such an assignment is routine procedure on the part of most hospitals at the time of admission. Hospitals often serve the attending physician or surgeon by also securing from the patient, at the time of admission, an assignment of benefits from the patient to the physician or surgeon.

The insured person under a commercial carrier's group insurance policy must usually make a positive voluntary assignment of benefits. Otherwise, the policy provides that benefits are payable to the insured. This is one of the key differences between the medical expense coverage written by commercial health insurance carriers and that written by Blue Cross associations.

AUTHORIZATION TO RELEASE MEDICAL INFORMATION

Authorization by the insured person to release medical information to the insurance carrier is also provided for on most claim forms used in connection with both hospital and physician care.

The insured's signature on the authorization form enables the carrier to secure additional medical information from the hospital or physician if the insurer deems it is needed to process the claim. For example, some group plans provide lesser benefits (or no benefits) for conditions deemed preexisting in accordance with the contract language used by the carrier in the particular policy. In such cases, the hospital or physician, if authorized, can supply the carrier with information about the patient's previous medical history.

Medical information on an individual is highly personal. It should be treated with maximum confidentiality. There are growing pressures, many at the state and federal legislative levels, on carriers to provide further safeguards for confidential medical information. The carrier should restrict the use of the medical information to processing the claim and should not reveal this information to any other person or organization without the expressed written consent of the patient.

PAYMENT OF THE CLAIM

Once the information initially received or subsequently developed by the claims department of the carrier is adequate, the amount of liability payable under the policy for the proof of expenses submitted is calculated.

When this has been done, regardless of the degree of sophistication of the systems used by the carrier, a check or draft is drawn for payment. Details of the payments made under the specific group policy are retained for three reasons. First, the checks drawn must be charged against the carrier's banking account. Second, the benefits paid must be charged against the proper group policy. Third, the details of the expenses that resulted in the payment must be retained for statistical purposes by the carrier.

The introduction of automation into the claims process has allowed carriers to fulfill these requirements accurately and quickly.

The degree and types of automation used by carriers are extremely diverse. At the lower end of the scale the claims examiner uses a substantially manual procedure coupled with entry of that data and its processing in the batch mode by the carrier, producing a computer-printed check and explanation-of-benefit-payment document. At the higher end of the automation scale, television-like display screens known as cathode ray terminals (CRTs) are used by the claims examiner. The displays are directly linked to the computer. Through sophisticated programming, the computer leads the examiner through the total processing of the claim by screen displays at each step of the process.

EXPLANATION-OF-BENEFIT-PAYMENT

The claim payment is invariably accompanied by some type of explanation of payment. Depending on the sophistication of systems used by the carrier, the explanation-of-benefit-payment document can be a copy of the work sheet used by the claims examiner or a computer-printed form of the type reproduced in Figure 25-9.

Though certain basic information needs to be given to the policyowner, and in the case of a claim, to the insured employee, the manner in which this information is produced by the carrier varies widely among carriers.

DEVELOPMENT OF STATISTICAL DATA

The claims process represents by far the most important area of the carrier's operations for capturing statistics relating to the insured group. The sophistication and extent of the way in which this information is captured has a direct impact on the underwriting and actuarial departments of the carrier's group division. These statistics, derived from claims processing and payment, are essential when the group underwriting department reviews the adequacy of the premium rates charged under the policy and when the group actuarial department determines the experienced-rated premium refund or dividend that may have been earned by the policyowner. Such statistics also help to detect experience trends in the total group medical expense business in force with the carrier.

Many group policyowners, especially those with large numbers of employees, and their brokers or consultants, have developed increasing expectations about the quality of statistical data the carrier

FIGURE 25-9

Explanation of Benefit Payment Form

Pilot Life

PO Box 20727
Greensboro, NC 27420

Group Claims, Dept. 579

Explanation Of The Benefit Payment

Item No. 000000	Person Insured JOHN E. DOE 000000001	Patient MARY E. DOE DEP.- WIFE	Policy No. 00000	Branch 00
Date		Policyholder XYZ COMPANY		

Itemization Of The Policy Liability

Liability Computation for Medical Expenses

	Date of Service	Amount Charged	Basic Plan Amount	Code	Major Med. 80% Amount*	Code	Other Amount	Amount Not Considered Amount	Code	Code
RM	11-01-78	1000.00	940.00	RM				60.00		LI
EX	11-01-78	2000.00	1900.00	EX				100.00		SC
SU	11-02-78	500.00	400.00	SU				100.00		SC
PH	11-01-78	100.00			80.00					
D RN	11-10-78	250.00			120.00					
RX	10-30-78	60.00			40.00			10.00		NC

Totals and Adjustments

Basic	3240.00
Maj. Med	240.00
Other	
Dis-ability	
Sub Total	3480.00
Less	
Less	
Amt. Due	
Amt. Toward Deductible	100.00

Disability Benefits

Date Disability Begins
Days to Eliminate
Date Payment Begins
Date Through Which Payment is Being Made
Number of Weeks Being Paid ___ Wks ___ Days
Amount Payable Per Week
Amount of This Payment
Total Weeks Paid To Date ___ Wks ___ Days

*Represents amount payable after subtraction of deductibles and application of coinsurance percentage. If your plan has major medical expense coverage and if no such payment is shown this means the covered expenses did not exceed the deductible amounts.

Payment Of The Policy Benefits Due

The checks listed below have been issued in payment of this claim.

Check Number	Amount	Payee
A000000	2840.00	Columbia Hospital
A000001	400.00	Dr. John Johnson
A000002	80.00	Dr. Bill Smith
A000003	160.00	John E. Doe

Comments

SC - See Letter on R & C
SC - $75 Blood, $20.00 Tele., $5.00 TV
    See Letter about Blood

NOTE: If employee returned to work before the last date paid (see above), please return check (with the proper date) for correction. If a form is attached for an updated doctor's report please have it completed and return

OT - Other, Spec., or Misc. Charges

D - Part or all used for Major Medical Deductible

See Code Explanation on Back of This Page

G-3310

should furnish at intervals during the policy year or at the end of the policy year. The statistics developed and retained during the claims process constitute an extremely large part of the statistics that interest the group policyowner.

CLAIM ADMINISTRATION FOR UNINSURED PLANS

Employers considering the administrative services only (ASO) alternative may secure a proposal from the present carrier or secure competitive bids from a number of carriers for a contract for claims administration services in conjunction with the uninsured benefits.

A carrier that offers these services administers claims on the uninsured plan in much the same way as it administers insured benefit plans. The major difference is that the claims check or draft usually is drawn against a checking account identified with the employer rather than with the carrier. In addition, the explanation-of-benefit-payment forms and other forms used by the carrier in the administration of claims indicate in most cases that the employer is responsible for the benefit payment rather than the carrier. It is primarily in the accounting area that the handling by the carrier of an ASO plan differs from procedures used for that carrier's own insured business. Because the carrier is usually drawing checks or drafts against the employer's checking account in payment of claims, a system must be established to insure that the employer will keep that account funded. The carrier usually accomplishes this by a daily report to the employer concerning checks or drafts drawn against the account.

The carrier charges no premium on the coverages being administered in this way, and thus has no inherent source of funds to cover the expenses of the administrative service. Therefore, a fee for the carrier's service is negotiated with the employer. In setting the fee, the carrier attempts to leave a margin of profit for itself after reimbursement of the actual expenses incurred in performing the service.

Processing Other Health Coverages

Specialized coverages require the use of distinct claims forms, particularly if they are written as separate coverages under the group policy. In the absence of provision for these types of expenses by separate specific coverages under the group policy, there is usually some form of coverage for such expenses under the major medical expense insurance. For dental and vision care, the coverage under the major medical insurance is less comprehensive than that provided when separate coverages for these types of expense are included in the group policy.

DENTAL EXPENSES

A special claim form has been developed by the Health Insurance Association of America in conjunction with the American Dental Association for use on dental expense claims. An example of the form is reproduced in Figure 25-10.

Along with the general considerations that apply to the processing of all claims, there are special considerations that apply to dental

FIGURE 25-10
Dental Expense Claim Form

ATTENDING DENTIST'S STATEMENT—INSURANCE CLAIM **UNIFORM REPORT FORM**

1. Employee Name
2. Social Security No.
3. Name of Group Dental Plan
4. Employee Mailing Address
5. Policy Number
6. Union Local No.
7. City State Zip Code
8. Employer Name
9. Patient Name
10. Patient Relationship to Employee
11. Patient Birthdate Month | Day | Year
12. Date Patient First Visit (Current Series)
13. Dentist Name
14. License No.
15. Is Patient Covered by Other Plan? (Name Other Plan) Yes | No
16. Dentist Mailing Address
17. Phone No.
18. Is Any of Treatment for Orthodontic Purposes?
19. City State Zip Code
20. Treatment Result of Accident?
21. Result of Occupational Injury?
22. If Prosthesis, is this Initial Placement? ▢ YES ▢ NO (If No, Reason for Replacement)
23. Date of Prior Placement

25. Examination and Treatment Record—List in Order from Tooth No. 1 through Tooth No. 32

Tooth # or Letter	Surfaces	DESCRIPTION OF SERVICES (Including X-Rays, Propylaxis Materials Used, etc.)	Date Service Performed Mo.	Day	Yr.	Procedure Number	Fee	Do Not Use This Column

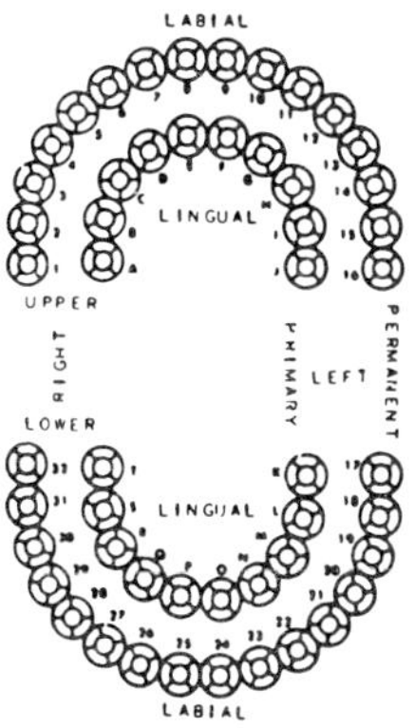

*Indicate Missing Teeth With an "X"

26. Remarks for Unusual Services

ORTHODONTICS *(Give diagnosis, class of malocclusion and described appliance(s) in above treatment section)*

Date First Appliance Inserted ______________

Date Last Appliance Removed ______________

Treatment Period *(Number Months)* ______________

Total Fee $______________

Total Fee Actually Charged

I hereby certify that the services listed above have been performed.

Tax Identification Number

DENTIST SIGNATURE ______________ DATE ______

I hereby authorize payment directly to the above named dentist of the group insurance benefits otherwise payable to me, but not to exceed the charges shown above. I understand that I am financially responsible for any charges not covered by this authorization.

EMPLOYEE'S SIGNATURE ______________ DATE ______

G—1780D

Approved by the Council on Dental Care Programs of the American Dental Association July, 1967

claims. For this reason, many carriers, particularly those with a large volume of dental expense insurance in force, have established separate dental claim processing units.

One special consideration that generally applies to claims for reimbursement of dental expenses is the requirement by the carrier that if the dental expense to be incurred exceeds a given dollar amount (usually $100), the dentist must file a treatment plan with the carrier before beginning the patient's treatment. This is usually called a predetermination dental procedure.

The purposes of this requirement are two-fold. The first is to give the carrier an opportunity to refer the treatment plan to a dental consultant to see if the plan is reasonable and effective. The second is to let the dentist and the employee know the extent to which charges for the proposed treatment will be covered by the dental expense plan under which the patient is insured.

In the processing of dental expense claims, there tends to be closer control in relation to benefit payments than is usually exercised by the carrier in the payment of medical expense claims. For example, it is not unusual for the carrier to request to see X rays made by the dentist, usually in conjunction with the proposed treatment plan. Alternatively, in cases where the carrier is exercising quality control, X rays taken before and after treatment may be requested. This requirement by some carriers has given rise to resistance among dental societies in some states. A special committee of industry representatives, formed under the Consumer and Professional Relations Division of HIAA, has negotiated with state societies on this and similar issues in Wisconsin, Indiana, and other states.

Some states, such as Pennsylvania, require that the carrier be responsible for checking the quality of the work done by a dentist on an insured patient or one of his dependents once it has been completed. This has provided carriers yet another reason to retain the services of a dentist as a consultant on such matters. In some states, state dental societies have formed claim review committees to which the carrier may refer claims where the carrier questions the fairness of the fee, or the advisability of the mode of treatment or extent of treatment given by the dentist.

VISION CARE

Vision care coverage is described in Chapter 14. Since the comprehensiveness of benefits under various plans differs considerably, this type of coverage may also require specialization on the part of the claims examiner.

PRESCRIPTION DRUG PLANS

Prescription drug plans are also described in Chapter 14. No uniform claim form has yet been adopted for claims for payment for prescription drugs. Given the relative high frequency of claims for this benefit and the general lack of ability by the carrier to exercise any meaningful controls other than the broad controls incorporated in the policy, an increasing number of carriers are entering into contracts with administrators who specialize in the initial administrative paper work involved and who have the ability to exercise controls by or through a direct relationship with pharmacies that have agreed to participate in plans administered by such special administrators. In such cases the carrier usually agrees to pay the special administrator a stated fee for each prescription processed. As part of the service and that administrator's agreements with pharmacies, an identification or embossed credit card is issued by the prescription drug administrator to the carrier for each employee insured for this coverage under group policy.

The participating pharmacy uses this credit card in billing the special administrator. Typically, the carrier furnishes the administrator with drafts on its bank for use in self-reimbursement for the bills paid to the pharmacies. The administrator usually bills the carrier directly for the fee, or has the authorization of the carrier to draw a draft in the administrator's favor for such fees. The administrator furnishes the carrier with a monthly computer listing of prescriptions processed and paid to the pharmacy.

The control aspect and the advantages that accrue to the carrier in using such specialist administrators are that the administrator, in making arrangements with participating pharmacies, requires that the drug or medicine be billed at cost plus an agreed-upon professional fee for each prescription by the pharmacy. Many companies in the industry believe that the use of such special administrative facilities results in cost savings because the controls exercised by the special administrator result in savings that substantially exceed the special administrator's fee for the service.

RELATIONSHIPS WITH PROVIDERS

It is obviously necessary for the commercial health insurance carriers to have a liaison with the providers of health care. This relationship benefits the carrier, those whom it insures, and the provider. For many years the Health Insurance Council, a part of the Health Insurance Association of America and now the Consumer and Professional Relations Division of HIAA, has worked through national committees of industry members and particularly through councils and committees established at the state level to secure agreement with providers on the use of standard claim forms and to establish claim review facilities as part of the structure of organized medicine.

Broadly, these activities have fallen into four major areas: hospital relations, physician relations, dental relations, and allied medical health service relations. The latter include relations with providers in the chiropractic and podiatrist professions, among others.

With the introduction of the Medicare program in 1965, the

federal government through the Department of Health, Education and Welfare (HEW) established Professional Standards Review Organizations (PSROs). The purpose of these physician organizations is to evaluate the necessity and appropriateness of the care given to Medicare (federally funded) and Medicaid (state funded) patients for benefit purposes. This evaluation is called peer review. Through the HIAA, many private insurers have contracted with these PSROs on a specified fee-per-patient basis to have the PSROs review the appropriateness and necessity of the care given their privately insured patients. This review is conducted while the patient is still in the hospital.

In addition, other peer review committees, either at the metropolitan, county, or state level are prepared to render objective, informal, professional advice on questions submitted by insurers, physicians, and patients that involve fees, procedures or treatments that appear unusual or in situations where the insurer and the provider do not agree about the appropriateness or necessity of care given or of the fee charged.[6] This is done retrospectively, after the patient has left the hospital, using the patient's medical record as evidence. The carrier then makes a decision as to the appropriate benefit payment, incorporating the advice of this committee along with other information relevant to the case.

Short-Term Disability Claims

The standard attending physician's claim form used for short-term disability claims calls for the attending physician's statement of the medical information necessary for the carrier to ascertain that the claimant was unable to work at the claimant's usual occupation. This information, in conjunction with the employer's statement, which is also provided for on the form, usually constitutes sufficient proof of claim for the payment of benefits.

As with medical expense claims, the claims examiner has to establish whether the injury that resulted in the disability arose out of or in the course of the claimant's employment, since most coverage of short-term disability is on a nonoccupational basis.

Two other considerations must be taken into account by the claims examiner. The first is whether the claim now being processed relates to a disability for which benefits were previously paid. In this respect, it is important to know whether the current disability is due to the same or a related cause as the previous disability. In such instances it is a question of determining whether the employee returned to active full-time work for a certain minimum period of time between the end of the previous disability and the onset of the current disability if the cause is the same or a related one. The second consideration is

---

[6]Health Insurance Association of America, *op. cit.*, p. 223.

the date on which the employee sought medical care for the condition in relation to the date on which the employee last worked. The contract provisions of most carriers require that the insured person be under the regular care of a licensed physician. Therefore, these two dates are important in establishing whether the insured person now making claim sought medical care coincident with or immediately following the date on which the claimant ceased work.

Disability income claims have to be processed promptly, since the employee-claimant is relying on the insurance benefits to partially substitute for the loss of income occasioned by the inability to work. The same attending physician's claim form may be used both for the purpose of claiming medical expense benefits and for the authorization of the payment of disability income benefits. The processing of the disability income payment should not be delayed if additional information is needed by the examiner only for processing the medical expense benefits claim.

SHORT-TERM CREDIT DISABILITY CLAIMS

Under credit disability insurance, the entity making claim is the lending institution, that is, the group policyowner. The purpose of this coverage is to replace by insurance the monthly installment payable by the borrower when the borrower becomes totally disabled. Such plans usually require a stated minimum period of time during which the borrower must be totally disabled before becoming eligible for benefit payment.

The special claim form used for this purpose is filed by or through the lending institution. It must contain medical evidence of total disability satisfactory to the carrier and a statement by the lending institution as to the amount of the monthly installment on insured loans of that particular borrower.

It is more customary to find this coverage in force under single premium plans, in conjunction with which individual rather than group policies are used. However, there is a total disability feature used by many carriers in conjunction with group credit life plans that serves a similar purpose. This is used more frequently in plans for the protection of members of credit unions. The elimination period in group coverages is usually longer than that used in the single premium-individual policy plans. Where credit disability coverage is in effect and a claim is received for processing, one feature to which the claims examiner should be alert is whether the disability existed at the time the loan was made by the insured borrower.

Long-Term Disability Claims

There are several ways the examination of long-term disability claims differs from short-term claims. Under long-term policies, income from certain other sources is usually taken into account and results in an adjustment of the monthly benefits payable under the group policy to the insured. These sources may include salary continuance by the employer, other group insurance income benefits, pension disability benefits, workers' compensation and compulsory state nonoccupational disability benefits, Social Security and Railroad Retirement disability benefits, and any benefits other than from individual policies that are payable from other sources as a result of the insured person's disability.

Another difference is the greater potential for malingering when long-term benefits are available. The high level of benefits provided by long-term income replacement insurance may serve to deter the insured's desire to return to work, especially if there is no job to which to return or if the insured is only a few years away from retirement. Still another difference between long-term disability income benefits and the short-term variety is that benefits under long-term disability are usually payable monthly, while the short-term benefit is usually payable on a weekly basis.

Because of the different nature of long-term coverage, the need for more complete medical substantiation of disability, and the information called for as a result of the effect of income from other sources during disability, a special claim form is used for this type of coverage.

The elimination periods used in plans of long-term disability insurance are typically longer than those used for short-term disability coverage. Thus, the first notice of claim received by the carrier may arrive as long as six months after the disability actually began. Since one of the main sources of other income for coordination of benefit purposes is the disability benefit under Social Security, the claims examiner should secure information as to whether the claimant has yet submitted a claim for the Social Security benefit. Where the claim is received at a point when the claimant has had time to have filed for Social Security benefits but no indication is received with the claim that this has been done or no determination has been made by the Social Security Administration, the carrier often uses an estimated Social Security disability benefit until the matter is settled. Instead of using an estimated Social Security disability benefit, some carriers secure a signed agreement from the claimant to repay any excess benefits paid under the group policy pending receipt of the Social Security Administration's decision as to whether or not Social Security disability benefits are awarded to the claimant retroactively.

The contractual definition of total disability narrows at the end of two years. Therefore, the requirements and definition of total disability for claims payment eligibility usually fall into two segments. The first typically covers the first two years of benefit payment. (This period may be longer in some policies.) The contractual provision usually states that the definition of total disability during this period is the inability of the insured person to perform each and every duty of his or her occupation. The second segment, which begins at the expiration of the first period of benefit payment, is based on the inability of the insured person to engage in *any* occupation for which he or she is reasonably suited by experience, training, or education, for gain or profit. In securing medical substantiation through the claimant or by independent medical examination paid for by the carrier, the main consideration during the first period of benefits is related to the inability of the claimant to perform occupational duties. However, most group policies also contain a provision that should the claimant of his or her own volition engage in any gainful occupation during this period, he or she is no longer eligible for the continued payment of disability benefits under the policy.

An exception is when the person returns to, or engages in, only part-time duties. Many group policies have a rehabilitation provision that, in such circumstances, provides for the payment of 50 percent of the regular benefit. This can be in addition to or instead of the payment of benefits under the rehabilitation benefit described below.

Therefore, the carrier will make, during the first payment period, periodic checks through field investigative facilities or a reporting service to determine the claimant's actual activities. Of course, the seriousness of the disability condition determines whether these checks are necessary and their frequency.

Just prior to the end of the first benefit period, it is usual to inquire more closely into the medical status of the claimant to determine whether the claimant's condition prevents him or her from engaging in any gainful employment, as described above. The frequency with which the carrier requires the claimant to furnish medical information substantiating total disability is a matter of judgment related to the nature of the disabling condition.

REHABILITATION

It is for the claimant's benefit as well as the carrier's to consider the potential of the claimant for rehabilitation. Authorities in this field state that this potential should be considered as early as possible after the onset of the disability. There are service organizations specializing both in investigating cases where there may appear to be a rehabilitation potential and, on the insurer's behalf, making arrangements for the steps necessary to accomplish rehabilitation. Some carriers with a large amount of long-term disability insurance in force have established their own in-house specialized units for this purpose.

Although the nature and severity of the claimant's disability is a key factor, equally important is the attitude of the claimant and the claimant's family toward consideration of a program of rehabilitation. Despite medical proof and evidence of total disability, the efforts that the claimant is willing to make to resume a productive role in society are based on extremely personal attitudes and vary widely among individuals.

In attempting to interest suitable claimants in a program of rehabilitation, the insurer will frequently offer to pay for the expenses of additional corrective surgery needed if the claimant has no resources out of which to finance the surgery. The carrier may also offer cash payments or cash advances in suitable cases to furnish the claimant with capital to start a business. If such arrangements are offered by the carrier, they are in the form of a written agreement that also guarantees to the claimant that, should he or she be physically incapable of carrying through the attempt at a gainful occupation for reasons related to the disabling condition, the claimant again becomes eligible for benefit payments.

SUMMARY

This chapter has described the processing and payment of claims under group life insurance and under group health insurance. The basic claims payable under group life were presented, including death claims on dependents, death claims payable under accidental death and dismemberment insurance, credit life insurance, and other benefits. For health claims, the basic methods of payment (by the home office, by company field offices, and by the policyowner or third party) were discussed and the details of processing medical expense claims were set forth. Health claims under short-term and long-term disability coverage were also described.

CHAPTER 26

GROUP REINSURANCE

INTRODUCTION

As the previous chapters have demonstrated, group insurance has been one of the most vital lines in the insurance industry, both in the United States and Canada. Particularly since the end of World War II, there has been an enormous expansion in the aggregate amount and in the kinds of coverage provided. Concomitant with the expansion of group insurance there has been an increase in the size and significance of group reinsurance as the means by which one insurer transfers part of the risk represented by a group to another insurer or insurers.

This chapter provides an overview of group reinsurance, with particular reference to the United States. This chapter begins with a discussion of the growth of group reinsurance and a brief description of how group reinsurance is arranged. The chapter then reviews the major kinds of group reinsurance coverages, with particular attention to the reinsurance arrangements appropriate to them.

THE GROWTH OF GROUP REINSURANCE

Since the end of World War II, reinsurance of the various group lines appears to have grown rapidly, both in aggregate total and in the kinds of group coverages reinsured. This growth pattern seems to have accelerated during the 1960s and continued subsequently. In effect, the growth of group reinsurance since 1945 has roughly paralleled the growth and development of group insurance itself.

Unfortunately, we have to say "seems" and "appears" because specific data about the growth of group reinsurance are sparse. However, the data showing a growth of Canadian group reinsurance coverage by three major reinsurers from less than $83 million at the end of 1963 to more than $733 million by the end of 1973 are suggestive of the likely trends in the American market.[1] Similarly suggestive is the

[1]See Chapter 28.

by
CHARLES A. DIFALCO, *Vice President, Group Department, North American Reassurance Company, New York, New York*

estimate by Goodrich that the reinsurance market in the United States grew from about $100 million in net written premiums after retrocessions in 1946 to more than $600 million by 1960 and his further comment that "of the $500 million increase, over two-fifths was produced by companies who had entered the American market after the second World War."[2]

There are several reasons for the relatively late emergence of group reinsurance as a significant aspect of the group insurance scene. First, until fairly recently the average size of a group life certificate was quite modest (only about $4,000 as late as 1960), and the levels of other benefits were comparable. As a result, the risks and the consequent pressures for spreading risk through reinsurance were also relatively low.

Second, for the larger risks covering a number of employees for substantial aggregate amounts, it was believed that physical dispersion of personnel both on and off the job sufficiently decreased the possibility of a significant number of deaths or injuries occurring from a single accident. The reasoning was that as the size of the group increased, the lives were spread out in different buildings, plants, or cities and lived in widely dispersed urban and suburban locations, thus preventing a high concentration of exposure and risk. Group insurance companies did, of course, recognize the concentration of exposure and risk in particularly hazardous industries such as underground mining and the manufacture of munitions. Intercompany pooling of risks was often undertaken to cope with such special circumstances.

Finally, until the 1960s, the great bulk of group insurance was written by a few large companies with substantial accumulated group and general surpluses that were available in the event of an unexpected major catastrophe. Thus, in 1931, 86.8 percent of the group life insurance in force was written by only four mutual and two stock companies. In 1951, these same six companies still retained just under 80 percent of the total group life insurance in force, and their collective share of the market did not drop below 70 percent until 1956. Today, although the 141 companies with $1 billion or more group insurance in force have 90 percent of the business, there are about 800 companies selling group insurance.[3]

In effect, although some group reinsurance has existed since the inception of group insurance itself, until fairly recently, this device was neither perceived as needed nor widely employed to absorb fluctuations in mortality or morbidity.

Even in the relatively early days of group insurance, however, there was some demand for reinsurance. Some large policyowners felt

---

[2]John B. Goodrich, "The Growth of the American Reinsurance Market," Unpublished M.S., Library of the College of Insurance, New York, May 1964, p. 1.
[3]*Best's Insurance News Digest*, August 14, 1978.

financially safer having the risk spread among several carriers. Furthermore, some policyowners of substantial size wished to direct their business to more than a single group carrier. The outstanding example of the latter is the Federal Employees Group Life Insurance program (FEGLI) that reflects the desire of the U.S. government to avoid favoring any single carrier.[4]

Another reason was that a policyowner sometimes wished to consolidate its group benefit package (the components of which were formerly carried with two or more insurers) while still keeping all the companies in the plan. Under such circumstances, the policyowner would place the complete package with one insurer and direct that the other insurer or insurers be permitted to participate.

Finally, some policyowners wanted to obtain advice from two independent sources. These policyowners felt that it was reasonable to expect a show of greater interest in offering such advice if each company had, in fact, a financial interest in the plan.

To sum up, the dramatic growth in group insurance—manifested in the rise in benefit levels in both life and health insurances, in the appeal to and coverage of a large and ever-increasing proportion of the population, in the proliferation of new coverages, and in the entry into the field of many new smaller companies—has increased the importance of group reinsurance. The many and varied aspects of the growth of group insurance have been amply described and analyzed in preceding chapters. The point here is that this growth adds up to an increased need and demand for group reinsurance.

REINSURANCE ARRANGEMENTS

If it is assumed that it is desirable to share the group insurance package among a number of companies, there are, in theory at least, four possible methods:
1. Dividing the package by geographic location of those covered;
2. Dividing the package by type of coverage;
3. Coinsurance, a limited variant of reinsurance in which each company issues and administers its own policy providing a share of each benefit; and
4. Reinsurance proper, in which one company issues a policy providing the entire benefit package and cedes to (i.e., reinsures) a share of the benefit package with one or more additional insurance companies as directed or agreed to by the policyowner.

Each of the first three theoretical possibilities poses serious administrative problems that detract from its suitability as a solution.

---

[4]Robert D. Eilers and Robert M. Crowe, *Group Insurance Handbook* (Homewood, Illinois: Richard D. Irwin, Inc., 1965), p. 162.

Thus, when several companies divide the package, the lack of uniformity in their procedures is likely to increase costs. Geographic location as a criterion for dividing the package becomes complicated—and expensive—because of the frequent changes those covered make in their jobs and residences. Dividing the package among carriers by type of coverage is difficult because some coverages consistently produce more favorable underwriting results than others and thus are more attractive to carriers.

Coinsurance is also not usually a satisfactory solution. Group commissions are generally paid on a graded scale. If each company pays commissions from the top of its scale for its share of the coverage, the total commissions payable will add up to more than would result from lumping the premiums for the entire package. Furthermore, there is likely to be an increased aggregate risk charge, since the smaller the case, the lower the credibility and the higher the risk charge. Finally, the premium base in any one company will be narrow, and thus the experience rating may not afford as great an opportunity for savings as under group reinsurance. Thus, the simplest solution is group reinsurance.

Reinsurance Treaties

The arrangements for group reinsurance are generally formally incorporated into an agreement, called a "treaty," among the participants. There are two general forms of reinsurance treaties where the writing company cedes a share of the entire benefit package. These are referred to as the "Hartford" style and the "New York" style.

THE HARTFORD STYLE

In the Hartford style treaty, the direct writing company establishes the net cost in accordance with its own rules and rating levels, and the reinsuring company shares in such on a net cost basis. Thus, the reinsuring company is compensated for assuming a share of the risk in accordance with the experience rating formula of the writing company. The net rates the policyowner pays under the Hartford method depend solely upon the experience rating formula of the direct writing company.

THE NEW YORK STYLE

Under the New York style treaty, the direct writing company and the reinsurer are individually responsible for determining the premium rates and the experience rating adjustments on their respective shares of the package. Mutual companies, which must follow their own dividend formulas, typically use the New York style.[5]

---

[5]Donald D. Cody notes that, "Under the New York Method, the reinsurer introduces administration and acquisition expense charges made by the ceding company into its

Terminology

Most of the terminology and techniques used in the reinsurance of an insurer's ordinary business apply also to its group line of business. A company's retention limit is the dollar amount of risk it is willing to carry on any one case. Automatic reinsurance agreements provide that the direct writing company must cede and the reinsurer must accept all the coverage over the direct writer's specified retention limit up to a specific amount. Under a facultative agreement, the reinsurer can decide which cases it will accept and which it will decline.

Reinsurance plans can be proportional or nonproportional. With proportional reinsurance, the reinsurer's potential liability is a known percent or portion of the risk accepted by the direct writer; with nonproportional reinsurance, it is not. Quota share reinsurance is the most obvious example of the proportional type, stop-loss of the nonproportional. The former type is described later.

STOP-LOSS COVERAGE

As its name indicates, under stop-loss reinsurance coverage the reinsurer agrees to reimburse the direct writing company for any excess beyond a predetermined limit of total claims over total portfolio in any given year. In theory, this form of reinsurance coverage can be applied to any group benefit or combination of benefits. In practice, however, stop-loss reinsurance coverage is apparently neither easily arranged nor widely used. It is difficult to negotiate, the reinsurance premium tends to be modest relative to the potential loss, and the reinsurer tends to set the "deductible level" (the point at which the reinsurer commences payment) high enough to moderate the frequency of claims and thus allow the direct writer to recover only in the event of extreme underwriting losses. Because there are almost no pertinent published statistics about stop-loss coverage, these statements are of necessity tentative. A possible explanation for the paucity of data is that stop-loss coverage is almost always hand-tailored for an individual situation and thus does not lend itself readily to statistical collection or categorization.

---

own dividend formula in place of similar charges normally made and adds charges for commissions paid, sales overhead, federal income tax, risk and profit. These latter charges are not made by the ceding company for the reinsurer's share of the risk. The resulting dividend is then paid to the principal insurer, which adds it to its own dividend—similarly determined—and pays the combined dividend to the policyholder, noting the respective parts. With the Hartford Method the reinsurer is charged for 50 percent of the dividend determined by the ceding company as if there were no reinsurance. The Hartford Method binds the reinsurer to the risk and profit charges, sales overhead charges and federal income tax charges of the principal insurer, whereas the New York Method does not." Eilers and Crowe, *Group Insurance Handbook*, pp. 371–372.

CATASTROPHE REINSURANCE

The concentration of risk in group insurance that exists simply because it is *group* insurance has been dramatically increased by modern technology and social customs, especially the widespread use of high-capacity airplanes for travel and the concentration of employees in giant office buildings and factories. Combining such developments with the increased levels of benefits available under many kinds of group coverages has concentrated risks to the point that a disaster could seriously drain the surplus of a single insurance company and perhaps even threaten its solvency. To obviate such a possibility, most companies writing group life policies obtain catastrophe reinsurance.[6]

Such insurance is obtainable from three sources. The first is a single reinsurer that assumes the risk, although it often retrocedes a share of the coverage to a second company. Under this arrangement, the ceding company needs to deal only with the prime reinsurer.

The second major source of catastrophe reinsurance is the "reinsuring company," which is much like the single reinsurer but is actually a pool of participating companies each of which assumes some stipulated share of a specific catastrophe risk or a number of such risks. A single company is designated as the "manager," and portions of each risk are automatically assigned to each company participating in the pool.

The third source is the assessment pool in which two or more companies are brought together to share in the catastrophic losses that may be incurred by all pool members according to a previously established and agreed formula. The initial cost covers expenses incurred in establishing and administering the pool; the ultimate costs include a specified portion of members' catastrophic claims that are assessed against those companies.

Under catastrophe reinsurance arrangements made with single reinsurers or with several reinsuring companies, the ceding company will purchase reinsurance for a specified dollar amount or for a high percentage of a specific dollar amount in excess of an amount that the ceding company would pay in the event of a catastrophic accident. A catastrophic accident is defined as an accident or series of accidents arising out of a single event or occurrence that results in the death of at least a prescribed minimum number of persons. An aggregate loss for any single contract year and a maximum loss on any one life are usually stipulated.

---

[6]For an excellent discussion of catastrophe reinsurance, see the article by Edward A. Green, "Concentration of Risk and the Catastrophic Accident Hazard," *Transactions of the Society of Actuaries*, Vol. VI (1954), pp. 506–511 and the continuing discussion on pp. 512–517. Green points out that the catastrophic accident hazard is undoubtedly greatest in the field of group insurance." He adds: "Since concentration of risk and catastrophic accident hazard cannot be eliminated by practical methods, a life insurance company has the choice of carrying the risk itself or reinsuring all or part of it."

For example, a ceding company might purchase catastrophe reinsurance that would pay up to the first $500,000 arising from each and every catastrophic accident—that is, each and every accident or series of accidents arising out of one event that results in the death of five or more insured individuals. The coverage might also specify that it would not apply to any loss in excess of $200,000 on any single life and would be subject to the typical exclusions described below. A premium expressed as a contingency charge (or "flat charge") plus a stipulated rate multiplied by the mean amount in force during the contract would be payable.

Typical exclusions include claims:

1. Arising out of or contributed to by declared or undeclared war, invasion, civil war, or any acts of a foreign enemy;
2. Arising out of or involving atomic energy plants or processes; and
3. Arising under any policy or certificates that cover occupational accidents and that are issued to an individual as an employee or member of a group or association that is involved in activities such as caisson work, explosives and munitions manufacturing, underground and underwater mining, operation of airlines, or as a member of a professional sports team while traveling as a group. Claims arising from accidents occurring while the individual is engaged in any of these activities are excluded.

In theory, with the development of experience tables on which to base premiums, catastrophe reinsurance coverage could be extended to such otherwise excluded areas.

REINSURANCE COVERAGES

In the following pages, this text will discuss the various types of coverage obtainable under group reinsurance. These will include accidental death and dismemberment, group weekly indemnity and basic hospital and surgical coverages, group major medical and group comprehensive major medical, group long-term disability, group creditor insurance and group dental, group podiatry, and group vision care coverages.

Reinsurance of Group Life, Group Accidental Death and Dismemberment Coverages

There are two different situations in which reinsurance coverage is provided for group life and group accidental death and dismemberment: when evidence of insurability is not required and when such evidence is required. These two methods will be considered separately.

EVIDENCE OF INSURABILITY NOT REQUIRED

Where evidence of insurability is not required, the reinsurance of group life and group accidental death and dismemberment coverage can be obtained either on a quota share (pro rata) basis or on an individual excess basis.

Under the quota share (pro rata) approach, the writing company reinsures a percentage share of the entire schedule of benefits. This percentage share is established so that the maximum retained risk on any one life does not exceed the maximum retention level established. For example, if a schedule of benefits provides a maximum of $50,000 on any one or more lives, and the writing company wishes to retain no more than $15,000 on any one life, a 70 percent quota share of the entire schedule is reinsured. Clearly, this gives the reinsuring company, in proportion to its share, the identical risk that the writing company undertakes. The two general forms of reinsurance treaty, the New York and Hartford styles, are applicable to reinsurance on a quota share basis. Reinsurance can be on a facultative or automatic basis.

Under the individual excess basis approach, the writing company retains, for its own risk, up to some stipulated dollar amount on each life and reinsures the excess amount. The writing company and the reinsurer agree on gross issue limits for any given case. To the extent that the writing company issues a schedule of benefits in accordance with such limits, it retains up to an established maximum on each life and reinsures the excess amount on each life. Such reinsurance is generally on an automatic basis unless the writing company seeks to exceed the preestablished gross issue limits for any given case. Thus, the reinsurer assumes amounts on relatively few lives, each of which is eligible for the higher benefit amounts provided by the schedule of benefits. Under this arrangement, it is possible that the reinsurer's experience will be quite different from that of the ceding company.

EVIDENCE OF INSURABILITY REQUIRED

The situation is different when amounts of insurance on individual lives are above the levels permitted under any reasonable set of group underwriting rules. If complete ordinary-type evidence of insurability can be obtained, almost any reasonable amount on an individual life can be reinsured on virtually the same basis as a comparable amount of ordinary insurance. This situation usually requires the introduction of two new elements not generally found in a group policy. These elements, applied to the individually underwritten group amount, are:

1. An ordinary-type suicide clause; and
2. A provision to permit carry-over of any substandard rating upon conversion of the group life term amount to permanent insurance.

Reinsurance of Group Weekly Indemnity and Basic Hospital and Surgical Coverages

The total benefits afforded under these coverages are relatively modest. Therefore, fluctuations in financial results are not caused by a few above-average claims. Instead, when such fluctuations occur, they usually result from multiple relatively modest claims. These claims may arise from inadequate rate levels, imprudent underwriting, or insufficiently stringent claim controls.

The only method of reinsurance (except for stop-loss) that can apply to these coverages is the quota share approach, in which a percentage of the entire benefit schedule is ceded. Under this circumstance, reinsurance cannot play its proper technical role of levelling swings in claim fluctuation from year to year.

Companies just beginning to write coverages in these areas often seek the guidance of reinsurers about policy forms, rating materials, sales literature, and the like. Furthermore, to dampen or minimize possible negative effects of these coverages on its total writings (assuming the company has already established that no more than a specified percentage of its total premium income is to stem from group weekly indemnity and basic hospital and surgical coverages), the neophyte company may seek to reinsure a quota share of its coverages in these areas.

Because of continuing unsatisfactory financial results for these coverages, especially hospital and surgical coverages, it has become increasingly difficult to find reinsurers willing to participate. Possibly the major motivation inducing a reinsurer to do so would be its hope of also assuming a sufficient amount of group life reinsurance, expecting that the profits from the latter would balance the likely losses from the health lines. However, such an expectation is at best tenuous.

Reinsurance of Group Major Medical and Group Comprehensive Major Medical Coverages

Until the middle 1970s there were few calls for maximums for group major medical and group comprehensive major medical coverages in excess of about $25,000. The vast majority of cases offered maximum benefits of significantly less than $25,000. Accordingly, there was no technical need for reinsurance, except, as was also noted above, for basic hospital and surgical coverage, where the company sought to control the portion of its total premium dollar income stemming from these coverages or where a neophyte company sought guidance from a reinsurer.

However, the continuing substantial upward spiral in the cost of medical services in the 1970s created a need and demand for higher maximum benefits ranging from $100,000 to $1 million and even, in some instances, to unlimited coverage. Such amounts cause a proper concern over the possibility of significant fluctuations in losses occurring because of a few claims of very substantial size. Reinsurance has a significant contribution to make under these circumstances.

Such reinsurance coverages can be purchased on an "extended deductible" basis where the writing company pays all claims on each life up to some stipulated maximum, that is, the "deductible." Typical deductibles range from $25,000 through $100,000. Amounts in excess of the stipulated deductible are paid by the reinsurer. From the viewpoint of the reinsurer, which wishes to maintain claims control, it would be desirable to have the writing company retain liability for some modest percentage share of the excess over the deductible. However, in practice, the idea of requiring the writing company to coinsure a share of the excess amount has not been favorably received.

Several reinsurers seek group major medical and group comprehensive major medical coverages. Premiums are quoted on a "per person" basis, with separate rates for employees and dependents, both experience rated and nonexperience rated. The available information suggests that the experience refunds have been quite modest. This reflects the genuine possibility of severe claim fluctuations and the need for the reinsurer to establish substantial claim reserves.

Reinsurance of Group Long-Term Disability Coverages

Group long-term disability is probably the most rapidly expanding of all group benefits on the market. Reinsurance has a very significant role to play in this coverage given the obvious need of the direct writer to dampen possible loss fluctuations. Such fluctuations are distinctly possible given the rather modest premium levels, the substantial individual claim amounts, the changing economic climate that makes accurate projections difficult, and the sharply increasing maximum monthly indemnity amounts ($2,500 was common and $3,500 not unheard of in the late 1970s). Table 26-1 presents a hypothetical example that clearly shows this by examining the reserve requirements. The levels of loss become very large quite rapidly.

Group long-term disability coverages are also very complex, so writing companies often turn to reinsurers not only for risk sharing but for counseling about problems of underwriting, rate setting, and claim adjudication.

Group long-term disability reinsurance is usually available on a quota share basis, to a more limited extent on an excess basis, and also

TABLE 26-1
Disabled Life Mean Reserves per $100 Monthly Indemnity
1964 Commissioners Disability Table—2½% Interest

Age at Disablement—42

Duration from date of disablement to date of valuation	Benefit to expire within ____ years of valuation date	Reserve/$100
More than 6 mos. but less than 12 mos.	10	4,569
	To age 65	6,694
	Lifetime	7,525
1 year but less than 2 years	10	5,934
	To age 65	8,716
	Lifetime	9,908
2 years but less than 3 years	10	6,572
	To age 65	9,622
	Lifetime	11,121
3 years but less than 4 years	12	8,022
	To age 65	10,317
	Lifetime	12,129
4 years but less than 5 years	11	7,956
	To age 65	10,598
	Lifetime	12,685
5 years but less than 6 years	10	7,647
	To age 65	10,608
	Lifetime	12,946
6 years but less than 7 years	9	7,187
	To age 65	10,457
	Lifetime	13,040

SOURCE: 1964 Commissioner's Disability Table, Vol. I, Valuation Net Premiums Active and Disabled Life Reserves.

on what might be called an "extended elimination" basis. The quota share approach is similar to that described above for group life and group accidental death and dismemberment coverages. For group long-term disability coverage, the reinsurer anticipates morbidity levels identical with those of the ceding company. The excess basis for coverage has not proved very popular because it is extremely difficult to predict loss levels for the relatively limited exposure at the top of the benefit scale for any given case or group of cases.

The extended elimination basis is an approach under which the writing company pays claims for benefits through a designated period. Examples include "two years for disabilities incurred for accident or sickness," and "two years for disabilities incurred for sickness and five years for disabilities incurred for accident." The reinsurer then reimburses the ceding company for payments made for claims continuing beyond the period stipulated in the reinsurance agreement to the end of the benefit paying period.

The reinsurer is interested in claims control, and therefore usually wishes to have the writing company retain the liability for some modest share of losses beyond the end of the extended wait period. Thus, some small percentage of the monthly benefit will continue to be paid by the writing company. A disadvantage for the reinsurer in this form of reinsurance is the modest premium income relative to the potential substantial losses.

Reinsurance of Group Creditor Insurance Coverage

There are marked differences between the two different forms of group creditor insurance and corresponding differences in their reinsurance implications.

Consumer credit generally involves loans of modest size repayable over a relatively short period of time. Such credit includes modest cash loans, furniture installment loans, automobile installment loans, and the like. By the late 1970s, inflation had pushed the level of such loans as high as $10,000 or so, repayable over a five- or six-year period. Mortgage credit, on the other hand, involves much larger loans, ranging as high as $50,000 and beyond, payable over for longer intervals— from 25 to 30 years or even longer.

Reinsurance of consumer creditor insurance is rarely motivated by a need for risk sharing because the loans are relatively small and of short duration. Given reasonable participation by the eligible debtors, quite accurate predetermination of mortality and morbidity levels is possible, and substantial fluctuation in such levels is unlikely. The basis for consumer creditor reinsurance is the need of the direct writer to have the reinsurance company shoulder the strain on surplus associated with single premium credit insurance, which is the way most such insurance is written. The commission level, and the requirement in a number of states to set up the gross unearned premium as a reserve, can necessitate a substantial surplus commitment. Shifting this strain can be accomplished by reinsuring a portion or all of a specific block of business.

By contrast, reinsurance is sought for group creditor mortgage loans—both life and accident and health—to temper possible fluctuations in mortality or morbidity results. Excess basis reinsurance is feasible if adequate individual underwriting is done and if the rates charged vary with age. If either is absent, reinsurance can only be provided on a quota share basis. Of course, stop-loss coverage is also possible, but it would have to be custom-tailored for each individual case.

Reinsurance of Group Dental, Group Podiatry, and Group Vision Care Coverages

These relatively new coverages have yet to be marketed to the extent that the traditional forms of group insurance have been. Because they are new and experimental, they have generally been written by the substantial group writers. Thus, reinsurance has not been much in demand for them. In addition, the benefit amounts of these coverages are relatively modest, so fluctuations in claim levels do not pose significant problems.

A neophyte company seeking to provide these coverages might look to a reinsurer for guidance and might also want the reinsuring company to share in its fortunes by reinsuring a quota share of the coverage. Stop-loss coverage would be possible but would have to be custom-tailored. Reinsurers can and often do aid the direct writer in formulating and administering programs in these areas through such services as product development (policy forms, setting rates, devising sales materials), identifying the markets, and administration (underwriting, claims, and actuarial).

SUMMARY

This chapter has briefly surveyed the growth of group reinsurance and the major arrangements under which it is provided. It has also examined the major kinds of group reinsurance coverage, including catastrophe reinsurance and stop-loss coverage.

Just as was its past, the future of group reinsurance is tied to the future of group insurance proper. Given the likelihood of continued expansion of all forms of group insurance, it appears probable that the need for and the amount and scope of group reinsurance will also increase.

PART 5

GROUP INSURANCE IN CANADA

CHAPTER 27

GROUP INSURANCE IN CANADA

INTRODUCTION

Group insurance in Canada has developed generally along the same lines as in the United States. The major differences in Canadian practices are the direct result of different legislation, particularly greater government involvement in health care. The so-called Uniform Life Insurance Act and Uniform Accident and Sickness Act of the provinces of Canada, which are in force everywhere except Quebec, have relatively few restrictions on group insurance.[1] In general, they provide the legal basis for insuring individuals under a group contract. These Uniform Acts require the provision of a certificate or other document to the individual setting out the amount of his or her insurance (or the formula to determine the same), the basis for termination of insurance, and the individual's rights, if any, upon termination. Unlike legislation in the various states in the United States, the uniform acts do not set out any underwriting requirements, such as types of groups permitted, minimum participation requirements, or maximum amounts of insurance.

In Canada, group insurance remained relatively free from provincial regulation until 1971, when the Association of Provincial Superintendents of Insurance issued "Rules Governing Group Life Insurance," setting out in some detail the types of groups that qualify for group insurance, the schedules of insurance that are permitted, and the requirement of a conversion privilege. Although these Rules do not have the force of law, the insurance companies, brought together through the Canadian Life Insurance Association, have agreed to abide by them.

---

[1]Blair C. F. Fraser, ed., *The Uniform Life, Accident and Sickness Acts of the Provinces of Canada Except Quebec* (Stone & Cox, Ltd., 1972).

by
JOHN CARTMELL, FLMI, *Group Insurance Executive, The Canada Life Assurance Company, Toronto, Ontario*

Agreements between the provincial and federal governments (under which all provinces now provide hospital and medical coverage) have had the greatest effect on group health insurance. Insurers in Canada are prohibited from offering basic hospital and medical insurance; group health insurance plans are therefore limited to covering the so-called fringe benefits not covered by the basic government plans.

The Canada Pension Plan and the Quebec Pension Plan provide disability benefits in much the same way that the U.S. Social Security program does. In addition, the Canadian federal government included sickness benefits in the Unemployment Insurance Act of 1971, thereby affecting the short-term disability market.

During the past few years, most of the provinces have passed human rights legislation under which an employer may not discriminate in terms or conditions of employment because of age, sex, or marital status. None of the legislation made specific reference to group insurance, and it was largely ignored until Ontario introduced legislation specifically dealing with discrimination in group insurance plans.[2]

This chapter will discuss these Canadian practices in some detail, beginning with a description of how group insurance is marketed in Canada. This will be followed by a discussion of the Superintendents' Rules and how they affect group insurance; tax policies; survivor income benefits; the complex questions of group health care and the government's deep involvement in it; unemployment insurance; pension plans; the taxation of disability benefits; recent human rights legislation; and some significant trends and changes.

MARKETING

Until recently all provinces except Quebec required that all individuals selling insurance be licensed through a single company. This situation still prevails in most provinces. Theoretically, therefore, there have been no independent brokers in Canada. In practice, however, firms specializing in employee benefits have developed, and although licensed through a single company, have been free to place business with any company, provided a letter of permission is obtained from the licensing company.

Employee benefit consulting firms now control most of the larger groups and have been showing an increasing interest in smaller cases. The majority of smaller groups, however, are still handled by agents representing a single company.

---

[2]Part X (Section 34) of the Employment Standards Act, 1974, came into effect on November 1, 1975.

Industry Organizations

There are relatively few life and health companies operating in Canada. By far the majority of these have their head offices in Ontario, particularly in Toronto. This geographic concentration has facilitated the development of a strong industry association, the Canadian Life Insurance Association (CLIA) with virtually 100 percent membership of eligible companies. The Group Insurance Committee of CLIA is one of many standing committees and is specifically charged with monitoring all matters pertaining to group insurance and with presenting the industry position to the superintendents of insurance and to governments.

The Canadian Association of Accident and Sickness Insurers (CAASI) is also located in Toronto. In addition to most life insurance companies, it includes among its members many general insurance companies selling accident and sickness insurance. CAASI has been heavily involved in dealing with both provincial and federal governments as they increasingly move into the health care field.

SUPERINTENDENTS' RULES GOVERNING GROUP LIFE INSURANCE

The Association of Provincial Superintendents of Insurance, at their fall 1970 meeting, established a code entitled "Rules Governing Group Life Insurance," and all member companies of the CLIA have agreed to accept them. The principal advantage to the companies in agreeing to follow the Rules rather than pressing for the enactment of legislation to do the same thing is that the Rules can be more easily changed. In fact, the Rules have been amended almost annually since 1971.

The Rules became effective January 1, 1971 for all group policies issued on or after that date. Group contracts already in force were not required to comply with the Rules until such time as the benefits were substantially amended. For the greater part, the Rules enunciated underwriting and administrative practices already followed by most companies. For example, a conversion privilege became mandatory for employees under age 65 whose group life insurance coverage was discontinued because of termination of employment. It had, in fact, been standard practice for all companies to offer such a provision.

The Rule that proved most troublesome was one that limited voluntary additional insurance. A few professional associations had developed successful group plans under which their members were offered a choice of amounts of insurance, usually subject to evidence of insurability. Relatively few employer groups offered employees a choice of amounts of insurance. The 1971 Rules stipulated that the schedule "may provide members with the right to select either a basic benefit or another benefit not exceeding double the basic benefit." This limitation was largely the result of pressure from the Canadian Life Underwriters Association, which contended that voluntary additional group insurance would erode the individual market. Following the establishment of the 1971 Rules, there was an increasing interest in optional or voluntary additional coverage among employer groups and association plans. The Rule limiting optional coverage was gradually liberalized and finally removed entirely from the Rules on January 1, 1975.

The Association of Provincial Superintendents has revised the Group Life Rules each year since 1971. Effective January 1, 1976, the association also issued Rules governing group accident insurance and group sickness insurance, which for the most part parallel the group life Rules. The principal changes to the Rules, apart from the removal of the limitation on optional coverage, took place in 1974 and 1975. Only minor revisions to the Rules were made in 1976 and 1977.

The 1974 Rules included one dealing with a claimant's rights upon termination of a group contract. This Rule attempted to assign liability when one contract was replaced with another. In essence, the superintendents said that the original insurer must assume liability for a claim, provided the event giving rise to the claim occurred while the contract was in force. The insurer cannot apply more stringent requirements after a contract is terminated than would have been applied on a contract in force. When coverage is transferred, the original carrier is still liable if the event giving rise to benefits takes place while the original contract is in force. The new carrier, however, cannot deny benefits to employees insured under the original contract solely by reason of their not being actively at work when the new contract becomes effective.

The 1975 Rules included a revised Rule for group creditors insurance. The superintendents had become concerned at the reverse competition inherent in many creditor plans, where the full amount of the premium is paid by the borrower but any dividend or experience refund is paid to the creditor policyholder. The new Rule prohibited the payment of experience refunds or dividends where "a specific charge is levied against the debtor to pay the whole or part of the cost of the insurance." In addition, the Rule provided that "the policyholder may be reimbursed for reasonable and actual expenses incurred in connection with the contract [and stated] that the amount of reimbursement:

1. for the collection of premiums shall not exceed 5 percent of the premiums collected less 5 percent of any premiums or portions thereof refunded; and

    2. for any administrative expenses shall be related to the ser-
vices provided and not be calculated as a percentage of or
otherwise related to the premium for the insurance."

GROUP LIFE

    The group rules define eligible groups much along the lines of
legislation in many of the states. A contract of group insurance may be
issued to cover employees of the same employer or a number of
associated employers, or members of a professional or occupational
group,, trade union or credit union. The group must be formed for a
specific purpose other than to obtain insurance and the schedule of
benefits must be nondiscriminatory among members of the same
class. As in the United States, the great majority of group life contracts
are with employers to cover their employees. Groups down to ten lives
are usually underwritten without any evidence of insurability requirement, provided at least 75 percent of the employees eligible participate
in the plan. Amounts of insurance above the insurer's normal group
underwriting maximum are often offered subject to evidence of insurability. Several companies offer coverage on groups of less than ten
lives down to two lives, subject to evidence of insurability. Most
employer group plans provide for an amount of insurance based on a
multiple of the employee's annual salary. Coverage is normally terminated or substantially reduced at retirement. Most plans also provide
for a reduction of coverage at age 65 even if the employee continues
employment beyond that age. Human rights legislation generally prohibits discrimination by age up to 65 but still permits termination
or reduction of insurance at ages 65 and over.

Optional Group Life

    For several years a number of professional associations have
sponsored group life insurance for their members. Members are offered one or more units of insurance subject to a maximum number of
units. Issuance is subject to evidence of insurability. Since the premium is fully paid for by the member, a unit of insurance usually
provides a level amount of insurance to a certain age, with premium
rates increasing with age, often in five-year intervals. At the older
ages, the premium remains constant, and the amount of insurance
reduces each year with coverage terminating at a specified age, such
as 75.

    Prior to the 1971 Group Rules, no limits were placed on the types
of schedules that could be offered. The only restrictions were those
enforced by the insurer. Many of these plans have been most success-

ful, and amounts of insurance in excess of $100,000 are now often available. Since the association has no direct financial involvement in the plan, dividends and refunds are often applied to provide bonus additions to insured members, further increasing the insurance available. The 1971 Superintendents' Group Rules, with the limitation on optional coverage, immediately restricted the expansion of these plans. At the same time, the limitation on options seemed to generate an interest in optional coverage by employer groups. The Rule limiting options was subsequently liberalized and totally removed effective January 1, 1975.

The interest of employer groups in offering optional coverage was given further impetus by human rights legislation and a desire to allow employees to elect optional insurance as determined by their own needs.

Optional group insurance added to an employer group plan differs somewhat from professional association group insurance. The amounts available are usually more modest and the options restricted. A typical plan might offer optional coverage equal to 100 percent or 200 percent of annual salary, or a choice of fixed amounts of $10,000, $20,000, or $30,000. Coverage usually terminates at age 65. Premium rates are often age graded in five-year age intervals, and the issuance of coverage is usually subject to a health questionnaire or other evidence of insurability.

The employer collects the premium from employees by payroll deduction and handles the administrative details. Since the employer usually makes no financial contribution to optional insurance the coverage is often excluded from the calculation determining the dividend or experience refund.

There has been a steady interest in optional group insurance because it offers employees what is essentially term-to-65 insurance at rates lower than can be obtained on an individual basis.

Group Creditors Insurance

Group creditors insurance in Canada falls principally into two categories: (1) arrangements by the large chartered banks for life insurance coverage on personal loans, with no direct identifiable charge being made to the borrower; and (2) the offering by finance companies and other lenders of life insurance and sometimes disability coverage on an optional basis, with the borrower paying the full premium.

The Superintendents of Insurance have expressed concern for a number of years over group creditors insurance where the premium is paid by the borrower and any refunds or dividends are paid to the creditor policyholder. They have contended that this represents reverse competition, where it is in the policyholder's interest to place the business with the company having the highest rates, and hence the highest dividends.

In 1973 the Ontario Department of Insurance began an investigation of group creditors insurance, and the CLIA formed a committee on creditors group insurance. The purpose of the committee was to work with the Ontario Department of Insurance and to express the insurance industry's point of view on any proposed regulations or legislation. Several schemes for monitoring premium rates and loss ratios were proposed, but the decision finally taken by the Ontario Superintendent of Insurance was to prohibit any refunds or dividends under creditors group insurance contracts:

> . . . except under those contracts where the premium is paid wholly from the funds of the creditor without a specific charge to the debtors for the insurance. The contract may, however, provide for experience refunds or dividends where such experience refunds or dividends are paid retroactively to the debtors, are applied to reduce premiums, or are set aside as a special fund to be held by the insurer for the purpose of reducing future premiums. In no event shall any monies in the special fund referred to above be directly or indirectly paid to the creditor during the existence of the contract or after its termination.[3]

In addition, any single premium paid by a debtor must be turned over immediately to the insurer. It had been the practice of many creditors to charge a single premium, but to pay the insurer monthly. The expense allowance payable by the insurer to the creditor policyholder is limited to 5 percent of premium for premium collection, plus the payment of other expenses "reasonable in relation to the services performed." To monitor loss ratios and the charges made, all insurers are required to submit detailed annual reports on Ontario creditor groups.

Other provinces quickly followed Ontario's example and the Superintendents included the position taken by Ontario in their 1975 Group Rules.

More recently, consideration has been given by the superintendents to further limiting any expense allowance paid by insurers to creditor policyholders. Both Ontario and Alberta have now established minimum loss ratios for creditors group insurance of 80 percent for life and 75 percent for disability insurance, with some allowance for lower ratios on smaller groups.

---

[3]Letter from Ontario Superintendent of Insurance to insurers dated November 30, 1973.

TAXATION AFFECTING GROUP LIFE INSURANCE

All provinces levy a tax of 2 percent of the premium. Ontario increased the premium tax to 3 percent in April 1976. But after considerable pressure, particularly from Ontario insurance companies who were concerned at retaliatory measures that might be taken by other jurisdictions, the rate was dropped back to 2 percent in March 1978.

There is very little self-insurance of group life insurance benefits in Canada because, under the Federal Income Tax Act, any self-insured death benefits payable by an employer on the death of an employee are taxed as income to the employee to the extent that they exceed the lesser of the employee's annual salary or $10,000.

Benefits payable under an insured group plan are not taxable as income to the deceased employee or beneficiary, but employer contributions on sums assured in excess of $25,000 must be included as income to the employee and are subject to the payment of income tax by the employee. The amount of employer contributions to be taken as income to the employee is determined by applying the average net rate for the group policy to the sum assured in excess of $25,000. This is then reduced by any employee contributions that are applicable to the sum assured in excess of $25,000. To reduce employer contributions that are subject to tax, it is permissible to apply employee contributions first toward sums assured in excess of $25,000. Group life survivor income benefit plans have created a further complication in determining employer taxable contributions. The amount of group life insurance required to fund the survivor benefits must be included with all other group term coverage in determining the sum assured in excess of $25,000. Particularly on larger groups, detailed accurate survivor figures are not always maintained on each employee, particularly if the group is self-administered.

SURVIVOR INCOME BENEFITS

Since the middle of the 1960s, there has been considerable interest in providing survivor income benefits funded through group life insurance. A number of factors have influenced this trend:

1. To qualify for special tax treatment as a registered retirement savings plan, group pension plans must limit survivor income benefits to 50 percent of the accrued pension benefit at the time of the employee's death.
2. Survivor benefits from a group pension plan are fully taxable to the beneficiary, whereas survivor benefits from group life in-

surance plans are taxable only on the interest portion of the annuity.

3. Many employers feel it is in the interest of the beneficiary to have the benefit payable as an annuity rather than in a lump sum.

Many employers have thus removed survivor income benefits from their group pension plan and now provide a group life survivor income benefit plan in addition to basic group life insurance. Others have revised their basic group life insurance plan, reducing the lump sum benefit while adding a group life survivor income benefit plan.

Most group life survivor income benefit plans provide a benefit to the surviving spouse of 25 to 40 percent of the employee's salary, usually with a children's benefit of 5 to 10 percent per child up to a maximum of 15 or 20 percent. The spouse benefit usually terminates at the earlier of death or remarriage and often is reduced by any survivor benefits payable under the Canada or Quebec Pension Plans. There is frequently a one- or two-year lump sum "dowry" benefit payable upon remarriage.

A group survivor income benefit by its very nature requires benefits to be paid to the surviving spouse and children. The Uniform Life Insurance Act, however, gives the group life insured the statutory right to appoint anyone he or she so wishes as beneficiary. A group contract cannot therefore provide that the beneficiary will automatically be the surviving spouse and children. For example, a group life insured could name a person other than a spouse to receive the spouse's benefit.

In the vast majority of cases, the group life insured designates the spouse and/or children as beneficiary. Furthermore, many companies have taken various steps to minimize the possibility of contesting beneficiaries. The simplest way is to have the employee designate his or her spouse as irrevocable beneficiary. This assures that the designation is not to be changed, but the provision can cause problems if the employee and spouse separate. Many plans include a period certain, whereby the benefit is payable for the guaranteed period to the named beneficiary, but beyond that time only if the surviving spouse is the beneficiary, is still alive, and has not remarried. The Superintendents of Insurance are now considering revisions to the Uniform Life Insurance Act and to the Uniform Accident and Sickness Act. It is probable that some action will be taken to permit beneficiaries under group life survivor income benefit plans to be designated by contract.

HEALTH CARE COVERAGE

The provision of health care in Canada falls under provincial jurisdiction. In 1948, however, the federal government began making a series of grants to the provinces to assist with various health programs.

This culminated with the Federal Hospital Insurance and Diagnostic Services Act, which became effective January 1, 1958. Under this act, the federal government offered financial assistance to those provinces providing hospital and diagnostic services to all residents on uniform terms and conditions established by the federal government. This legislation required the provinces to join a government hospital insurance plan on the terms set by the federal government if they wished to obtain federal assistance. Between July 1, 1958 and July 1, 1959 all provinces, except Quebec, established qualifying plans. Quebec finally joined the plan on January 1, 1961.

Government Hospital Insurance

To qualify for federal assistance, a provincial hospital plan must offer to all residents full basic hospital coverage including all necessary services and supplies. The additional cost of semi-private or private room accommodation over and above the hospital's usual charge for standard ward accommodation is not covered.

In the case of out-of-province emergency treatment, the provincial plans will pay the hospital charges for insured services in full. For elective out-of-province treatment, most provincial plans restrict the amount of benefits payable. For example, Ontario will pay only 75 percent of the hospital charges for insured services.

Some provinces provide the coverage automatically to all residents from tax revenues while others make a specific premium charge. In the latter case, coverage is usually mandatory for employer groups, which assures a high level of participation among the total population.

With the introduction of government hospital insurance, private insurers were prohibited from insuring any hospital services covered by the government scheme. As a province entered the national plan, insurers had to amend their group health plans by deleting any basic hospital coverage.

Insurers are permitted to offer insurance to cover the cost of room and board accommodation in excess of standard ward level. Originally, most companies offered supplementary hospital coverage up to a fixed dollar limit per day, designed to cover the cost of semi-private or private room accommodation. More recently it has become common practice to offer insurance to cover the cost of semi-private accommodation without reference to a fixed dollar amount.

Since the bulk of hospital costs are covered by the government hospital plan, group health plans in Canada have not been subject to the same inflationary pressures as in the United States. However, the daily cost of semi-private accommodation (differential between standard ward and semi-private) has been increasing steadily in the 1970s. Rapidly increasing health care costs, and the difficulty provincial governments have in absorbing them, now appears, however, to be resulting in substantially increased costs for semi-private and private room accommodation. For example, the additional daily charge for semi-private accommodation in 1978 in Ontario is $12 to $25.

Government Medicare Insurance

Following the introduction of what in effect was a national hospital plan, there was substantial growth in surgical and medical insurance. Groups that previously had a hospital plan barely covering the cost of ward accommodation and a limited surgical plan now requested semi-private hospital coverage and full coverage of all surgical and medical expenses.

In Canada most provincial medical associations publish recommended fee schedules. These provided a basis for offering full coverage plans. Nonprofit organizations, including some sponsored by medical associations, offered full surgical and medical coverage with payment being made directly to participating doctors. A very high percentage of doctors participated in these plans and agreed to accept the plan payment, usually 90 or 95 percent of the provincial fee schedule, as payment in full for their services. To compete with such plans, many insurers offered comparable coverage, but with payment at 100 percent of the provincial fee schedule also being made directly to the doctor if so arranged by the employee.

EXPANSION

Even with a large segment of the population insured under full coverage plans, there was continuous political pressure to make government medicare coverage available to all, regardless of physical condition. In 1963 Saskatchewan unilaterally established a provincial medicare plan covering all residents. This had relatively little impact on the group insurance market because Saskatchewan was primarily agricultural.

Two provinces, Alberta and Ontario, tried to provide access to coverage for all residents while still maintaining private insurance. The Alberta Medical Plan was established in 1963. It required all insurers to offer two basic contracts to all residents. One plan was designed to supply full first dollar coverage, and the other offered benefits subject to deductible and coinsurance. A compulsory pooling arrangement was established to cover poor risks, and government subsidies were made available to those with low incomes. The Canadian Health Insurance Association (which later became the Canadian Association of Accident and Sickness Insurers) handled all arrangements, including the pooling device, on behalf of the insurers.

In 1966, Ontario introduced the Ontario Medical Services Insurance Plan (OMSIP). This was a government-operated plan that made available full first dollar coverage on an individual basis only, with subsidies for low-income residents. Both the Alberta and Ontario plans operated successfully. By combining the best features of private insurance and government involvement, these plans provided residents with access to full basic coverage without disrupting the many group health plans that were in force.

FEDERAL CRITERIA

Despite the success of the two plans, the pressure to move to full government medicare continued. The federal government encouraged the provinces to fall into line by promising financial assistance only to those provinces that established a medicare plan that met the following criteria:

1. The plan must cover all doctors' services, including specialists;
2. The plan must be universal (this was subsequently interpreted to mean that at least 95 percent of the population must be covered);
3. The plan must be administered by the province or a provincial agency; and
4. The plan must provide transferability, that is, must cover individuals moving from one province to another.

Some provinces, such as Ontario and Alberta, felt they already had adequate health insurance plans and wished to apply their financial resources to other priorities. However, since provinces not offering plans that met the federal criteria would not receive any financial assistance (although they would be contributing through taxation to the federal assistance being granted to other provinces), the provinces had no genuine alternative but to comply with the federal criteria.

Provinces entered the federal scheme over a period of two and one-half years. British Columbia and Saskatchewan qualified on July 1, 1968, and the Province of Quebec finally introduced a plan on January 1, 1971. Since to qualify, a plan must be administered by the province or a provincial agency, provinces were faced with serious administrative problems when establishing a plan. Many provinces turned existing nonprofit organizations into provincial agencies. Ontario initially utilized the services of the insurance companies to collect premiums and administer claims through an administrative arrangement known as Healthco Limited. This was essentially a temporary measure until the province could set up its own organization and combine both the hospital and medicare plans.

The introducton of provincial medicare plans thus legislated private insurers out of the basic health insurance market entirely. All basic surgical, medical, and diagnostic plans had to be terminated and major medical plans amended to remove coverage of any services provided by the government plan. Private plans may cover only such expenses incurred outside Canada to the extent that they exceed the amount payable by the provincial plan. No excess charges made for services received in Canada may be covered.

Most of the provincial plans pay doctors a percentage of the provincial fee schedule (usually 90 percent). Doctors may bill the government plan directly and must then accept the plan's payment as payment in full for their services. Alternatively, doctors may bill the patient directly but may charge the patient more than the provincial fee schedule only if the patient is so advised beforehand.

With nearly all hospital, surgical, medical, and diagnostic services covered by government plans, major medical plans now cover principally prescription drugs and private nursing. The pressure for first dollar coverage has continued, however, and many major medical plans in Canada now have no deductible and no coinsurance.

With the rapidly increasing costs of health care in recent years, serious financial problems are developing with the provincial plans. The federal government is now limiting its financial assistance and throwing the full impact of the increasing costs on to the provinces. Some suggestions are now being made to introduce a deductible in the government plans to curb excess or unnecessary usage of the plans.

Blue Cross

Blue Cross and comparable organizations operated plans across Canada prior to the introduction of government hospital and medicare insurance. Some of these organizations, particularly those which were doctor-sponsored and provided only surgical and medical coverage, ceased to exist when the government plans came into being. Blue Cross and many other organizations, however, still offer semi-private hospital coverage, major medical coverage, and even dental plans.

The largest of these organizations is Ontario Blue Cross, which provides both group and individual coverage. Through an arrangement with the provincial government, semi-private coverage may be included in the Ontario Health Insurance Plan (OHIP). The provincial agency collects the premium and includes a semi-private code on the OHIP identification card. Blue Cross pays the hospital directly for any semi-private charges incurred.

Ontario Blue Cross also offers major medical coverage, pay-direct drug plans, and pay-direct dental plans and is, in fact, one of the largest dental insurers in the country.

Dental

Dental insurance has been the most rapidly growing segment of group health insurance in the last few years. One major provision in Canada, which simplifies the operation of dental insurance, is that provincial dental associations publish recommended fee schedules, which provide an acceptable basis for benefits and facilitate the payment of benefits directly to dentists.

Group dental plans are offered by many insurance companies as well as by Blue Cross and similar organizations. Most plans cover basic preventive treatment with payment at 100 percent of the provincial dental fee schedule. Additional benefits to cover such items as prosthodontics and orthodontics may be included subject to coinsurance and an annual or lifetime maximum.

Many plans base their benefits on the current provincial fee schedule. Whenever a fee schedule is changed (and in recent years of high inflation most provincial dental associations have changed their fee schedules annually), benefits are automatically increased, and the insurer usually has the right to adjust premium rates coincident with the increase in benefits.

In the early 1970s it seemed probable that the provinces would proceed with government dental insurance. The escalating costs of existing government health insurance plans, however, appear to have delayed any such move. Instead, many provinces have been moving cautiously to provide dental care to children under a certain age, generally through dental units working within the school system. For example, dental services for children under eight years of age became covered in Quebec on May 1, 1974. The age limit has gradually been increased, and by 1978 children up to 14 years of age were covered.

Drug Benefits

Although prescription drugs are covered under major medical plans, and in fact are now the major item of expense under such plans, a number of new plans covering only prescription drugs have been developed. These plans, with claims being paid to the pharmacist, have been pioneered by Blue Cross and similar organizations. A number of companies have also developed comparable plans with a pay-direct facility.

Prescription drug plans usually provide for the insured to pay a dispensing fee of 35 cents, with the pharmacist billing the insurer for the cost of the prescription. Such plans require the insurer to enter into an agreement with participating pharmacists, and the operation of the plan is limited to these participating pharmacists. The insurer issues each participant with an identification card and must maintain some arrangement with participating pharmacists to check the validity of claimants. These plans are popular with employees, particularly with union groups, because of the ease of claims procedure.

Many provinces are now covering prescription drugs on some basis. Most provinces supply free prescription drugs to all residents over age 65, but Saskatchewan and Manitoba have extended the prescription drug plan to all residents. In Saskatchewan the province operates a plan covering all residents for prescription drugs subject only to the payment of a dispensing fee. Under the Manitoba program the province pays 80 percent of the cost of prescription drugs over $50 a year for each family unit in the province.

Private insurers are virtually excluded from covering prescription drugs in Saskatchewan and Manitoba. On national plans with some residents in Manitoba it is usual to allow the first $50 of prescription drugs (the deductible under the government plan) to be included under the major medical plan.

DISABILITY INSURANCE

In 1970 the federal government published a white paper entitled "Unemployment Insurance in the 70s." In addition to proposing many far-reaching changes to the existing Unemployment Insurance Act, the report indicated an intention to include coverage of unemployment due to accident, sickness, or pregnancy.[4]

This proposal caused considerable concern to insurers and to employers with group disability plans. The Canadian Association of Accident and Sickness Insurers submitted alternate proposals that would not disrupt existing group plans, while still extending coverage to all workers. Sections of the revised act relating to disability coverage became effective January 2, 1972. They provided that all employees who had worked at least 20 weeks during the preceding 52 weeks would be eligible for up to 15 weeks of benefit after a 2-week waiting period if absence was due to accident, sickness, or pregnancy. The level of benefit is 66⅔ percent of the employee's average weekly earnings, with maximum insurable earnings in 1978 being $240 per week. The Unemployment Insurance Plan is always the "last payer," so that if a private insurance plan is maintained, unemployment insurance benefits are payable only after the benefits of the private plan have been exhausted.

The representations made by the Canadian Association of Accident and Sickness Insurers and other groups had some effect. Provision was made for employers to register disability plans with the Unemployment Insurance Commission and those plans that met certain standards received a rebate by means of reduced unemployment insurance contributions. The principal criteria for a plan to qualify for registration are:

1. Benefits must commence no later than the fifteenth day of disability and continue for at least 15 weeks.
2. The benefit level must be at least 66⅔ percent of earnings, based on maximum insurable earnings at least as high as for the Unemployment Insurance Plan. If there is no employer contribution to the disability plan and the benefit is therefore

---

[4]*Unemployment Insurance in the 70's* (Ottawa: Queen's Printer for Canada, 1970).

nontaxable, the benefit level may be at least 60 percent of earnings.
3. All employees working at least 20 hours per week must be eligible after completing no more than 3 months of service.
4. At least 95 percent of eligible employees must be covered.

Industry fears that many disability plans would be discontinued proved groundless. In fact, the majority of plans have stayed in force, and many were upgraded to qualify for registration. Many disability plans previously provided for a maximum benefit of only 13 weeks. Virtually all of these have been increased to provide a benefit for at least 15 weeks. It had been usual to limit pregnancy benefits to six weeks. Most plans now exclude pregnancy benefits since the Unemployment Insurance Plan provided a benefit of 15 weeks. Plans excluding pregnancy coverage have qualified for registration, but effective October 1, 1976, amended regulations require disabilities resulting from pregnancy to be covered except during a 17-week period surrounding the date of delivery, or during maternity leave.

The initial contribution rate to the Unemployment Insurance Plan was established at 90 cents per $100 of earnings paid by the employee and $1.26 paid by the employer. If an employer registered a qualifying disability plan, the contribution rate for the ensuing calendar year was reduced by 40 cents per $100 of payroll. In turn, the employer was required to pass on to employees five-twelfths of this rebate either in cash or through improved benefits.

The level of unemployment has been particularly high during the 1970s, and premium rates have been increased. In 1978 the contribution rate was $1.50 per $100 earnings paid by the employee and $2.10 paid by the employer. For employers with a qualifying disability plan, the employer's contribution rate was reduced by 42 cents to $1.68 per $100 of earnings.

The level of maximum weekly insured earnings has been increased each year. To qualify for registration, the level of insured earnings under private plans has also been increased. This has caused a substantial volume of plan amendments to be effected each January first and has been a continuing source of increased business. The maximum insurable earnings for 1978 were $240 per week, with maximum weekly benefits being $160 for taxable plans and $144 for nontaxable plans.

THE CANADA PENSION PLAN AND THE QUEBEC PENSION PLAN

The Canada Pension Plan (CPP) became effective January 1, 1966. It operates in all provinces except Quebec, which established its own comparable program, the Quebec Pension Plan (QPP). The two plans are closely coordinated and tend to operate as one plan, subject to a few differences in benefit levels. The combined plan covers virtually all employees and self-employed persons on a compulsory basis. The plan is intended to provide benefits based on the average industrial wage. Each year, a yearly maximum pensionable earnings figure is established under the plan (YMPE), and maximum contributions on benefits are based on this figure. Both employer and employee contribute 1.8 percent of the employee's earnings up to the YMPE ($10,400 in 1978) in excess of a deductible amount of $1,000. For self-insured persons, the contribution rate is 3.6 percent.[5]

The plan provides six benefits:

1. Monthly retirement pension;
2. Monthly disability pension;
3. Monthly benefit for children of a disabled contributor;
4. Lump-sum death benefit;
5. Monthly pension for surviving spouse; and
6. Monthly benefit for children of deceased contributor.

The YMPE and maximum benefits for 1978 are as follows:

	CPP	*QPP*
YMPE	$10,400.00	$10,400.00
Retirement pension	194.44	194.44
Disability pension	194.02	269.42
Disabled contributor's child benefit—each child	48.19	29.00
Death benefit (lump sum)	1,040.00	1,040.00
Surviving spouse's pension		
under age 65	121.11	196.51
over age 65	116.66	116.66
Surviving children's benefit—each child	48.19	29.00

Many group survivor income plans provide a higher level of benefits for salaries up to the YMPE, but with the actual benefit being reduced by CPP/QPP survivor benefits. Survivor benefits to children are also often offset by CPP/QPP benefits. In virtually all cases the offset is established when the benefits become payable, and any subsequent cost-of-living increases in CPP/QPP benefits are not taken into account.

Most long-term disability plans are offset with the CPP/QPP primary benefit, but the secondary or childrens' benefits are usually ignored, or are only subject to an "all source" maximum. As with the survivor income benefit offset, any cost-of-living increases in CPP/QPP benefits are not taken into account.

---

[5]Students and others working for a relatively short period of time during the year do not have to contribute if earnings are less than the deductible amount.

TAXATION OF DISABILITY BENEFITS

Prior to the promulgation of the federal budget of June 18, 1972, all benefits paid under insured disability plans were tax-free to the claimant. In the federal budget of June 18, 1972, benefits from disability plans issued or amended after that date became taxable as income to the claimant. Benefits from all plans already in force on June 18, 1972 became taxable from January 1, 1974. The only plans not affected by the budget legislation are those where 100 percent of the premium are paid by participants in an employee group.

As a result of the change in the taxable status of disability plans, many employers have arranged a redistribution of the cost-sharing basis with employees to provide the greatest tax advantage to them. For example, it is now advantageous for employee contributions to be directed to disability plans to ensure that benefits remain tax-free, and to apply employer contributions to the first $25,000 of group life insurance and to other health benefits. On this basis employer contributions are not taxed as income to the employee.

Where employers have continued to contribute to disability plans, it has been necessary to provide a higher level of benefits, since these are now taxable, to maintain the same level of after-tax benefit that was provided before the legislation became effective. Schedules providing up to 80 percent of earnings are not uncommon if the benefit is taxable.

Insurers are required to issue a statement of benefits paid to each claimant under taxable plans on the appropriate federal income tax reporting form.

For Quebec residents, insurers must withhold provincial income tax and the payroll tax for government hospital and medicare insurance. Federal tax withholding is not required, but is permitted if the policyholder so requests. Some union plans, in particular, have requested federal tax withholding so that members are not faced with substantial tax arrears if they have received several weeks of benefits from which tax has not been deducted at source.

HUMAN RIGHTS LEGISLATION

During the early 1970s most provinces enacted human rights legislation prohibiting discrimination in terms and conditions of employment because of race, creed, age, sex, or marital status. Although a great many group plans did include discriminatory features, in the absence of specific legislation dealing with discrimination in group plans, both employers and insurers were unsure how to proceed. The legislation was generally ignored as far as group plans were concerned.

The Ontario Human Rights Code Amendment Act of 1972 recognized the special problems of discrimination in group plans, and the amendment exempted these plans from the operation of the act. Meanwhile, a provincial task force was established to consider discrimination in group plans and to make recommendations. The recommendations of the task force were finally included as Part X of the Ontario Employment Standards Act, which required all plans to comply by the first anniversary date of the policy after November 1, 1975, or in the case of plans subject to union bargaining agreements, by the first bargaining date after November 1, 1975, but in no event later than November 1, 1977. The purpose of Part X is to define what is deemed to be discrimination in group plans with respect to age, sex, and marital status.

Two aspects of the legislation have proved particularly troublesome. The task force held that dependents' benefits must be made available to a common-law spouse on the same basis as a legal spouse but failed to define "common-law spouse." The usual definition followed by insurers provides that a person with whom the employee has cohabited for a specified period, and whom the employee represents as his or her spouse, be deemed the employee's spouse.

Pregnancy must be treated like any other disability for health benefits, but may be excluded from disability coverage during the period of maternity leave of absence. The employee is entitled to this leave under the Ontario Employment Standards Act. The problem arises because the starting date of the maternity leave is left largely to the employee's discretion. The act provides that an employee with 12 months and 11 weeks of service prior to the estimated delivery date is entitled to a leave of absence of at least 17 weeks, commencing during the period of 11 weeks preceding the estimated date of delivery and extending to the later of 6 weeks after the actual delivery date or 17 weeks from the beginning of the leave of absence. An employee can choose as the starting date any date within this 11-week period or any earlier date mutually agreed upon between herself and the employer. However, the employer may insist that the employee go on leave at any time within the 11 weeks prior to the estimated delivery date if the performance of her work is materially affected by the pregnancy.

The Canadian Association of Accident and Sickness Insurers has recommended that contracts stipulate that benefits will not be payable at any time when the employee is on pregnancy leave or could be placed on pregnancy leave by the employer. With this provision, pregnancy benefits would be payable under a disability plan until the eleventh week prior to delivery. At this point, benefits would be suspended for the duration of the pregnancy leave. Of course, if an earlier starting date has been agreed upon, then that date would be used as the cutoff date for the disability benefits.

It is not required that maternity leave of absence be provided to an employee who would not be employed for at least 12 months and 11 weeks before the estimated date of delivery. The employer has the right to terminate such an employee rather than grant maternity leave. Since the new regulations permit the exclusion of disability income benefits only while the employee is on maternity leave, most insurers provide in their contracts that benefits will not be payable for a disability resulting from a pregnancy for which the employee fails to qualify for maternity leave solely because of failure to meet the length-of-service requirement.

In view of the exhaustive study made by the Ontario task force, it is probable that other provinces will follow the task force recommendations and that more uniformity among the provinces may ensue.

TRENDS AND CHANGES

The insurance legislation in the Province of Quebec was rewritten during 1976 and became law on October 21, 1976. The general result has been to bring insurance law in Quebec much closer to the Uniform Act in the common-law provinces. Included with the new act were group regulations that generally followed the Superintendents' Group Rules. The principal difference was in the conversion provision. The Quebec regulations now require group policies to allow a terminating employee to convert to an individual policy that provides coverage comparable both in amount and duration to the coverage terminated under the group contract. In the case of group survivor income benefits, the terminated employee will be able to convert to a family income policy providing the same monthly benefit until age 65, subject to a minimum period of 10 years. If a company does not offer an individual policy providing comparable coverage then an individual policy to age 65 of equivalent value must be offered.

The Superintendents of Insurance of the other provinces at their fall 1976 meeting amended the group rules dealing with conversion to bring them closer to the new Quebec regulations. New group policies issued on and after July 1, 1977 and existing policies renewing after that date must permit terminating employees to convert to an individual policy of either whole life or term to age 65.

In October 1975 the federal government established an anti-inflation program to regulate the earnings of employees in firms with 500 or more employees during the following three years. In determining earnings all forms of compensation must be taken into account, including fringe benefits. This has restricted the growth of group coverage to some extent, since many employees have preferred to take any increase in earnings as take-home pay, rather than in benefits.

Extremely high inflation in recent years, particularly in health care, has created severe financial problems in many provincial hospital and medicare plans. Additional financial assistance by the federal government has not been forthcoming, so that the full cost of inflation has been borne by the provinces. Further governmental involvement in drug and dental benefits in the near future is likely to be similarly inhibited.

High bank interest rates are causing larger employers to place more emphasis on interest credited by insurers to group reserves. On many large plans, interest is being credited on cash flow and all reserves at current competitive rates of interest. There has been limited interest in administrative services only arrangements, and only a few relatively large plans are being operated on this basis.

In recent years most changes in group insurance plans have resulted directly from increasing government involvement in the provision and financing of health care. Even without new government plans, changes and amendments to existing government programs will require further adjustment of, and integration with, private plans.

SUMMARY

This chapter has provided an overview of Canadian group insurance practice, noting both the similarities to and differences from U.S. practice. The major differences result from different Canadian legislation, especially in the area of health care. Marketing methods and insurance organizations in Canada were described. The Superintendents' Rules that regulate group life insurance were presented in some detail, since they provide the context within which group life operates in Canada. The various aspects of group health care, including hospital insurance, medicare insurance, Blue Cross, dental insurance, and prescription drug benefits, were discussed with special reference to the powerful influence of the federal and provincial governments. Finally, consideration was given to unemployment insurance, the Canada Pension Plan and the Quebec Pension Plan, human rights legislation, and salient trends and changes.

CHAPTER 28

GROUP REINSURANCE IN CANADA

INTRODUCTION

This chapter discusses several aspects of the reinsurance of group insurance, with particular attention to how they apply to the Canadian market. The three major methods of group life reinsurance used in Canada are identified and illustrated, and then several problems are discussed as they relate to group reinsurance, including reinsurance cost, experience refunds, experience rated or "retention" cases, stop loss and catastrophe reinsurance, and amounts in excess of no-evidence limits.

The application of the three major methods of group reinsurance to various kinds of group coverage are considered, including survivors income benefit, association group business, group creditor insurance, group accidental death and dismemberment benefits, group long-term disability business, group weekly indemnity, and group dental insurance. Other aspects of the group reinsurance business discussed are reinsurance treaties, the spreading of risk among several insurers, and the use of the professional reinsurer. The chapter concludes with a brief discussion of reinsurance contracts, legal requirements, and reporting to supervisory authorities.

GROUP REINSURANCE

Parallel with the growth of group insurance in Canada, there has been a corresponding growth in the use of reinsurance and hence a substantial increase in the amount of reinsurance ceded. For example, at the end of 1966, the total group life reinsurance in force of three major reinsurers operating in the Canadian market amounted to $154 million. By the end of 1976, the total group life reinsurance in force for these three organizations had risen to over $1,958 million. This reflects

by
G. R. MINNS, FIA, FCIA, ASA, *President, Munich Reinsurance Company and The Victory Insurance Company Limited, Toronto, Canada*

not only the growth of group business but also the significant increase in the size of available group benefits.

The Professional Reinsurer

Many of the larger companies in the Canadian market exchange reinsurance on their individual business on a reciprocal basis. This method works satisfactorily because there is seldom competition among the companies involved for the particular case. This is not true, however, for a large group case which is usually offered to many direct writing companies to ascertain who can offer the most advantageous terms. Thus, it is not common for reinsurance on group business to be offered to another direct writing company; reinsurance is usually offered to a professional reinsurer who does not compete directly for the business. The particular advantage is that the direct writer avoids sharing any of its own ideas and philosophies with a competitor. Although the professional reinsurer may be approached by more than one company regarding the same business, this does not create problems since the reinsurer normally endeavors to offer equivalent terms to all companies, leaving the direct writers to compete for the business.

The reinsurance terms that a company can obtain will be important in determining the price it charges in the marketplace. Obviously the higher the proportion of business reinsured, the more significant the reinsurance cost becomes.

USE OF REINSURANCE IN SMALL COMPANIES

The services provided by professional reinsurers extend beyond carrying surplus risk. Professional reinsurers have a wide knowledge of the market, which, combined with their technical expertise, enables them to provide considerable advice and assistance to small and new companies. These companies often rely heavily on the assistance they receive from their reinsurers. This arrangement is mutually beneficial, because the reinsurer is able to encourage sound underwriting practices by the ceding company; at the same time, the ceding company obtains the advantage of the reinsurer's expertise.

The problems that face a small life insurance company are significantly different from those facing a large company. A large company probably has a higher retention limit, therefore, its reinsurance needs are more limited. On the other hand, the small company, with its lower retention limit, may need a substantial amount of reinsurance if it is to be able to operate competitively.

The reinsurer can also supplement the expertise of the smaller company. This assistance can take the form of advice on items such as policy wording, underwriting standards, no-evidence limits, and possibly renewal underwriting. Hence, the reinsurance terms and conditions that it can obtain and the services that can be provided by its reinsurer are very important in enabling a small direct writing company to maintain a competitive position in the marketplace.

SPREADING OF RISK AMONG SEVERAL INSURERS

The large insurance company usually has little need for reinsurance. Nevertheless, from time to time the group policyholder may request that two or three insurance companies participate in the underwriting of its group life program. Sometimes the reason for this is that a very large group is involved, and in the event of a disastrous occurrence the amount of liability may be considered by the consultant to the policyholder to be too large for any one company to handle. However, the more usual reason is that for business reasons the group policyholder wishes to favor certain insurance companies, and hence the risk will be spread among several companies.

One insurance company will usually be named as the prime carrier. That company is responsible for allocating reinsurance as determined by the group policyholder. Each participating company receives its percentage of the total premium and is responsible for its share of the claims, reserves, and any dividends. To simplify administration, each is normally expected to follow the experience rating procedures of the primary company rather than apply its own procedure. The primary company is responsible for the administration of the group policy. In return for providing this service, it receives a greater share of the expenses than do the other participating companies.

REINSURANCE OF GROUP LIFE COVERAGES

The most common use of reinsurance in Canada is in group life insurance. Many of the considerations involved in the reinsurance of group life business is also applicable to the reinsurance of other coverages.

Three Methods of Reinsuring Group Life Business

There are basically three methods of reinsurance generally in use in Canada at the present time for the reinsurance of group life business: the quota-share method, the surplus method, and a combination of the two called quota-share and surplus.

QUOTA-SHARE METHOD

The quota-share method is the most popular for group life business. Using this method, the reinsurer insures the same percentage of each risk covered under a group life contract. The expense loadings contained in group life premiums are usually small; it is therefore important to minimize the costs of administration. This factor makes the quota-share method attractive because it is both easy to understand and simple to administer.

SURPLUS METHOD

The surplus method is an arrangement whereby the reinsurer accepts reinsurance of all amounts in excess of the retention limit of the ceding company. While this method comes closest to meeting the needs of the ceding company, if often creates difficulties for the reinsurer.

One problem is a case where one or two of the senior people in the company covered by the group life contract are either uninsurable or highly substandard. Even though there is a limit imposed on the maximum benefit, if the reinsurer accepts reinsurance on a surplus basis, the reinsurer may find itself carrying the risk on only the two or three lives with the largest benefits. If any of these individuals are substandard risks, then the reinsurer would be reinsuring poor risks whereas the direct writing company would be retaining a good spread of risk. Generally then, the use of the surplus method is feasible only where the reinsurer can obtain an adequate share of the risk. The determination of what constitutes an adequate share is a matter of judgment for the reinsurer. This method has a large measure of appeal to the ceding company, since it can retain the maximum spread of risk for itself at the same time as it minimizes its reinsurance premium outlay.

QUOTA-SHARE AND SURPLUS METHOD

This method combines the quota-share method and the surplus method so that the reinsurer receives a fixed percentage of each risk until the ceding company has reached its maximum retention. Thereafter, it reinsures all amounts in excess of the retention of the ceding company. The quota-share applies effectively to the smaller amounts of insurance, but once the ceding company has reached its maximum retention then the arrangement actually becomes a surplus arrangement. This method is obviously a compromise between the quota-share method and the surplus method, with some of the advantages of both. The reinsurer can obtain a reasonable share of the total risk, whereas the ceding company minimizes the amount of business that is necessary to reinsure.

The application of these three methods is illustrated in Table 28-1.

Thus, if the amount of insurance is $20,000, the amount of reinsurance would be $12,000 if the quota-share method at 60 percent is used, nothing if the surplus method is used, and $5,000 if the 25 percent quota-share and surplus method is used ($20,000 × .25). If the amount of insurance is $50,000, the amount reinsured under a 60

TABLE 28-1
Examples of Three Methods of Reinsurance Used in Canada for Group Life Business

Maximum Retention of Ceding Company $ 40,000
Maximum Benefit $100,000

Amount of Insurance	Amount of Reinsurance		
	60% Quota Share	Surplus	25% Quota Share and Surplus
$ 10,000	$ 6,000	$ —	$ 2,500
20,000	12,000	—	5,000
40,000	24,000	—	10,000
50,000	30,000	10,000	12,500
75,000	45,000	35,000	35,000
100,000	60,000	60,000	60,000

percent quota-share arrangement will be $30,000 ($50,000 × .60); under a surplus arrangement, $10,000 ($50,000 − 40,000); and $12,500 under the combination method ($50,000 × .25 = $12,500). Since the direct writer keeps $37,500, an amount still under its retention limit, the reinsurer's share is $12,500.

STOP-LOSS

The methods of reinsurance discussed so far are referred to as proportional methods, since the reinsurer accepts a proportion of the risk. There are also nonproportional methods, and the best known of these is stop-loss. Under stop-loss reinsurance coverage, the reinsurer agrees to reimburse the direct writing company if the total amount of claims within the total portfolio exceeds a predetermined limit in any single year. A typical coverage might provide that the reinsurer pay claims in excess of 120 percent of expected mortality up to a maximum of $2 million. This approach has a great deal of theoretical appeal, because it should stabilize the experience of the direct writing company. Also, the cost often appears to be very attractive.

However, little coverage of this nature has been written in Canada because of certain problems. These include:

1. The reinsurers' liability arises only for amounts in excess of the predetermined limit. The direct writer is still liable for claims in excess of the expected mortality up to the predetermined limit;

2. Any reduction in the predetermined limit dramatically increases the premium;

3. The reinsurer determines the maximum amount it will cover on any one life under the stop-loss arrangement, and therefore surplus reinsurance may be required; and

4. Since the reinsurer determines a total maximum claim it will pay, the coverage is not complete and any claims in excess of this upper limit are the responsibility of the direct writer.

GROUP LIFE INSURANCE PORTFOLIO

The comments above could apply equally to the reinsurance of a single group life insurance policy. However, quite often one reinsurer will assume the risk for all of the reinsurance arising out of the group life portfolio of a company. The most appropriate method of reinsurance depends on the distribution by amount of the business written by the ceding company. The important consideration to the reinsurer is to receive an adequate share of the total portfolio and thus obtain a reasonable spread of risk.

THE CATASTROPHE RISK

There is always a risk of catastrophic situations in both individual and group business, but the risk is much greater with group life insurance given the potential concentration of risk in one location, whether it be an office, a factory, or a chartered aircraft. A disaster of catastrophic nature involving many deaths could result in a serious drain on the surplus of the insurance company and possibly even threaten its solvency. For this reason, most group writing companies obtain catastrophe reinsurance. This coverage provides for the reinsurer to pay a large proportion of the claims resulting from a single event, usually in excess of a single deductible amount and subject to an overall maximum. The single event is usually defined as a specific minimum number of lives lost.

A typical arrangement might be for the reinsurer to pay 90 percent of all claims in excess of a total of $200,000 involving 3 or more deaths from a single occurrence, subject to an overall maximum payment of $2 million. This coverage may include group life claims only or may be expanded to include accidental death coverage.

The price of this catastrophe cover is very sensitive to the amount of deductible and also the minimum number of lives required before the catastrophe cover takes effect. The coverage is normally written on a one-year basis, renewable at the option of both the direct writing company and the reinsurer. The coverage could apply to only one large group, but normally it would apply to all groups in the portfolio of the direct writing company.

Reinsurance Cost

There are essentially two methods used to determine the cost of the reinsurance of group life business: group reinsurance premium rates and coinsurance.

Some reinsurers have developed their own group life "reinsurance premium rates." These are applied to the sums reinsured to develop the cost of reinsurance. This is essentially the same method as the yearly renewable term (YRT) method, the most common method used for the reinsurance of individual business. However, if the reinsurance premiums of the reinsurer do not provide for exactly the same type of benefit as that offered by the ceding company, it is necessary for the reinsurance premiums to be adjusted. Partly for this reason, but mainly to reduce administrative costs, the coinsurance method, using the premium rates of the ceding company, is generally more appropriate. The reinsurer will normally quote coinsurance terms sufficient to cover the agency commission costs and also contribute to the expenses of the direct writing company, since the administrative expenses of the direct writing company would be greater than those of the reinsurer. For example, if the total agency cost is 6 percent of premiums and the reinsurer offered a further 4 percent as a contribution to the expenses of the direct writing company, then the coinsurance allowance would be quoted as 10 percent. The reinsurer would then receive 90 percent of the gross premiums reinsured.

The particular advantage of the coinsurance method in combination with the quota-share method is that the determination of the reinsurance cost is straightforward. For example, if the total premium for the group is $100,000, if 60 percent of the group is reinsured, and if the coinsurance allowance is 10 percent, then the gross reinsurance premium is $60,000, and the reinsurance premium net of the coinsurance allowance is $54,000. Using the premium rates of the reinsurer would involve the calculation of a reinsurance premium for each individual, the sum of these being the total premium paid to the reinsurer.

If reinsurance is to be on a surplus basis, it is necessary for separate calculations to be made for each life reinsured, because the distribution of the reinsured business by both age and amount is unlikely to be the same as that of the whole group. Thus, some of the advantages of coinsurance would be lost.

EXPERIENCE REFUNDS

Reinsurance may be arranged on either a participating or a nonparticipating basis. If reinsurance is participating, a formula is agreed upon between the ceding company and the reinsuring company whereby in the event of favorable experience a refund is made to the ceding company. Because the business may produce profits in some years and losses in other years, the reinsurer will usually require the establishment of a contingency reserve within the refund formula so that only part of the profit is released to the ceding company in any single year. A reinsurer that does not follow this practice might find itself in the position of paying experience refunds for several years when the experience of the business is favorable and then incur losses when the experience turned unfavorable. Even though the overall experience may have been profitable, such a reinsurer could eventually end up in a loss position because of the experience refunds paid in the early years of the agreement.

The exact terms of refund formulas vary because the formula is usually a matter of negotiation between the reinsurer and the ceding company. The overall principle involved is that there should be both a sharing of profits and a sharing of losses.

EXPERIENCE-RATED OR "RETENTION" CASES

If a group is sufficiently large so that its mortality experience can be expected to be reasonably stable, it is frequently written by the ceding company on an experience-rated or "retention" basis. Given the expected stability in the experience-rated portion of the group, the need for reinsurance is usually minimal.

Where reinsurance is desirable, it is normally on a quota-share basis. The usual arrangement is for the direct writing company to establish an experience rating refund formula with the client. Through the formula, the reinsurer then participates in its share of premiums, reserves, claim expenses, and dividends. The expenses of the reinsurer should be less than those of the direct writer because the latter is involved in such additional administrative costs as issuing the individual certificates and preparing the master policy. Therefore, the reinsurer receives a smaller share of the expense charges than does the direct writing company. The exact allocation of expenses between the direct writer and the reinsurer is negotiated between the two parties.

Reinsurance of Survivors Income Benefits

Reinsurance of the survivor income benefit can be arranged on a full coinsurance basis, with the reinsurer paying its share of the income each month to the ceding company. However, this method involves additional administrative costs. The more common approach is for the direct writing company to calculate the commuted value of the benefit and then reinsure this amount in exactly the same way as group life coverage. As an example, if the commuted value of the benefit in the year is $100,000, and 40 percent of the benefit is reinsured, then the reinsurance cost would be based on a sum reinsured of $40,000. In the event of a claim, the reinsurer will pay its share of the commuted value of the death benefit, namely $40,000, to the ceding company and would have no further liability. Thereafter, the direct writer gains or losses depending on the adequacy or otherwise of the commuted value.

Reinsurance of Waiver of Premium Benefits

Disability benefits, such as waiver of premium, are usually reinsured in proportion to the life risk. The cost of this benefit is usually included in the group life premium and the cost is small. Hence reinsurance in proportion to the life risk reinsured simplifies administration.

Amounts in Excess of No-Evidence Limits

From the point of view of an employer, it is desirable that as far as possible, all individuals should be covered under a group life plan without medical selection, since the plan is more readily acceptable to the employees, and the inconvenience of a medical examination is removed. However, if the amount of coverage available is large or if the number of lives insured in the group is very small, it is necessary for the direct writing company to set a no-evidence limit. Amounts of insurance in excess of this limit are then subject to individual underwriting. From the reinsurance point of view, these amounts are similar to individual policies, although it is possible that the underwriting standard may be more liberal than that for an individual policy.

There are two methods of reinsurance normally used in this situation: (1) the coinsurance method can be used wherein the reinsurance premium consists of the premiums of the direct writing company less a coinsurance allowance, or (2) alternatively, the yearly renewable term method of reinsurance can be used, with premiums the same as those for individual business. The latter method is equally appropriate, provided similar standards of selection are applied.

Conversion Options

In the event that an individual exercises the conversion option under a group life policy to convert his or her coverage into a new individual policy, the reinsurer will usually continue to reinsure the same proportion of the coverage. Reinsurance of the new policy will probably be based on the same method, either yearly renewable term (YRT) or coinsurance, as the direct writing company uses for its individual business.

Reinsurance of Association Group Business

The method of reinsurance to be used for association group business depends mainly on the extent of underwriting. Where an association group obtains a high percentage participation of potential members, it can be considered very similar to an employer group. In that event, coverage is usually offered without evidence of insurability, and reinsurance becomes essentially the same as for an employer group case.

However, enrollment in association group cases is frequently low, resulting in potential antiselection if evidence of insurability is not obtained. Where evidence is obtained, this type of business is somewhat similar to individual business, and for reinsurance purposes could be reinsured on a YRT basis in the same manner as the direct writing company's individual business. Alternatively, for administrative reasons, it may be simpler to work with the gross premiums of the ceding company and to reinsure on a coinsurance basis. Whichever method is used, the reinsurance costs should be actuarially equivalent.

Although an arrangement on a surplus basis may seem preferable from the point of view of the ceding company (the volume of reinsurance would be less), reinsurance is frequently effected on a quota-share basis to simplify administration.

Reinsurance of Group Creditor Insurance

Because the amounts available for group creditor business are usually small, there is very little reinsurance developed. If reinsurance is required, it would probably be for reasons other than stabilization of mortality experience. As an example, if a company wishes to write this class of business but has little experience or expertise, the company might reinsure a share of the business in order to have access to the experience and expertise of the reinsurer. Reinsurance would probably be arranged on a quota-share basis, using the coinsurance method to minimize administration costs. Since evidence of insurability is not normally obtained, the business becomes somewhat similar to employer group business for reinsurance purposes.

REINSURANCE OF OTHER COVERAGES

Much of what has been said concerning reinsurance methods and premium rates can be applied to the other coverages subject to reinsurance: group accidental death and dismemberment, group long-term disability, group weekly indemnity, and group dental insurance.

Group Accidental Death and Dismemberment Benefits

There is obviously scope for selection against the insurance company with group life business where evidence of insurability is not obtained. Although evidence of insurability for group accidental death and dismemberment benefits is not required, the element of adverse mortality selection has been removed to a large extent, and therefore the considerations for the reinsurance of these benefits are somewhat different.

The problem of antiselection can usually be solved to a large extent by the group underwriting approach, because groups involving hazardous occupations are usually either rated or declined. There is, of course, always the possibility that an individual with, for example, a clerical occupation may indulge in a hazardous avocation, such as parachuting, but today this type of risk can occur among the employees with small benefits as well as the employees with large benefits. For this reason the use of the surplus method is desirable. This enables the direct writing company to retain its maximum share of the risk.

However, if the basic group life treaty is reinsured on a quota-share basis, for administrative reasons it may then be easier to reinsure the accidental death and dismemberment benefits in the same proportion. From the point of view of the reinsurer, this method has the additional advantage of reducing the possibility of antiselection.

The comments above apply where the accidental death coverage is mandatory. If part or all of the coverage is voluntary, there is real possibility of antiselection and the quota-share approach is then probably essential for the reinsurer.

PREMIUM RATES

Premium rates for group accidental death and dismemberment benefits are usually independent of age. This means that the calculation of reinsurance cost is facilitated since the rate is simply applied to the volume of reinsurance. The reinsurance cost might be quoted as a flat rate, for example, $0.72 per thousand or on a coinsurance basis such as $0.80 per thousand with a coinsurance allowance of 10 percent to produce the same net cost to the ceding company of $0.72 per thousand.

To further simplify administration, the reinsurance rate might be applied to the average volume of reinsurance in force during the year. As an example, if the volume of reinsurance in force on January 1 is $950,000 and the volume in force on December 31 is $1,050,000, then the average in force might be determined as $1,000,000. The reinsurance cost for the year is therefore $1,000,000 × $0.72 per thousand, or $720.

Reinsurance of Group Long-Term Disability Business

Paralleling the growth of group life business in Canada has been a substantial growth in the amount of group long-term disability coverage. Benefits provided under long-term disability contracts range from 2-year benefits up to benefits payable to age 65, which could mean benefits payable for 40 or more years for a young life.

THE PROBLEM OF DISABLED LIFE RESERVES

One of the main problems in the direct writing of this class of business is that substantial disabled life reserves are required where the benefit is potentially payable for a long period. This factor, combined with high benefit levels, produces very substantial liabilities. Therefore, many companies look to the reinsurance market to reduce their potential liability. This is particularly true for the smaller companies, because the experience of the whole product line may be affected by such factors as economic conditions. These factors, combined with a lack of experience with the product, may in turn cause the smaller company to seek to reduce its exposure to the effects of this volatility through reinsurance.

An important factor for the reinsurer to bear in mind is that disablement rates and duration of claims often tend to increase as the total amount of benefits increases, especially where the benefit available represents a high percentage of total regular income. Hence unless the quota-share method is used, the experience of the reinsured business may be different from that of the business as a whole.

PROPORTIONAL AND NONPROPORTIONAL APPROACHES

There are two quite different approaches to the reinsurance of group long-term disability business: the proportional approach and nonproportional approach. Under the proportional approach, reinsurance is usually on the quota-share basis using the coinsurance method. The reinsurer receives a share of each risk in the group and grants the ceding company a coinsurance allowance to cover its expenses. An alternative approach is reinsurance on the surplus basis, but the premium calculation is more complex. Also, as mentioned above, the experience among the larger risks may be significantly different from the experience of the group overall, so that the experience of the reinsurer for a group could be different from that of the direct writer if the surplus method is used. This could create problems at the time of renewal underwriting. In general, for both administrative and technical reasons, the quota-share approach is more common.

In the nonproportional approach to reinsurance, the extended wait method can be used. Under this method, the reinsurer is responsible for a low percentage of benefit payment for a certain period and a much higher percentage of benefit payments thereafter. For example, the reinsurer may be responsible for 20 percent of the benefit during the first 2 years of payment and 80 percent of the benefit thereafter. It is, of course, desirable that the ceding company have a continuing interest in the claim throughout the duration of its payment. The particular advantage of this method for the ceding company is that it reduces potential losses on the larger benefits and at the same time removes the need to establish large reserves for long-term claim payment situations. This can be a significant factor for companies beginning to write this class of business which do not have the necessary resources to absorb the strain of the reserving requirements. The main disadvantage of this method is that it is a more sophisticated approach and therefore can create additional administrative problems.

Reinsurance of Group Weekly Indemnity and Group Dental Insurance

Although a substantial volume of weekly indemnity business is written in Canada, the need for reinsurance is limited because the claim reserves required for these short-term benefits are much smaller than for group long-term disability insurance. Furthermore, the benefit levels are generally somewhat lower than for the long-term benefits.

Group dental insurance is a small but expanding market in Canada. However, little reinsurance is required because the nature of the coverage is such that annual premium income should be sufficient to cover claims and expenses in any year. Thus the experience should be relatively stable.

If reinsurance is used, it is probably done more to obtain the knowledge and guidance of the reinsurer than to attempt to stabilize experience. When it is used, reinsurance is usually on a quota-share basis using the coinsurance approach.

REINSURANCE TREATIES

Reinsurance treaties for group business may be arranged on either an automatic or facultative basis. If the treaty is on a facultative basis, then each group to be reinsured is submitted to the reinsurer for prior approval and agreement of the reinsurance terms. If, however, the direct writing company is likely to need reinsurance for a substantial number of groups, it is normal for that company to enter into an automatic treaty arrangement with the reinsurer. Under this arrangement, the direct writing company is able to cede business automatically to the reinsurer on a predetermined basis. One common method is for reinsurance to be on a quota-share basis, the quota-share being determined by the ratio of the maximum retention of the company to the maximum benefit under the group. For example, if the maximum retention of the ceding company is $50,000 and the maximum benefit under the group is $75,000, then the direct writing company would reinsure one-third of all risks with the reinsurer.

The normal arrangement is that the underwriting of the ceding company is based on its group underwriting manual and its standard policy wording, both of which are reviewed by the reinsurer before entering into a treaty arrangement. The group underwriting manual would provide information on the method of calculation of premiums, no-evidence limits, and the general underwriting practices of the direct writing company. Provided the direct writer does not deviate from this manual, reinsurance can be ceded automatically. Otherwise, reinsurance would revert to a facultative basis.

Reinsurance Contracts

The type of reinsurance documentation used depends on whether the reinsurance is carried out under an automatic or facultative arrangement. If reinsurance is handled on a facultative basis, it is likely to be transacted through an exchange of correspondence. No formal documentation is developed. However, if the reinsurance is ceded under an automatic treaty, a treaty document is required. This document is comprehensive and outlines the scope of the automatic coverage, the commitments of the ceding company and the reinsurer, and the procedures to be followed for underwriting, claims, and accounting. If the agreement is on a participating basis, the experience refund formula would be included in the treaty. The document is usually signed by two officers of the ceding company and two officers of the reinsurance company. The agreement, although legally binding, is intended to be a "gentlemen's agreement." It relies on the good faith of both parties to ensure a workable arrangement.

LEGAL REQUIREMENTS

There are no special legal requirements for reinsurance under the various insurance acts in Canada. Reinsurers are subject to the same legislation as are the direct writing companies; they can be licensed to write business by either the federal or provincial governments. However, since a direct writing company can take credit for reserves on reinsured business only if the reinsurer is also licensed in the same jurisdiction, all professional reinsurers in Canada operate under federal licenses.

All reinsurance companies are required to file an annual statement of their business with the supervisory authorities in the same way as the direct writing company. This statement presents the financial picture of the company, incorporating details of business in force, movement of policies, the actuarial valuation, the actuary's certificate and details of investments.

MAINTENANCE OF RESERVES

Provided the reinsurer's license is good in the appropriate province or territory, the direct writing company can take credit for the reserves of the business reinsured. The direct writing company is required to calculate reserves on a gross basis, but it is able to deduct the reserves established by the reinsuring company from its liabilities and therefore is required only to maintain reserves on a net-of-reinsurance basis rather than on a gross basis. This is a very important consideration for the small company with limited resources where the amount of reinsurance is large.

Although unlicensed reinsurance is possible, it does create difficulties, primarily because it is not possible to deduct the reserves held by such a reinsurer from the direct writer's own liabilities. As a result, the ceding company must establish gross reserves. This problem can be overcome by having the reinsurer deposit assets equal to the reserves with the ceding company. However there are some administrative problems, not the least of which is that in the event of the insolvency of the ceding company the reinsurer may have difficulty recovering part or all of this deposit.

SUMMARY

This chapter has considered many different aspects of group reinsurance as it applies to Canada. The discussion began by identifying the three main methods of group life reinsurance, the quota-share method, the surplus method, and the quota-share and surplus method. A variety of aspects of the reinsurance business as they apply to the Canadian market were then explored, including reinsurance cost, experience refunds, experience rated cases, stop loss, and amounts in excess of no-evidence limits. Group reinsurance arrangements for a wide range of benefits were also discussed, among them survivors income benefit, association group business, group creditor insurance, group accidental death and dismemberment benefits, group long-term disability, group weekly indemnity, and group dental insurance. The chapter concluded with a discussion of reinsurance contracts and certain legal requirements.

PART 6

GOVERNMENT INSURANCE PROGRAMS

CHAPTER 29

FEDERAL SOCIAL INSURANCE PROGRAMS

INTRODUCTION

The first section of this text analyzed the devices used to provide a measure of economic security for working men and women through employee benefit plans. The motivating factors behind the initial development and subsequent growth of employee benefit plans were discussed as were the specific vehicles used to protect workers and their families against the hazards of premature death, sickness, unemployment, and the cessation of income because of retirement. It was observed that employee benefit plans may be provided through either public or private channels. This text has been primarily directed toward those benefits provided through the private sector of the economy, specifically through the medium of group insurance.

A true understanding of employee benefit plans, however, cannot be gained without at least a brief analysis of related governmental activity. Federal and state governments play an expanding role in providing economic security for their citizens. Not everyone agrees about the desirability of this expansion, but regardless of the observer's political philosophy, an investigation of only private plans in this text would provide a very incomplete and misleading picture of the group insurance world.

The three chapters in the last Part of this book will be devoted to the activities of the federal, state and local governments in the United States in providing life insurance, health insurance, and to some degree, pensions. Retirement pensions have been purposely excluded from the subject matter of this text, and have been given only passing and very general references up to now. Yet, the old-age pension component of the Old-Age, Survivors, Disability and Health Insurance (OASDHI) cannot be separated from other coverages in a comprehensive survey of this huge federally administered program. Therefore, in

by
ROBERT W. BATTEN, FSA, *Professor of Actuarial Science and Head of The Actuarial Science Program, Georgia State University*

this chapter only, the concept of benefit plans must be expanded to include consideration of this public pension system.

SOCIAL INSURANCE AND PUBLIC ASSISTANCE PROGRAMS

Activities of governments in providing a degree of economic security for their citizens through insurance are often loosely referred to as social insurance plans. However, government-sponsored plans include true group insurance plans as well as plans designed largely to promote certain social ends. Several characteristics generally attributed to social insurance will help to identify and characterize the various insurance plans associated with governmental rather than private sponsorship. These characteristics were suggested as the defining properties of social insurance by the 1964 Commission on Insurance Terminology, operating under the aegis of the American Risk and Insurance Association.[1] (Other definitions of social insurance suggested do not significantly disagree with the definition of the 1964 Commission.) These characteristics include:

1. All eligible persons must be covered, with rare exceptions;
2. Eligibility for benefits results from contributions made on behalf of the claimant; benefits are received as a matter of right rather than as a result of demonstrated need;
3. The benefits are in an amount prescribed by law; they are not necessarily determinable directly by the total contributions made on behalf of any claimant. This characteristic of social insurance has often been described as an emphasis on "social adequacy" over "individual equity." Social insurance plans often act as redistributors of income. Thus, they may sacrifice the individual equity characteristic of private insurance in favor of providing larger benefits to those with lower income than could be justified by their contributions;
4. While some contributions may be made from general revenues, the bulk of all contributions are scheduled to be made by participants and/or their employers;
5. The plan is at a minimum supervised, and often directly administered, by the government concerned;
6. To qualify as social insurance, a plan must not be so structured as to provide benefits only for employees of the government; and
7. The financing of social insurance plans is designed in a way

---

[1]John G. Turnbull, C. Arthur Williams, Jr., and Earl F. Cheit, *Economic and Social Security*, 4th ed. (New York: The Ronald Press Company, 1973).

that would be expected to be adequate under long-range considerations, rather than necessarily producing short-term equality of income and outgo. This differs sharply from the carefully reserved plans of private insurance in which all participants are theoretically assured of their earned benefits even in the absence of continuing contributions from present and future generations.

The federal OASDHI program has each of these seven characteristics and is generally considered the prototype of social insurance in the United States. On the other hand, programs such as Federal Employees Group Life Insurance and the various insurance plans of the Veterans Administration display some of these characteristics but cannot be considered as social insurance because they fail to meet at least one of the defining criteria.

Another important distinction that should be kept in mind is the basic difference between social insurance programs and public assistance programs. Public assistance programs tend to have more in common with charity than with insurance. Eligibility is based solely on need. Benefits are funded from general governmental revenues rather than from funds directly traceable to contributions or to taxes paid specifically to fund the plan in question. The estimates of future amounts that will be necessary to fund certain public assistance plans are much more difficult to forecast than the amounts needed to fund social insurance programs, because eligibility is so closely tied to variables such as the national (or local) economy and the political climate. Changes in these variables often result in sudden changes in the availability and the amount of benefit payments.

This last Part will discuss social insurance programs and other devices through which governmental units utilize insurance techniques to some extent to provide various types of economic benefits. Public assistance plans will be alluded to only when there is an inseparable relationship with plans of social insurance, for example, where provision for both is found in a single piece of legislation. An investigation of governmental plans of insurance would be doubly meaningful if the relationships between public and private plans could be closely examined as, for example, any effect that the availability of old-age payments under OASDHI might have upon the demand for private pensions. Even though it may seem evident that expanding social insurance programs would reduce the demand for similar products available through the private sector, unfortunately, such relationships have not yet been thoroughly studied quantitatively.

Some analysts believe that social insurance plans have stimulated interest in, and sales of, private plans. These analysts reason that social insurance heightens public awareness of financial needs and

causes some people to realize that the benefits provided are not as
much as they need or desire. People are thus led to seek additional
insurance both through individual policies and through group plans.
Hopefully, future researchers will study this important and largely
overlooked measure of how private plans may be affected by the very
existence of governmental plans.

Although several insurance programs sponsored by the federal
government provide a degree of economic security for certain groups,
all pale in comparison with the mammoth Old-Age, Survivors, Disability, and Health Insurance system, often referred to as "social security," or OASDHI. The term "social security" in principle should be
used in connection with any governmental system designed to provide
economic security for its citizens, but, deferring to common usage,
this book will refer to the OASDHI system by its widely accepted
name—social security.

Specific groups, such as railroad workers, veterans, civil service
employees, and armed services personnel are covered by one or more
forms of government-underwritten coverage. This chapter, however,
will discuss the two federal programs generally considered to be true
social insurance, the OASDHI and the Railroad Retirement Systems.[2]
The important financial interdependence of these systems, in addition
to their social insurance character, requires that they be handled
together.

THE OASDHI SYSTEM

The present-day structure of the OASDHI system can be understood only by surveying its historical origin and development, the
coverage and benefits it provides, and the method of financing these
benefits. This chapter emphasizes the system's underlying philosophy
and the mechanics through which this philosophy is translated into the
provision of benefits. Some attention will be given to the specifics of
the system and the details of coverage and benefit payments, but such
details are secondary in importance to a description of the nature and
purpose of OASDHI.

Origin of OASDHI

The well-documented shift in the United States from an agrarian
to an industrialized economy was probably the first of many social

[2]For a detailed treatment of social insurance and other governmental programs,
including actuarial analyses and an overall analysis of the several means through
which economic security is provided in the United States, see Robert J. Myers, *Social
Security* (Homewood, Ill.: Richard D. Irwin, Inc., 1975) and John G. Turnbull, C.
Arthur Williams, Jr., and Earl F. Cheit, *Economic and Social Security*, 4th ed. (New
York: The Ronald Press Company, 1973).

changes leading ultimately to the passage of a comprehensive social security package by the Congress in 1935. The same stimuli also led to much activity in the sphere of private insurance, but the failure of private plans to provide adequately for all segments of society resulted in pressures that propelled Americans to press for governmental action. Sentiment for action was especially strong in the areas of old-age dependency and the plight of the needy unemployed.

By the early 1930s, many states had initiated systems of payments to certain needy segments of the population, notably the blind, the orphaned, and the elderly. However, these plans often degenerated into a hodgepodge of complicated and harsh eligibility conditions, inadequate benefits, and inconsistent administration. Probably the greatest weakness in these plans was the lack of widespread and consistent coverage. Some plans were administered by counties, others by states. There was little or no assistance available to the unemployed. As the country moved toward and into the Great Depression of the 1930s, the various systems of assistance to the needy proved chaotic, inefficient, and often inequitable.

This climate of inadequate assistance for the needy, coupled with desperation and despair spawned by the greatest economic crisis in American history, provided a fertile ground for the implementation of comprehensive federal social programs. An already unsatisfactory network of state and local plans was crippled at the onset of the depression as the number of "eligible" recipients skyrocketed. In June 1934, President Franklin D. Roosevelt appointed a blue ribbon Commission on Economic Security chaired by Secretary of Labor Frances Perkins. The commission included three other cabinet members and was assisted by a 23-member Advisory Council of representatives from labor, management, and the public. The commission was charged with the task of probing, through a comprehensive analysis, the state of economic security in the United States. Its recommendations formed the substance of the social security legislation proposed to the Congress in early 1935. In August of the same year, the Social Security Act of 1935 was approved by both houses, placing on the statute books what may have been the most significant piece of social legislation ever passed in this country.[3] In the succeeding four decades, the initial legislation has been amended numerous times. Each amendment has expanded the scope of the system until over $84 billion was paid out in 1977, excluding payments made for health benefits. This figure

---

[3]An interesting footnote to history is that a large number of Congressmen found the benefits provided by the original bill to be too liberal for their tastes. Yet, many cast affirmative votes against their true sentiments, motivated by the widespread belief that the Supreme Court would rule the entire act unconstitutional. However, in 1937 the Court ruled for the government in a six-to-three decision that effectively ended any uncertainty about the permanence of the system.

contrasts with slightly less than $274 million paid in 1945 to retirees, their families, and their survivors.[4]

The 1935 Act was a comprehensive one, containing many provisions. Most of its provisions concerned programs of public assistance rather than social insurance. These programs included aid to the blind, to dependent children, and to the needy. In addition, the act authorized grants to the states to be used in providing certain health services, unemployment compensation payments, and vocational rehabilitation. None of these programs, however, really used the insurance mechanism. The portion of the act that did and is therefore relevant to this text authorized a system of federally administered old-age benefits and established a financing system for such benefits through payroll taxes on both workers and their employers. This old-age insurance feature, almost an afterthought in an act that was basically a public assistance vehicle, represented the first seeds of what is referred to in the United States as "social security."

Insofar as old-age pension features of the social security program was concerned, the initial legislation was seemingly quite modest. The tax was 2 percent on the first $3,000 of income (one half paid by the employee and one half by the employer). The maximum monthly benefit that could be paid to a retired worker was $85, a figure that only young workers with relatively high salaries could ever hope to reach. Lump-sum death benefits were originally, and continue to be, a minor feature of the system.

Social Security Amendments

Through numerous amendments to the original act, the social security system has expanded from a relatively insignificant old-age cash benefit program to a gargantuan structure that affects every resident in the United States. Expansion has occurred in the categories of eligible individuals, the types of coverage available, and the amounts of benefits.

Extension of the categories of individuals eligible for coverage was incorporated into several of the amendments. These include:

1939—Made specific categories of dependents and survivors—wives, widows, dependent parents, and minor children—eligible for cash payment benefits;

1950—Added about 10 million workers to the system by extending coverage to several new categories of employment, including nonfarm self-employed individuals and United States' citizens working for United States employers abroad;

---

[4]American Council of Life Insurance, *Life Insurance Fact Book* (Washington, D.C.: 1978), p. 51.

1954—Extended coverage to include self-employed farmers and gave local and state governments the option of enrolling their employees;

1956—Expanded system to include self-employed professionals (other than physicians);

1958—Expanded disability component by providing that dependents of disabled beneficiaries be eligible for benefits;

1965—Extended benefits to include self-employed physicians; and

1966—Expanded eligible category to include certain individuals over age 72 who would otherwise not be eligible for benefits.

Amendments which expanded the types of benefits available include the following:

1956—Provided cash benefits for workers who were totally and permanently disabled;

1958—Expanded the disability component by providing benefits for dependents of disabled beneficiaries;

1965—Created the Medicare program to provide health care benefits for the elderly (thus establishing the HI component of the OASDHI system). These benefits include Part A (a true social insurance program), which provides in-hospital and certain post-hospital benefits, and Part B (a governmental insurance program) to cover physician and other medical expenses; and

1972—Expanded the Medicare program by extending coverage to disabled beneficiaries under age 65 and to individuals needing kidney transplants or renal dialysis, regardless of age. This amendment also made coverage under Part B (for which the individual must pay a nominal fee) automatic unless it is specifically rejected.

Increases in the amounts of benefits paid were incorporated in the amendments of 1950, 1952, 1954, 1958, 1960, 1961, 1965, 1967, 1969, 1971, and 1972. The 1972 amendments were especially important in that they made future benefit increases (as well as increases in the taxable earnings base) automatic when justified by a rise of 3 percent or more in the Consumer Price Index (CPI).

As a result of congressional concern about the financing of these vastly expanded programs, the 1966 amendments provided, for the first time, that the newly authorized benefits for individuals over the age of 72 would be paid out of general revenue funds. The 1972 amendments addressed the problems of financing the program by tying increases in the taxable earnings base to the CPI. The 1977 amendments went still further. These amendments substantially increased both the tax rates and wage bases on which these taxes must be paid, reallocated income to the disability trust fund (which was threatened with bankruptcy by 1978) and stabilized benefit levels in relation to wage levels.

The remaining discussion of the OASDHI system will describe the coverage, eligibility, benefit, and financing features of the current system. Unless stated otherwise, the description is current as of the changes in the system effective in December 1977.

Cash Benefit Features

The discussion of the cash benefit features of OASDHI will consider coverage provisions; eligibility for benefits; payment of benefits to workers, dependents, and survivors; maximum monthly benefits; and death benefits.

COVERAGE PROVISIONS

In 1939 only 55 percent of the Americans who held civilian jobs were covered under the old-age provisions of the Social Security Act. State and local government employees, farm workers, and the self-employed were entirely excluded. By the late 1970s about 90 percent of the workers in the United States were contributing to the system, about one hundred million persons holding jobs that met the criteria for covered employment. All groups of nongovernment workers were covered, as were a substantial proportion of public employees. As of the end of 1977 approximately 153 million persons had at some time held employment covered under OASDHI. Of this number, about 83 million were still employed with coverage in effect.

The largest category of noncovered workers is represented by the approximately three million employees of the federal government who are covered by the Federal Civil Service Retirement System. Many observers have recommended that this substantial group be included in the future. A few other minor categories of federal workers, such as certain elective officials, are also not covered.

Employees of state and local governments are not generally covered, although there are many exceptions. How such governmental employees may gain coverage varies from state to state and with the category of employee involved, but in all cases approval of the government in question is required for its employees to be covered under OASDHI. Where there is no coverage available under a state or local retirement system for government employees, OASDHI coverage is mandatory. However, in most states in which employee retirement systems do exist, employees are also covered under social security only if a majority of the employees involved have voted in favor of such coverage. An exception to this retirement benefit eligibility exists in several states for members of police departments. In these states, police are not eligible for OASDHI coverage unless no other retirement system is available. It is estimated that more than half of the workers still not covered under OASDHI are employees of some governmental unit.

Self-employed individuals whose earnings from self-employment are less than $400 per year are excluded. Domestic employees other than farm workers are not covered if they receive less than $50 in cash wages in a given quarter from each of their employers. Thus, a domestic worker might earn $40 from each of several employers in a quarter, but, in that quarter, the conditions for coverage would not be satisfied. Nondomestic employees in other forms of casual work are treated in the same manner as nonfarm domestic workers. Persons engaged in employment on farms, whether or not their work is classified as domestic, are not covered unless they have cash wages in a year from any one employer of $150 or more, or unless they are paid on a time basis by any one employer for at least 20 days' work in a given year. There is one miscellaneous category of noncovered employees in business and commerce: such workers as newsboys under age 18, student nurses, and students waiting on tables in a college club or fraternity house. Other categories of excluded workers have only small numbers of workers in any one category.

In summary, total coverage under OASDHI is coming closer and closer. More important, perhaps, the majority of the workers not now covered by OASDHI are covered under some alternative plan providing similar benefits. The only significant exceptions involve some low-income or irregularly employed individuals. Many of these persons are beneficiaries of public assistance programs, leaving an extremely small number of workers who are not covered by some governmentally administered security program.

ELIGIBILITY FOR BENEFITS

The fact that an individual worker is presently being taxed under the Federal Insurance Contributions Act (FICA) is not in itself sufficient to guarantee eligibility for all the benefits that may be payable under the system. Various types of benefits are contingent upon the fulfillment of certain eligibility conditions. These conditions generally depend upon the duration over which a worker has been taxed at the time that the worker, his or her dependents, or his or her survivors would otherwise qualify for payments under OASDHI.

Types of Insured Status. The requirements for "insured status" are expressed in terms of "quarters of coverage." Quarters of coverage are defined slightly differently depending upon the classification of worker involved. Nonfarm workers receiving $50 or more in covered wages in a calendar quarter are credited with a quarter of coverage. Self-employed individuals are credited with a quarter of coverage for any calendar quarter in which they earn $100 in covered income from self-employment. A quarter of coverage for farm workers is defined as one in which $100 is earned in covered farm wages. Farm workers who earn more than $400 in covered farm wages for a calendar year are credited with four quarters of coverage regardless of how this total income was apportioned to the separate quarters of the year, as are the self-employed. Finally, if any person receives a total covered income during a calendar year (including both wages and self-employment income) that is as much as the maximum covered earnings for that year ($17,700 for 1978), the full four quarters of coverage are credited.

The terms "fully insured," "currently insured," and "disability insured" delineate the requirements for specific OASDHI benefits. The first is required for most old-age and survivor benefits; the second (in cases where the first is not satisfied) for certain survivor benefits; and the third for disability benefits.

A worker is deemed "fully insured" if he or she has been credited with 40 quarters of coverage. An exception is that fully insured status may be attained by a worker with as few as six quarters of coverage if the worker has at least one quarter of coverage for each year that has elapsed since 1950 or the year of attainment of age 21, whichever is later. Only years prior to the year of attainment of age 62, or prior to disability or death, are counted in the determination of the number of quarters credited.

"Currently insured" status, relevant only when a worker is not fully insured, is so defined as to require 6 quarters of covered employment in the 13-quarter period ending with the quarter of death or entitlement to old-age benefits.

A fully insured worker is considered "disability insured" as well if the worker has 20 quarters of coverage during the 40-quarter period ending with the quarter of disability. Workers who incur a disability prior to age 31 have somewhat less stringent requirements for disability insured status; blind persons merely must be fully insured to qualify for disability benefits.

A factor referred to as the "disability freeze" exists to ease the requirements for fully and currently insured statuses for workers whose coverage has been interrupted because of disability. If a worker is disability insured, any periods of disability of at least five months' duration are excluded in the determination of his or her insured status. Blindness is considered sufficient in itself for an individual's qualification for the disability freeze, whether or not the technical definition for disability discussed below has been satisfied.

The Earnings Test. In addition to the requirement that insured status be attained before eligibility for OASDHI benefit payments, a further condition is imposed for qualification. An "earnings test" prohibits payments from being made to certain categories of beneficiaries when such beneficiaries have specified amounts of earned income. For every dollar earned in excess of these amounts, benefits are reduced by fifty cents.

The specifics of the earnings test have been changed many times since it was first implemented in 1935. The original 1935 Act prohibited any old-age payments to persons engaged in "regular" employment, but there have been several liberalizations since then.

The Social Security Amendments of 1977 lowered the exempt age (that is the age when elderly individuals may receive full benefits without regard to their earnings) from 72 to 70 beginning 1982. The annual amount of earnings a beneficiary age 65 or over may have without any benefits being withheld is set at $4,000 in 1978, $4,500 in 1979, $5,000 in 1980, $5,500 in 1981, and $6,000 in 1982. Subsequent limitations are to be adjusted automatically on the basis of earnings levels. The annual exempt amount for beneficiaries under age 65 was retained ($3,240 in 1978), with subsequent increases determined automatically as wage levels rise.

Workers between the ages of 65 and 72 (between 65 and 70 after 1982) who annually earn in excess of the permitted amount not only must forego part or all of their monthly cash benefit otherwise available, but must continue to pay social security taxes on earned income, as must all other wage earners regardless of age. Because cash benefits are based on a complex formula reflecting average earnings under the social security system, taxation of such post-65 wages appears actuarially necessary for persons whose income is at or above their income level prior to age 65. However, criticism has been levelled against taxation of persons who are essentially retired but who continue to earn small incomes through part-time employment and who therefore do not stand to receive higher subsequent benefits because of these earnings.

The earnings test has been severely questioned and attacked by its critics since it was first introduced in 1935. Opponents hold that it discourages productive activity by elderly persons who wish to remain active and that the old-age benefit at 65—having been "paid for" through many years of contributions—is a matter of right. These opponents also argue that there should be no distinction between "earned" income and funds that are not considered as wages, such as investment income. Proponents counter that the earnings test tends to discourage continued employment by older persons, making room in the work force for younger workers. Congress has continually liberalized the test, but appears unlikely to abolish it.

Calculating of Benefits. With the exception of the health insurance benefits payable under Medicare, all social security benefits amounts are based upon the size of the worker's "primary insurance amount" (PIA). The PIA formula tends to treat lower paid workers more favorably than the higher paid. For example, a worker earning $6,000 per year (and therefore paying taxes on that amount) has a PIA which is much more than half of that of a worker whose annual wages are $12,000. The social security system undeniably favors the concept of social adequacy over that of individual equity. Many critics of the present system argue that such an arrangement borders on an outright income redistribution scheme; proponents point out that social adequacy is one of the basic purposes of social insurance plans.

The calculation of the PIA depends on the amount of "average monthly wage" (AMW). Both the PIA and the AMW are specified by law in detail. Here, only the basic principles will be presented.

The AMW is computed by determining the number of years that have passed between 1950 (or the year in which age 21 is attained, if later) and the year in which death, disability, or the attainment of age 62 occurs. This number may be reduced by five to soften the effect created by as many as five years of low or no earnings, but in no case may the number of years used in the computation be fewer than two. For old-age benefits, the number of years used in calculating the AMW must be at least five unless the requirements for the disability freeze have been met. The number of these years is called the "benefit computation years." The AMW is the average monthly covered wage over the number of years that is equal to the number of benefit computation years.

A key feature of the current formulas is the provision, adopted in 1972 and retained in the 1977 amendments, that payments to present beneficiaries are to be adjusted automatically to reflect increases in the Consumer Price Index. These increases are to be made in June of any year if the Consumer Price Index has increased 3 percent or more during the past year. The amount of benefit increases will be the actual rise in this index, rounded to the nearest 0.1 percent unless Congress has acted on its own to implement an increase. In years for which the automatic escalator provisions call for an increase in the maximum covered wage, an additional 20 percent of the increment is included as a component of the PIA. Workers with more than 25 years of coverage, but with low earnings during such years, are eligible for higher PIAs than the basic formula would produce.

PAYMENT OF BENEFITS

Once the calculations of the AMW and the PIA have been performed, the amounts of cash benefits available to the various classes of beneficiaries can be determined. As of the end of 1977, over 34 million persons were receiving monthly payments under OASDHI. Approximately $84 billion was disbursed in 1977 as either monthly payments or lump-sum benefits.[5]

Benefits to Workers. Upon reaching the age of 65, a fully insured worker becomes eligible for monthly retirement payments equal to 100 percent of his or her PIA. Should a worker choose to retire before age 65, payments may begin as early as age 62, but with a reduction of 5/9 percent for each month of age prior to age 65. A worker retiring at age 62, then, can receive monthly payments of 80 percent of the PIA.

The earnings test mentioned earlier prohibits payments to persons who, though past age 65, still earn in excess of a prescribed amount. This provision, however, is effective only in cases of persons

---

[5]*Ibid.*

younger than age 72 (age 70 after 1982). When a worker who has not drawn any retirement benefits attains the stipulated age, the benefits are based upon a PIA that is 107 percent of that which would be otherwise determined. Further, for any number of years, with a maximum of seven (five after 1982), during which a worker delays retirement benefits by continuing to earn income or by simply not claiming old-age payments, the PIA is increased.[6] For workers eligible for retirement before 1979 there is a 1 percent increase in the PIA applied. The Social Security Amendments of 1977 raised this retirement credit to an increase in the PIA of 3 percent per year beginning in 1979 as part of an effort to strengthen work incentives. This provision applies only to the old-age benefits of the insured worker, and not to any benefit amounts for the worker's dependents or survivors.

The other basic benefit available to the worker is income in case of disability prior to age 65. To qualify, a disability must be so severe as to prevent the worker from engaging in "any substantial gainful activity." The disability may be either physical or mental, but must be certified by a physician as likely to result in death or to last a minimum of 12 months. The disability must be of at least five months' duration. Thus, the first monthly payment for a qualified disability is made approximately six months after the disability occurs. To qualify for payments, the worker must be disability insured. As with retirement benefits, the monthly payments are 100 percent of the worker's PIA. Payments continue only until the attainment of age 65 by the disabled worker, when old-age benefits begin. One restriction on the size of disability payments is that the combined disability benefits and workers' compensation benefits may not exceed 80 percent of average earnings prior to disability. This "average earnings" figure is computed in a complicated but liberal manner and can in no case be lower than the worker's PIA. Further, this figure is automatically increased for changes in general earnings levels after the worker's disablement.

Benefits to Dependents. Dependents of workers who are receiving either old-age or disability benefits are eligible for benefits of their own, limited only by a ceiling on the amount that can be paid to any given family in a month. The payment amounts for such dependents are determined as a function of the PIA of the retired or disabled worker, or, stated more simply, as a percentage of the actual monthly payment being received by the worker.

---

[6]The rationale behind this delayed retirement increment is that persons working beyond age 65 continue to make contributions to the system and, obviously, will not receive as many old-age payments as if such payments had actually commenced at age 65. However, the increase in benefits so provided reflects less than one-sixth of the amount actuarially justified, unlike early retirements for which benefit payments are decreased on an actuarially equivalent basis. The system therefore clearly benefits from delayed retirements.

Benefits to Survivors. The architects of social security legislation have followed the philosophy that the death of a retired or disabled worker should not result in a cessation of benefits to the survivors. Further, it is felt that a worker who dies before the worker or the worker's dependents have received any benefits under the system should have monthly payments made, on the worker's behalf, to his or her survivors. The availability of such payments displays the genuine life insurance aspect of OASDHI far more clearly than do the nominal lump-sum death benefits.

MAXIMUM MONTHLY BENEFITS

Clearly, unless some limitations were imposed, the total monthly benefits to a retired or disabled worker and dependents could be several times the worker's PIA. Similarly, the survivors of a deceased worker could receive, in the aggregate, relatively large benefits. To guard against unduly large payments being made on behalf of any single worker, maximum family benefits are specified in the law. Such limitations have existed since the system's inception and have generally been related to both the AMW and the PIA of the insured worker. Currently, the maximum monthly family benefit is defined in a detailed manner in terms of the various layers of a worker's AMW. The net result is that this maximum benefit is always between 150 percent and 188 percent of the worker's PIA, with 175 percent of the PIA applying to all whose AMW exceeds $627.

The lower bound, or minimum, for family benefits is much less complex. In no case may family benefits be less than the minimum PIA. Such a provision applies only when there is a single surviving beneficiary. The only situation in which family benefits can be less than the minimum PIA is in the case of a widow or widower who claims benefits prior to age 62.

An additional limitation on benefits is simply that where one individual is eligible for more than one monthly payment, only the larger (or largest) of such payments may be received. This restriction applies chiefly in cases in which both a husband and wife are insured and the wife would otherwise be entitled to both a primary and a dependent benefit. This again illustrates the predominance of the concept of social adequacy over that of individual equity.

DEATH BENEFITS

For many years, the lump-sum death benefit payable at the death of a fully or currently insured worker has been $255 or, if less, 300 percent of the worker's PIA. If the surviving spouse had been living with the worker just prior to the worker's death, the spouse receives the full $255. Otherwise, the amount paid may not exceed the worker's burial expense. (The restriction is a remnant of earlier days when funerals were less expensive, but it has remained on the statute books.) The $255 maximum benefit has not been changed for more than 25 years, although early in 1979 some proposals to eliminate the feature were put before Congress.

Medicare

Although Medicare is an integral component of the present social security system, it is of a markedly different nature from the old-age, survivors, and disability components. The most notable difference is that the payments to Medicare recipients are spasmodic in contrast to the regular monthly payments associated with other coverages. In addition, one portion of the Medicare program is optional and is funded through participant premiums, much like private health insurance plans. Such premiums are, however, supplemented by general governmental revenues.

Payments are made to qualified recipients without regard to past monthly wages, primary insurance amounts, or, if over 65, present earnings. Yet, in some respects, especially eligibility, the Health Insurance (HI) component of social security is similar to the other features of the system. Because of the sharp distinctions between Part A, hospital insurance (HI), and Part B, supplementary medical insurance (SMI), the two will be treated separately.

HOSPITAL INSURANCE (PART A)

The Part A is that portion of Medicare that aids elderly persons with hospital bills and related items. It is similar in many ways to the other components of the social security system already discussed.

Coverage. All workers who are covered by Old-Age Survivors and Disability Insurance (OASDI) are automatically covered by Part A and are taxed to support the system. The reader will recall that OASDI coverage encompasses the majority of the United States work force. The only major exceptions are certain classes of government workers.

Eligibility for Benefits. The large majority of persons eligible for Part A benefits are those aged 65 and over, whether or not retired, who are eligible for either cash benefit payments from social security or are receiving annuity income from the Railroad Retirement System. In addition, persons under age 65 who have been receiving disability payments, whether through social security or Railroad Retirement, for a minimum of two years, are eligible. As discussed earlier, such persons include certain widows, widowers, and children, as well as the disabled workers themselves.

Persons attaining age 65 prior to 1968 but not otherwise eligible for social security benefits are included under the Part A component if they are citizens or lawfully admitted aliens who have resided in the United States continuously for five years. Further, persons who attained age 65 after 1967 but before 1975 were allowed to qualify with

fewer quarters of coverage than would normally have been required for
fully insured status.

The 1972 amendments to the Social Security Act made it possible
for persons over age 65 who are not covered under Part A to elect such
coverage on a contributory basis. The premium, $45 per month in
1977, but subject to periodic increases, is designed to bear the full cost
of the protection. The election of this coverage is available only to
persons who are also insured under Part B. The significance of this
amendment is that many government employees who would not otherwise qualify (through no fault of their own) are now allowed to
participate, although at a cost that is high for many retired persons.

Coverage was also extended by the 1972 amendments to fully or
currently insured workers under age 65 with chronic kidney disease
that requires either dialysis or transplant. Dependents of such insured workers or of monthly beneficiaries are also eligible.

Benefits. Persons covered under the Part A program are eligible
for three separate types of benefits. The first relates to costs actually
incurred in the hospital; the second to extended care services subsequent to a hospital stay; and the third to home health services received
after hospitalization.

A covered person is entitled to receive Part A benefits for up to 90
days of care in a hospital within any single "spell of illness." A spell of
illness is defined as beginning when a patient enters a hospital and
ending after he or she has been out of the hospital or a skilled nursing
or rehabilitation facility for 60 consecutive days. As soon as a given
spell of illness is terminated, another can commence with the next
entrance into a hospital. There is no limit on the number of spells of
illness for which a person can receive payments, although benefits are
only temporary where a patient is confined for an extended period of
time, and thus does not satisfy the requirements for the termination of
a spell of illness and hence the initiation of another.

All hospital services are covered other than private duty nurses
and physicians' fees. However, elective confinements, such as surgery
for purely cosmetic reasons, are not covered. Also, luxury services
such as private rooms (unless absolutely necessary), telephones, and
television sets are not considered reimbursable expenses. The patient
is required, beginning in 1979, to pay a total of $160 for the first sixty
days of services, and an additional $40 per day for the remainder of the
90-day period. These deductible ($160) and coinsurance ($40) charges
are subject to periodic increases consistent with rising costs of medical
care. A further expense that must be borne by the patient is the cost of
the first three pints of blood if transfusions are required.

It is conceivable that 90 days of coverage is insufficient in extended illnesses. For this reason, each Part A beneficiary is allotted an
additional 90 days of coverage as a "lifetime reserve," but with a daily

coinsurance charge of $80. In addition, there is a "lifetime maximum" of 190 days of coverage for psychiatric hospital care.

Services performed in skilled nursing facilities are covered, under the condition that the facility "qualifies" under the law. Confinement in such a facility must begin following a hospital stay of at least 3 days' duration within a 14-day period after release from a hospital. A special wing of a ward or hospital may qualify as well as the more traditional nursing home, but it must be demonstrated that confinement is necessary as a direct result of the condition prompting the initial hospitalization and that such confinement is justified by the need for skilled services on a daily basis. Care that is simply custodial is not covered.

Benefits are provided for up to 100 days in any spell of illness, with no deductible or coinsurance for the first 20 days of this period. From the 21st to the 100th day, however, the patient must pay a coinsurance amount ($20, beginning January 1, 1979). This figure is subject to periodic review. Basically, all services are covered, just as for inpatient hospital care. Such additional services as physical, occupational, or speech therapy are also covered.

The final type of coverage under Medicare Part A provides benefits for persons who are confined to their homes and cared for by qualifying home health agencies. Again, coverage is available only when such visits are subsequent to a hospital stay of at least 3 days' duration, and begin no more than 14 days after discharge from a hospital or skilled nursing facility. The need for such home visits must be documented by a physician's statement, and the visits must be made according to a plan developed by the physician. Further, they must be a direct result of the illness that required hospitalization or confinement in a nursing facility.

Coverage is available for up to 100 home visits within a one-year period after discharge and within a single spell of illness. There is no charge to the covered individual as long as the services received are of the type permitted in the law. Visiting nurse services and various types of therapy are covered. In certain instances, outpatient care at a hospital, nursing facility, or rehabilitation center may be covered as well. However, the law expressly forbids coverage for full-time home nursing, for the provision of meals, or for housekeeping or similar custodial care.

SUPPLEMENTARY MEDICAL INSURANCE (PART B)

The SMI component of Medicare, often referred to as Part B, provides payments for doctor's services and various other items not covered under Part A. Unlike Part A and the other benefits provided under social security, Part B is not mandatory and is much more closely related to private insurance than to social insurance.

Coverage and Eligibility. There is no provision for premium payment (taxation) for Medicare Part B prior to the age when a person is eligible for benefits. The reader will recall that the cost of SMI is partially borne by monthly premiums payable by those who are covered.

The same categories of persons are eligible for Part B as for Part A. The basic distinction is the procedure through which Part B coverage is effected. The reader will recall that coverage under Part A is automatic at age 65. Prior to the 1972 amendments, however, persons attaining age 65 were required to apply formally for Part B coverage. Since then, however, enrollment has been automatic although any person may refuse coverage (and hence the payment of premiums) if he or she so desires. The only eligible persons for whom automatic coverage is not effected are those who continue to work after age 65 and those who are residents of Puerto Rico or foreign countries. Such persons must request coverage if they desire to be included.

Approximately three months before an eligible person is to attain age 65 (or prior to the first month of eligibility for a disabled person), he or she receives information that describes the SMI program and explains the procedures to be followed by those persons choosing not to participate. Those persons who decline coverage, but who change their minds after a seven-month period beginning with their original notification by the Social Security Administration, may enroll later under certain restrictions. A penalty is incurred, however, of an increased monthly premium charge. Similarly, an enrolled person may terminate coverage and later reenroll subject to a penalty for each full year during which coverage was not in force. Such reenrollment is limited to one instance per individual. Of course, cancellation may occur upon request or as a result of failure to submit the prescribed premiums. The latter situation is rare, since the large majority of those covered under SMI have their premiums deducted from their regular monthly retirement checks.

Benefits. The major benefit component of SMI covers physicians' services. Such services are covered regardless of where they are performed (office, hospital, home, or elsewhere) and include medical supplies, drugs that can only be administered by the physician, and such expenses as ambulance service, equipment rental, and prosthetic devices. Certain oral and dental surgery and certain services of chiropractors and podiatrists are covered. Excluded are the costs of routine physical examinations, glasses and eye examinations, hearing aids and related hearing examinations, dentures and routine dental care, immunizations, and prescription drugs and patent medicines. Services not specifically necessary for the treatment or diagnosis of an illness or injury are likewise not covered. As with Part A, the cost of personal comfort items and the first three pints of blood in any year must be borne by the patient.

In addition to the basic costs of physicians' services, Part B covers home health services in much the same manner as does Part A. A major difference is that no preliminary three-day confinement in a hospital or nursing facility is required. Out-patient hospital services and out-patient physical therapy and speech pathology services are also covered. All of these coverages are contingent upon the definitions of such services carefully spelled out in the law.

The first $60 of covered charges in any calendar year must be borne by the individual. This deductible is applicable to all covered services except laboratory and radiological services performed by a physician while the patient is actually confined to a hospital. SMI payments are made, after satisfaction of the deductible, to the extent of 80 percent of the "reasonable charges" for covered services for the remainder of any calendar year.

The term "reasonable charges," the basis for all payments under SMI, is carefully defined in the law. Basically, reasonable charges are established for each participating physician, based upon the customary charges that the physician has set in the past for certain procedures and services. This customary charge is limited by the prevailing charge in the community by other providers of medical services and is further limited by the prevailing charge in the 12-month period from mid-1972 to mid-1973, increased by an economic index reflecting increasing earnings and costs of medical care. The rigid reimbursement schedule that has resulted has come under severe criticism by both individual physicians and the American Medical Association, because Medicare patients may not be billed on the same basis as other patients. A compensating feature, however, is the guarantee provided to the physician that payment will be made, eliminating the uncertainties involved when billings are made to individuals who may not be financially able to pay in full.

ADMINISTRATION

Unlike the cash-benefit components of social security, which are wholly administered by the Social Security Administration, an agency of the Department of Health, Education, and Welfare (HEW), the benefit payment aspects of Medicare administration are handled largely through private organizations.

Most Part A benefit payments are administered through designated "fiscal intermediaries," such as Blue Cross, health insurers, and state agencies. The use of Blue Cross organizations is by far the most common. Each institution that provides services covered under Part A is given the option of dealing directly with HEW or with such an intermediary. Where an intermediary is chosen, as occurs in the large majority of cases, the provider of services receives payments from, and is audited by, the intermediary. The basic functions of the intermediary are to review claims and provide safeguards against overutilization of services (usually through cost screens). The intermediary reimburses the providers of services on a reasonable cost basis as determined by the intermediary in a manner consistent with HEW guidelines. Of course, the intermediaries are in turn reimbursed by the Social Security Administration for the administrative costs incurred and for the benefit payments themselves.

In much the same manner, the administration of the Part B benefit payments depends heavily upon outside organizations. The so-called carriers, usually Blue Shield or insurance companies, are selected by HEW for specific geographical regions. These carriers are much like the fiscal intermediaries employed in Part A administration. They are responsible for reimbursing the various providers of services, and are compensated by HEW for both payment and their administrative expenses.

Financing

One of the distinctive characteristics of most social insurance programs is that the system is supposed to be largely self-supporting. In 1950, this principle was reaffirmed by Congress. Indeed, Congress decreed that the system should be completely self-supporting, with no payments made from general revenues. However, through the years, exceptions have been made, such as the 1966 Amendments that extended the availability of benefit payments to uninsured persons over age 72, financed by general revenues rather than payroll taxes. The most significant exception is the subsidization through general revenues of 50 percent of the cost of SMI, with the remainder being financed by the monthly premiums paid by covered persons.

CHANGES IN TAX RATES AND WAGE BASES 1937–1977

The first contributions to the system, made in 1937, amounted to 1 percent of the wages of covered workers, payable by the worker and matched by the employer. The total covered earnings were limited to $3,000, producing a maximum contribution by any individual of $30 per year. This earnings base was unchanged until 1951, when it was increased to $3,600 and the maximum employee tax was raised to $54, reflecting the 1950 change in the tax rate from 1 percent to 1.5 percent. Through the years, as benefits have been expanded and liberalized, the tax rate and the maximum covered earnings have risen. By 1978, those persons earning $17,700 or more were taxed a total of $1,070.85, an amount matched by their employers.

The Social Security Amendments of 1977, as part of their focus on strengthening both the long-term and short-range financial structure of the system, incorporated a series of yearly raises in both the employer tax rate and the wage base through 1987. Table 29-1 shows these increases.

TABLE 29-1
Employee Social Security Tax Rates and Wage Bases: 1978–1987

	Tax rate	Wage base
1978	6.05%	$17,700
1979	6.13	22,900
1980	6.13	25,900
1981	6.65	29,700
1982	6.70	31,800
1983	6.70	33,900
1984	6.70	36,000
1985	7.05	38,100
1986	7.15	40,200
1987	7.15	42,600

NOTE: After 1961, figures for the wage base are estimated.
SOURCE: U.S. Dept. of Health, Education, and Welfare.

RATES FOR THE SELF-EMPLOYED

Self-employed persons first became covered under the Social Security System in 1950. When they did, a dilemma of sorts was created with respect to the tax rate that should be applicable. It seemed unfair to require the self-employed to pay the combined employer-employee rate. However, the employee rate alone would be inadequate. A compromise was reached, and for many years the self-employed contribution rate was 75 percent of the combined rate, or, equivalently, one and one half times the employee rate.

However, the rates for the self-employed were allowed in later years to depart from this ratio. Thus, in 1977, for example, the rate applied to the self-employed was 7.9 percent or about two thirds of the combined employer-employee rate of 11.7 percent set for that year. The Social Security Amendments of 1977 restored the self-employment tax rate to its original level of one and one half times the employee rate, or 75 percent of the combined rate.

THE TRUST FUNDS

Four separate trust funds, maintained by the U.S. Treasury, have been established to pay benefits directly to recipients. Each fund has a separate board of trustees, although each is composed of the same members. The assets of each fund are invested in interest-bearing obligations of the United States. Tax receipts are allocated to the various funds in proportion to the estimated benefits that will become payable. The Old Age and Survivors Insurance Trust Fund receives the greatest proportion of income, while the Disability Insurance Trust

Fund receives slightly more than one tenth as much, a ratio indicative of the relative size of the benefit payments from the two funds.

Each component of Medicare also has its own trust fund. The Hospital Insurance Trust Fund is allocated, as of 1975, payroll taxes amounting to that which would be generated by a separate tax rate of 0.9 percent of covered wages on both the employee and employer. A self-employed person also pays at a rate of 0.9 percent into the HI Trust Fund.

The SMI Trust Fund, although structured identically to the other three, differs because its income comes directly from the participants and from the general revenues of the federal government. No payroll tax is levied to support SMI. The monthly participant contributions are determined by the Secretary of Health, Education, and Welfare, and remain level for an integral number of 12-month periods commencing on a July 1. In determining the participant premium, consideration is given to the requirement that participants (aged and disabled alike) pay for 50 percent of the benefit and administration costs for those 65 and over, in addition to a margin for contingencies. A limitation on any premium increase is that the percentage increase cannot exceed the percentage increase in cash benefit levels during the preceding 12-month period. As a result of this limitation, governmental contributions to SMI have become greater than 50 percent of the total cost, largely because of limitations on the premiums of disabled beneficiaries.

The monthly charge for SMI participants was $3.00 during the first two years of the program's existence. By 1978, a series of increases produced a $8.20 premium level. These SMI premiums are deducted from the monthly checks from OASDHI, Railroad Retirement, or Civil Service Retirement, where such checks exist. Otherwise, participants are billed periodically and are generally given a grace period of 90 days for payment to be made.

Present Status

Even before the passage of the original Social Security Act of 1935, the concept of government-supported social insurance in this country had been hotly debated. One group of persons and organizations has supported expanding the social security system. They have, for the most part, supported extensions of social security even beyond its present bounds. They advocate benefit increases, often far beyond the "floor of protection" level that was a trademark of the system for many years. It is largely through their efforts that the system presently has a benefit structure heavily weighted in favor of the lower salaried workers. This philosophy has emphasized the principle of social adequacy over that of individual equity. Direct governmental subsidies to the system are often advocated by the expansionists, who base their social security philosophy on humanitarian considerations.

Other persons and organizations oppose extensions of the scope of the system. Their arguments center around the contention that the bulk of the provision for the economic security of American families should be provided through private means and that government-supported systems should merely provide a floor of protection upon which other, elective, forms of insurance can be constructed. They believe that significant amounts of compulsory insurance for all citizens is inherently wrong. Thus, they contend, the OASDHI system should be limited in scope and apply basically only to those persons totally unable to make other provisions for their old age. These individuals and groups see the true purpose of social security as providing assurance that dependents and survivors will not be left penniless as a result of the breadwinner's untimely death or disability. Opponents of further expansion of the system point to the increasingly burdensome tax liability of recent years, a liability whose maximum more than doubled for individual workers between the years of 1972 and 1977 and will more than triple again by 1987. Observing that the tax burden on the employer has grown at the same rate, they argue that further rapid increases might impair the ability of private industries to continue to offer attractive benefit plans for their employees.

Neither group has been consistently successful in their efforts of recent years. Even though recent trends have, generally speaking, produced a system that is much broader in its coverages and benefits than it was a decade ago, it has not reached the scope advocated by many expansionists. Thus, expansion of OASDHI to include compulsory national health insurance has much support among expansionist groups but, at this writing, such support has not been translated into legislation.

Along with the philosophical question about what form of social insurance system best meets the legitimate needs of a highly industrialized country such as the United States, other practical questions of dramatic importance were widely discussed in the late 1970s. Most of these questions revolved about the financing aspects of OASDHI. The source of this rather sudden concern was the realization that the beneficiary rolls were increasing as expected, but that the worker rolls and hence tax revenues were not keeping pace with the projections that formed the basis for the present and future benefits levels. Several reasons were forwarded for this insufficient tax base. One major cause seems to be the decreasing birth rate coupled with the tendency of retired persons to live longer. These combined to throw the relationship of tax revenues to benefit payments out of balance. The situation was compounded because the financing of the system has always essentially been on a pay-as-you-go basis, with a resulting small balance in the various trust funds at any given time. Sharp and unexpected changes in experience, such as the one caused by the recessionary economy of the mid-1970s, unbalance the relationship between income and outgo. This imbalance creates immediate problems that would not be encountered if the system operated on the same actuarial basis as individual life insurance.

PUBLIC CONCERN AND THE 1977 AMENDMENTS

An important provision of the Social Security Act requires annual reports to Congress by the trustees of the various OASDHI trust funds. Such reports are required to include statistical data about past operations and actuarial analyses of cost estimates and financing recommendations. The report completed in the spring of 1974 was ominous. It indicated a 25 percent cost overrun relative to the tax income for the OASDHI component of the system. The actuarial imbalance reported in 1975 was even more alarming, indicating an actuarial deficiency of almost 50 percent of the average value of future taxes.

The 1975 report indicated that the Old-Age and Survivors Insurance (OASI) Trust Fund would be depleted in 1983, and the Disability Insurance (DI) Trust Fund in 1980, unless additional financing measures were taken. Some knowledgeable observers believed these projections far too conservative, predicting depletion of the funds even sooner if the rate of increase in income (and hence of taxable wages) lagged behind projections, as seemed likely in mid-1975. While few knowledgeable observers desired the system to be fully funded, essentially all agreed that the OASI Trust Fund had dipped to a dangerously low level.

The status of the two Medicare trust funds was and is not as insecure as was that of the OASI and DI funds, largely because as wage levels and earnings base have risen (producing an increase in taxes), benefit levels under Medicare have not risen as they have in the OASDI system. The SMI fund appears to be quite stable. It would be considered in actuarial balance even under the strictest standards of solvency. The HI fund, while not in the same state as its SMI counterpart, does not appear to be in any danger of insolvency in the foreseeable future.

Congress responded in 1977 to the alarming trustee reports and to widespread public concern by raising the taxable wage base and tax rate itself over a ten-year period beginning after 1978 as described above. These increases were designed to reduce the projected 1978 and 1979 annual deficits in the cash benefit program and to provide excesses of income over expenditures starting in 1980. The 1977 amendments were designed to assure that for the remainder of this century the trust funds will grow relative to annual expenditures and that the social security program will be soundly financed until well into the next century. The medium-range deficits over the next 25 years are eliminated in theory, and the long-range deficit reduced from over 8 percent of taxable payroll to less than 1½ percent (all of the latter deficit would occur in the next century).

Additionally, the 1977 amendments increased the allocation of OASDI income to the DI trust fund, thus putting both the old-age and survivors income and the disability components of the program on a sounder financial footing. Part of the previously scheduled increases in HI rates were reallocated to OASDI, since the higher contribution and benefit bases will result in additional income to the HI program.

The 1978 amendment to the Age Discrimination in Employment Act of 1967 approaches the problem from another direction. This amendment forbids the enforcement of a fixed retirement policy by private employers who engage in interstate transactions or employ at least 20 persons during the year, as of 1979. Exceptions are permitted for employees who have an annual retirement income of $27,000 or more. The impact of this amendment on the financial status of the Social Security System will, of course, depend on the proportion of employees who take advantage of this amendment to continue paid employment after the age of 65.

Whether the future of the system will be one of continued expansion, involving larger benefits, higher taxes, and additional dependence upon governmental revenues, or of retrenchment, with greater emphasis upon the responsibility of individuals for their own financial affairs, is not clear. Needless to say, the direction OASDHI takes in the short-range future will be watched carefully by individual family units, employers of American workers, and the group insurance industry.

THE RAILROAD RETIREMENT SYSTEM

The Railroad Retirement System covers barely 1 percent as many persons as its OASDI counterpart. However, its similarities to and interaction with the OASDI program make it an appropriate subject for discussion throughout the remainder of this chapter.

Origin of the System

Throughout the nineteenth century, the federal government showed itself as vitally interested in the systematic growth of the railroads of this country and went on record as being prepared to intervene when such action was deemed appropriate. One occasion to do so came as a result of the inadequacy of company-sponsored pension plans to cope with problems of the Great Depression.

The early 1900s had produced substantial activity in the area of company-sponsored pension plans for the highly unionized railroad workers. By the early 1930s, nearly 90 private plans had been established. Unfortunately, many of these plans had not been funded on a sound basis. Inadequate funding combined with the economic effects of the Great Depression to reduce pension payments in some instances and to end employer contributions in others. As unemployment grew, workers became apprehensive that layoffs would nullify their existing pension credits. A few railroads declared bankruptcy. Others incurred huge operating losses. The plans established by the unions themselves fared no better than the company-sponsored plans. The plight of the railroad workers' present and future financial security seemed dire.

Spurred by the railroad labor unions, Congress enacted a law in 1934 that provided for a single pension plan administered by a federal agency for all railroad employees. Fearing the economic impact of the act at a time when profits were low or nonexistent, the railroads vigorously opposed the act. Their objections were upheld by the Supreme Court, which found the act unconstitutional shortly after its passage. The Supreme Court not only felt that it was improper (even with the "commerce clause" as a justification) to impose a mandatory retirement system on employees engaged in interstate commerce, but was also unwilling to accept certain features of the act, notably one which required retirement at age 65.

THE RAILROAD RETIREMENT ACT OF 1935

Undaunted by this initial failure, labor organizations continued their efforts. In 1935, Congress created a system similar to that contemplated by the 1934 Act, but designed so as to circumvent the objections of the Supreme Court. Thus, the benefit and tax provisions were wholly segregated, provisions for compulsory retirement were eased, and employer contributions were set at a level equal to those required of workers. However, the plan remained compulsory, prompting another effort on the part of management to have it declared unconstitutional. Such a ruling was made by a lower court, but President Franklin D. Roosevelt, determined that some solution to the worsening problem be reached, called representatives of both sides into conference. As a result, the railroads dropped their formal opposition to the 1935 Act.

To gain this concession, the unions agreed to certain amendments that were enacted in 1937. The most important amendments provided that existing pensioners would be taken over by the government, with the costs of these benefits to be underwritten through general governmental revenues. This lifted a great burden from the railroads with existing plans, because the benefits rolls had swelled and the worker rolls had shrunk under the impact of the depression. Further, the compromises provided that there would be no deviation from a 50-50 split of contributions to the plan between the companies and the employees.

The 1935 act, as amended in 1937, is known as the Railroad

Retirement Act. The act created a Railroad Retirement Board head-quartered in Chicago. The Board's three members are appointed by the President and are charged with the administration of payments of retirement and disability annuities to railroad workers and to their supervisors and dependents.

Initial Provisions of the System

The Railroad Retirement Act was passed only two weeks after the Social Security Act and, not surprisingly, the provisions of the acts are somewhat similar. The coverage provisions of the Railroad Retirement Act, however, were quite simple and all-encompassing, unlike those of the Social Security Act. Essentially, all railroad workers in the United States have been covered from the start. Thus, while the history of the changes and liberalizations of the Social Security Act is filled with extensions of coverage to broader and broader classes of workers, Railroad Retirement provided total coverage from its inception.

Retirement income was available to persons retiring at age 65, or as early as age 60 if the employee had as many as 30 years of service and took a reduction in payment amount that approximated the actuarially proper reduction. Persons leaving the railroad industry who were not yet entitled to immediate benefits were given a deferred annuity, starting at age 65 but to begin and continue only if they satisfied strict requirements about subsequent employment after terminating their association with the railroad industry.

The benefit structure of the Railroad Retirement System was similar to that of social security at the start, and has remained so through the years. The initial maximum creditable wage was $300 per month, slightly more than the $250 of social security. Benefits for Railroad Retirement were weighted in favor of the lower paid workers just as were those of the social security system.

In contrast to the Social Security System, which incorporated disability benefits only after the system had been in effect for about 20 years, disability benefits for railroad workers were available from the beginning. These disability benefits were restricted to persons who either had 30 years of service at disability or were at least age 60. The latter group was required to absorb an actuarial reduction in payment amount.

There were originally no survivor benefits under Railroad Retirement, other than a guarantee that an employee's aggregate contributions, increased by a stated rate of interest, would be returned as a minimum benefit.

The original system was financed by 2¾ percent tax on the first $300 of monthly earnings, levied on the employee and matched by the railroad employer. The initial legislation prescribed increments of ¼ percent on both the employer and employee every three years, with a total combined tax of 7½ percent to be reached by 1949. This income tax was paid into the Railroad Retirement Account, from which were paid all benefits and administrative expenses.

CHANGES THROUGH AMENDMENTS UNTIL 1974

A long succession of expansionary amendments has sharply altered the features of the Railroad Retirement System over the last four decades.

The first significant change in the system occurred in 1946, when monthly survivor benefits were implemented in a form similar to those which had become a feature of social security six years earlier. In fact, the survivor benefit feature of Railroad Retirement was completely integrated with that of OASDI. Earnings records were combined so that survivors could not receive payments under both systems.

A significant change in the philosophy of the program occurred when the 1951 amendments introduced "financial interchange" provisions between the Social Security and the Railroad Retirement Systems. The impact of these provisions has remained highly important, and continues to underline the true interdependence of these two huge social insurance systems.

The financial interchange provisions placed two social security trust funds, the OASI trust fund and the DI trust fund, in such a position that transfers between the appropriate trust funds were to operate so as to negate the effect created by persons who had accumulated credits under both systems and who would therefore appear to be eligible for dual benefits.

In addition to the implementation of the basic financial interchange provision, the 1951 amendments provided that workers with fewer than ten years of railroad service would not be covered by railroad retirement in any way, but would have their payments made through OASDI and their contributions transferred to OASDI, an arrangement still in effect today.

Amendments to the Railroad Retirement Act between 1951 and 1974 liberalized benefit amounts, made adjustments in beneficiary categories parallelling those of social security, and expanded the available funds by increasing the contribution rates.

The Railroad Retirement Act of 1974

It was increasingly obvious for many years before 1974 that the railroad industry was not the vibrant, exciting, prosperous industry that it had been earlier in this century. In fact, the financial history of the industry has shown sharply decreasing revenues, numerous bankruptcies, court-appointed trusteeships, and increasing federal involvement. For the Railroad Retirement System, these facts meant decreasing railroad employment and a resulting shortage of funds with which to pay its current pensioners. A static situation with respect to benefit levels would have been serious enough, but significant increases in social security benefit levels placed the Railroad Retirement System under pressure to follow suit. By 1970, it was clear that to liberalize benefits under existing employment conditions would be to throw the actuarial balance of the system into complete disarray, practically inviting depletion of the system's assets. As a result, Congress approved a temporary benefit increase, while at the same time creating a Commission on Railroad Retirement to investigate the current status of the system and recommend changes that would place the system on a sound financial footing. A major consideration of this commission was the problem of dual benefit recipients and the resulting drain on the Railroad Retirement System. A further complicating factor was that the longer the commission deliberated, the more desperate the situation became.

The findings of the commission formed the basis for negotiations between representatives of labor and management that produced the provisions of the new act. In October 1974, the complete restructuring of the Railroad Retirement System was accomplished through passage, over President Ford's veto, of the Railroad Retirement Act of 1974.

The major effect on benefit payments of the 1974 Act was the phasing out of dual benefits through a large scale restructuring of the benefit system. Effective January 1, 1975, the benefits under OASDI and Railroad Retirement were completely coordinated through a two-tiered benefit system. Dual benefits for persons already eligible or vested for both types of payments were protected, but at public expense.

The two tiers created by the 1974 Act, acting in concert, permit benefits through both systems, but do not allow an individual retiring in the future to take full advantage of the favorable treatment previously accorded low-paid workers under the two systems.

The major financing change instituted through the 1974 Act was that certain benefits, both for beneficiaries already on the rolls and for new annuitants, are now funded through general revenues. Such infusion of general revenues into the Railroad Retirement System is anticipated to continue until the year 2000.

Present Features of the System

An examination of the specific benefit features and financing provisions of the Railroad Retirement System following the amendments of 1974 indicates that while the Railroad Retirement System shares many similarities with its social security counterpart, the two systems display differences as well.

BENEFIT FEATURES

The benefit features of the Railroad Retirement System, as amended by the 1974 Act, are similar to those of the OASDI system. Cash benefits are available to employees, their spouses, and their survivors. The reader will recall that health insurance through Medicare is provided for railroad workers just as for persons with no railroad employment. However, the cash benefits payable through the Railroad Retirement System are not calculated in a manner as favorable to lower-paid workers as are OASDI benefits. To a limited extent, though, the concept of social adequacy does predominate over that of individual equity. In addition, cash benefits depend upon the number of years of covered railroad employment. They are similar to those benefits generally available under private pension plans, but quite apart from those provided through social security. This has been justified because, as we have seen, railroad workers actually have a portion of their benefits determined by formulas prescribed in the Social Security law. Benefit amounts are generally somewhat larger than would be provided through OASDI, basically because the tax rate is higher.

The clearest quantitative evidence available of the degree of improvement in the financial condition of the system is the estimate that the actuarial deficiency of the system, 9.05 percent of taxable payroll prior to the passage of the 1974 Act, fell to less than 1 percent of taxable payroll afterwards. More concrete estimates, based on actual experience of the system after the end of 1974, will be available upon the completion of the next triennial valuation of the system's actuarial status.

FINANCING PROVISIONS

The present tax rate on employees is the same as the prevailing rate under social security. Employers are required to contribute the same amount plus an additional 9.5 percent. The maximum taxable amount, or tax base, for any individual worker, is one twelfth of the annual social security maximum. This rate of taxation produces different results in many cases from that of the Social Security System.

The drastic financial crisis faced by the Railroad Retirement System prior to the passage of the 1974 Act has now been largely eased. Three features of the 1974 Act contributed to this result. Most notable was the infusion of general revenues into the system to fund dual benefits. Other factors were the gradual phasing out of dual benefits and the lower benefit level that will ultimately prevail after a grandfather clause ceases to be effective in 1983.

SUMMARY

This chapter has described in appropriate detail the two benefit programs that are considered to qualify as social insurance programs of the federal government, the OASDHI and Railroad Retirement Systems. Topics presented about each system included its origins, its expansion through amendments, and its coverage, eligibility, benefit, and financing provisions. The old-age, survivors and disability benefits of the Social Security System were discussed separately from Medicare, with its separate hospital insurance and supplementary medical insurance components.

The OASDHI and the Railroad Retirement Systems are largely complementary in their operations and integrated in their underlying philosophies, but it must be borne in mind that the former is vastly larger in scope and coverage than the latter.

Most important, the student should comprehend the massive amounts of insurance protection available through these systems in addition to the retirement benefits that are usually considered the most important features of the plans. Through benefits payable to survivors, and the health insurance benefits payable through Medicare, it can be argued that these systems are this country's primary insuring institutions. Needless to say, the insurance industry will continue to view social insurance systems with a wary eye, especially when and if some form of national health insurance is implemented. The future direction of the vast insurance industry in the United States will continue to be considerably influenced by governmental activity in the area of providing economic security for its citizens through compulsory means.

CHAPTER 30

BENEFIT PROGRAMS FOR FEDERAL EMPLOYEES

INTRODUCTION

Many believe that the social security program, which touches the lives of almost every American, is the only significant way the government provides insurance benefits for its citizens. This belief is inaccurate, since federal, state and local governments all administer numerous plans for the insuring of certain risks. The federal government also is heavily involved in the insurance business, at least in a supervisory capacity. Major examples of this involvement are the Servicemen's Group Life Insurance plan and the Federal Employees Group Life Insurance plan.

The preceding chapter discussed the characteristics of social insurance and treated in detail OASDHI and the Railroad Retirement System. This chapter will survey those governmental activities that do not technically qualify as social insurance, but that provide insurance benefits for certain segments of the population. These segments are usually, but not always, composed of persons who are presently, or have been in the past, employed by a governmental body.

The first portion of this chapter discusses programs covering armed forces personnel and veterans. The second portion discusses benefit plans covering civilian employees of the federal government.

ARMED FORCES AND VETERANS PROGRAMS

Long before the pension and group insurance boom of the early and mid-twentieth century, the federal government decided that it owed a debt of gratitude, both moral and financial, to those persons

by
ROBERT W. BATTEN, FSA, *Professor of Actuarial Science and Head of The Actuarial Science Program, Georgia State University*

who aided in the country's defense during wartime. As early as 1792, Congress legislated pensions for veterans of the Revolutionary War. Prior to that date, those veterans were given land grants and bonuses, on the theory that they had not only contributed their time and labor, but probably had also foregone the opportunity to establish a personal economic base.

A federal Commissioner of Pensions, headquartered in the Department of the Interior, was appointed in 1849 to handle the various military pension laws then in effect. After World War I the handling of veterans' affairs was distributed among several governmental agencies. Consequent confusion of authority led to the formation of the Veterans Bureau in 1920. Ten years later the Veterans Administration (VA) was established by consolidating the Veterans Bureau and two other federal agencies. The VA is an independent agency of the executive branch of the federal government, charged with the administration of various benefits for veterans, their dependents, and their survivors. Of all the independent agencies of the federal government, only the postal service has more employees than the VA. In our discussion, veterans' benefits will be categorized as life insurance, survivor and dependent benefits, health insurance, and retirement and death benefits. Other benefits, such as those provided through the 1944 GI Bill of Rights and similar legislation, are not insurance benefits and will not be considered.

Life Insurance

Since the end of World War I, seven separate life insurance programs for veterans, in addition to the group life plans for those on active service, have been implemented. Most are no longer open to new issues but still have significant amounts of insurance in force. Each program operates independently, as if it were a separate life insurance company. These programs vary in the degree to which they are self-supporting. Though earlier programs were subsidized through general tax funds for administrative costs and the extra costs of insuring service-related deaths, more recent programs have been increasingly self-supporting. Each program has its own fund established with the United States Treasury.

The first two government life insurance programs, United States Government Life Insurance (USGLI), available from 1919 to 1940, for active service personnel and from 1928 to 1951 for veterans who had served in the period from 1917 to 1921, and National Service Life Insurance (NSLI), available from 1940 to 1951, shared many features:

1. They were available to veterans and active armed services members;
2. They had a maximum face amount of $10,000 (this restriction

also applied to the amount of insurance that could be purchased under USGLI and NSLI combined);

3. They provided for a choice of programs—five-year renewable
   and convertible term, ordinary life, and endowment policies;
4. They provided coverage on a net cost basis;
5. They were government subsidized for administrative costs and
   the extra cost of insuring service-related deaths; and
6. They offered disability income insurance at an extra premium.

Because of the huge increase in the number of people on active
military duty during World War II, approximately 22 million NSLI
policies were issued, 20 times as many as under USGLI. Premium
rates for NSLI policies were somewhat higher than those for USGLI
policies because the base premium provided for disability waiver of
premium as well as death protection.

A quarter of a century has passed since the last USGLI policy was
issued, so only a small fraction of issued policies remain in force; this
number is decreasing at a rate of approximately 7 percent annually. A significant block of NSLI business remains in force, and since
the average age of policyowners is approximately 60, the NSLI program will be in operation for many years to come.

SERVICEMEN'S INDEMNITY AND INSURANCE ACT

Concern among private insurers and others about the heavy subsidy of USGLI and NSLI by the federal government led to the enactment of the Servicemen's Indemnity and Insurance Act of 1951. This
act terminated the availability of new insurance in both of the existing
programs, based on the belief that continued federal subsidy of the
programs after a policyowner was no longer active in the service was
an unjustifiable public expense. The act provided for $10,000 of free
term insurance coverage for all active service personnel. This term
insurance terminated without value 120 days after separation from the
service. In no case was coverage to extend beyond the end of 1956.
The amounts of free insurance could not exceed a total of $10,000
when added to existing coverage under USGLI and NSLI. However,
provision was made for the temporary lapsing of existing coverage so a
member of the armed forces could take advantage of the free protection while maintaining his or her other rights to other government
coverage after returning to civilian life.

Veterans Special Life Insurance. The 1951 Acts also gave veterans
who were separated from active duty between April 1951 and the end
of 1956 the right to replace their free coverage with a five-year renewable but nonconvertible and nonparticipating term plan known as Veterans Special Life Insurance (VSLI). The VSLI policies were not such a
bargain for their owners as had been the earlier policies under USGLI
and NSLI. The premiums were calculated more conservatively and

were sufficient to cover service-related deaths as well as standard risks. The government still contributed to the program, but only to the extent of the costs of administration. The maximum coverage remained $10,000, including any other amounts of government life insurance in force at the time of application.

The five-year renewable term plans issued as VSLI proved less than satisfactory because the premiums increased relatively rapidly under such plans. For this reason, Congress passed legislation in 1958 allowing VSLI policyowners to convert these term plans to a lower priced term plan (nonrenewable after age 50) or to a permanent plan offered under one of the other programs. Two-thirds of VSLI policies that remain in force today are five-year term policies.

Service Disabled Veterans Insurance. The 1951 acts created the Service Disabled Veterans Insurance Program (SDVI) under which armed forces personnel discharged after April 1951 and suffering from service-connected disabilities were (and still are) eligible to purchase policies at standard rates. These policies, implemented to provide preferential treatment for disabled service personnel, are nonparticipating and must be applied for within one year of the date on which the VA determines that service-related disability actually exists. They are available in all plans except endowments in amounts up to $10,000. Because premiums are calculated at standard rates even though all policyowners are at least partially disabled, the plans are not self-supporting. Periodic grants by Congress are necessary to cover excess disbursements.

VETERANS REOPENED INSURANCE

Congressional action in 1964 provided for the reopening of the NSLI program for a one-year period beginning May 1, 1965. Plans issued as a result were called Veterans Reopened Insurance (VRI) and were available only to veterans of the 1940–1956 period who had a disability which resulted in their being ineligible for commercial life insurance. The premiums depended upon the severity of the disability and whether or not the disability was service-related. Some policies were issued at standard rates. For service-connected disabilities, premiums ranged from standard to triple the standard rate. Where the disability was not connected with military service, premium rates were in some instances much higher than triple the standard rates. The basic actuarial assumptions that were used resulted in low premium levels for veterans eligible for standard rates. The $10,000 restriction on all government life insurance continued to apply under VRI.

The VRI program contained three significant features:

1. All administrative costs were borne by the policyowner;
2. No term insurance was offered; and
3. All policies under the program were nonparticipating policies.

Because the VRI policies were nonparticipating, a method of setting equitable rates was needed. Therefore, the policies were subject to premium adjustments based on developing experience. Net premium rates were made subject to revision every two years, while the loading costs for administrative services were subject to revision every five years.

In practice, rates charged to individuals insured at standard rates have been reduced on two occasions; those charged to individuals having rated policies have been reduced once. Administrative costs have remained unchanged. Even though enrollment in the VRI program was available for only a single year, nearly $1 billion of insurance remains in force at the present time.

SERVICEMEN'S GROUP LIFE INSURANCE

The termination of free term insurance for armed forces personnel as of December 31, 1956 marked the temporary end of life insurance provided through the government for active service personnel. The government temporarily went out of the insurance business, at least with respect to new issues, except for certain categories of disabled veterans. Coverage for those in active service again became available in 1965, but this time the government supervised the program rather than provide the coverage directly. The Prudential Life Insurance Company, selected by the Office of Servicemen's Group Life Insurance as the primary insurer, administers the plan, which is actually underwritten by a reinsurance pool of nearly 600 private insurers. The availability of Servicemen's Group Life Insurance (SGLI) coverage to those in active service was therefore reinstated, but under a new philosophy that the government itself should not assume the role of insurer.

Originally, SGLI provided $10,000 of term life insurance to all active service personnel regardless of their state of health. The policies required contributions from the servicemen who were covered. The government contributed to the extent of the additional mortality resulting from the hazards of military service, but administrative costs were covered by the participants' premiums (originally $2 per month for the $10,000 policies). Those eligible were also given the option of selecting a $5,000 policy for half the premium or of rejecting the coverage altogether. Unlike other plans of insurance discussed thus far, SGLI is a true group life insurance plan.

Various amendments have produced several important changes in the original plan. In addition, the Veterans Insurance Act of 1973, effective May 24, 1974, expanded the original list of eligibles for SGLI coverage so as to include the following individuals:

1. Active duty servicemen and servicewomen, including academy members;
2. Ready reservists, including members of the National Guard

who may be required to perform active duty or who are on active duty for training;

3. Retired reservists who have completed 20 years of creditable service toward retirement and who have not attained age 65; and

4. Reservists not otherwise qualifying who perform authorized training (eligible for part-time coverage only).

This broadened definition of eligibility made SGLI the largest group life contract in the world. As of June 1978, 133,000 persons were insured under SGLI for an aggregate of $62.2 billion.[1]

The amount of coverage available to individuals is currently $20,000, or twice the original amount. The provision of coverage for the full face amount is automatic unless the participant elects, in writing, coverage for $15,000, $10,000, $5,000, or no coverage at all. The insurance is term coverage only and expires without value 120 days after a person leaves active duty. Conversion privileges available under the original SGLI program have been eliminated though conversion is still available in connection with the Veterans' Group Life Insurance (VGLI) program discussed below.

Premium rates, subject to periodic change to reflect current experience, were reduced to 15 cents per month per $1,000 of insurance in 1978 for those on active duty and retired reservists. Retired reservists are charged a somewhat higher premium that depends upon their attained age.

Veterans Group Life Insurance. The newest plan of government-administered insurance for veterans is Veterans Group Life Insurance (VGLI), established by the Veterans Insurance Act of 1973. The first policies were available on August 1, 1974 to veterans separated from the service on or after that date. Coverage typically begins after the 120-day period during which SGLI coverage is extended.

VGLI policies consist of 5-year, nonrenewable, term insurance with face amounts of $5,000, $10,000, $15,000, or $20,000, but may not exceed the amount of insurance carried by the terminating participant under SGLI. Originally, eligibility was extended to everyone terminating active service after August 1, 1974 who was insured under SGLI, and also to veterans who had been separated from the service during the preceding four-year period. This grandfather clause for recently terminated veterans expired a year later on August 1, 1975. Currently the only eligibles are those persons whose 120-day SGLI extension is expiring.

Premium rates for VGLI are similar to those for SGLI. The only difference is a doubling of the premium if the VGLI plan is issued at age 35 or over. Thus, the premium rate is currently either 17 cents or

---

[1]Veterans' Administration, Washington, D.C.

34 cents per month per thousand, depending upon the age of the person terminating active service. As with SGLI, these rates are subject to revision in light of developing experience. However, they have remained the same since the program's inception. Veterans with service-connected disabilities are given standard VGLI rates.

The right to convert VGLI certificates to plans of permanent insurance is a key feature of the program. During the final 120 days of the 5-year VGLI coverage, policyowners are informed of the right to convert to an individual policy at standard rates, regardless of health, with any of the SGLI-participating companies. Such converted policies may not contain any war risk or military exclusion clause and thus would provide valuable protection for veterans who later reenter the service. Retired reservists are eligible for neither VGLI nor the conversion privilege. Unlike other government-sponsored life insurance programs for veterans, VGLI is administered by a commercial insurer and is only supervised by the VA.

Within the first six months following the implementation of VGLI, approximately 46,000 persons enrolled for an aggregate face amount of $850 million. A large majority of those covered are insured for the $20,000 upper limit.

Veterans Mortgage Life Insurance. A small but important life insurance program available to service-disabled veterans is Veterans Mortgage Life Insurance (VMLI). Congressional legislation in 1971 provided for coverage on disabled veterans who had received VA grants for housing. The face amount of life insurance on any given case is the balance of the mortgage, with a maximum of $30,000.

Premiums, generally deducted from VA compensation checks, are sufficient to cover only standard mortality costs. Therefore, government subsidies are necessary to provide for excessive mortality costs and administrative expenses. These subsidies account for about 80 percent of the program's income. As of the end of 1978, only about 5,600 policies were in force under VMLI, with an average face amount of almost $25,000.[2] The program is administered by a private insurer and is supervised by the VA in the same way as the VGLI Program.

Survivor Benefits

The availability and the size of cash payments to survivors of disabled veterans depend on several factors. The date of the veteran's death determines under which legislation the payments are to be made.

Whether the disability was service-connected or nonservice-connected and whether the service of the veteran was during peacetime or wartime are also important considerations. The pay

---

[2] *Ibid.*

grade of the veteran, the degree of disability, and the financial condition of the survivors may affect the size of any payments that are to be made.

A distinction must be made at the outset between compensation payments and pension payments with respect to both death benefits to survivors and disability payments to disabled veterans and their dependents. Compensation payments are made in cases of service-connected deaths or disabilities. These payments are usually made without respect to the financial need of the recipients. Payments made to survivors on behalf of service personnel with no service-connected disability are referred to as pension payments. Pension payments are generally available only where the veteran involved served during wartime years as defined in the relevant legislation. Note that this use of the word "pension" differs from usual usage.

COMPENSATION PAYMENTS

Disability and indemnity compensation payments to the survivors of veterans whose deaths (after January 1, 1957) resulted from a disease or injury incurred or aggravated while on active duty training, or inactive duty training (as in the case of a reservist on weekend duty) or from an otherwise compensable disability, are made through a program known as Disability and Indemnity Compensation (DIC).

Eligibility for DIC payments depends on several factors. A widow's benefit is available only if she lived with the veteran from the time of their marriage until his death, unless a separation occurred in which no legal fault was affixed to the wife. A remarried widow is ineligible unless and until the remarriage is terminated. Benefits are payable on behalf of surviving children under the age of 18. Where total and permanent disability of a child occurs before age 18, payments continue indefinitely unless the child marries. Dependent parents are eligible for DIC payments only if their income is below a certain level.

PENSION PAYMENTS

Death pension payments are made to survivors of veterans who served the country in time of war but whose death was not service-related. Eligibility requirements for pension payments under the current program are essentially the same as for compensation payments except that parents are ineligible for benefits. However, because the size of pension payments in most cases depends largely upon financial need, the pension system is more like public assistance than is the DIC system, which makes payments regardless of need.[3]

---

[3]Benefits of some veterans of World War I and earlier wars are not related to need.

SURVIVOR INCOME

The types of survivor benefits discussed thus far are available only to survivors of veterans with service-connected disabilities or of those whose period of service fell during wartime. In addition to these compensation or pension payments available to survivors, the Survivor Benefit Plan (SBP) established in 1972 provides survivor income to spouses and/or dependent children of retired career military personnel. Maximum coverage under SBP is automatic upon the retirement of veterans who have at least one eligible dependent unless election of lesser coverage is made or coverage is rejected altogether.

The basic benefit under SBP is income of up to 55 percent of the deceased veteran's military retirement pay. The cost of the coverage, payable in full by the retiree, depends upon whether the dependents consist of a widow only, dependent children only, a widow and dependent children, or some other person with an insurable interest in the retiree. Both premiums and benefits are automatically adjusted for changes in the Consumer Price Index. Approximately 37 percent of the total cost of the program is borne by the budget of the Defense Department. SBP is thus supported through general revenues.

Disability Benefits

Disability benefits, payable to a disabled veteran and his or her dependents, are divided into two classes, depending upon whether the disability was or was not service-connected. Many features of the disability benefit system resemble those of the death benefit structure outlined above.

COMPENSATION PAYMENTS

Veterans disabled by personal injury suffered or disease contracted in line of duty, or by aggravation of a preexisting injury or disease while in the line of duty, are eligible for disability compensation regardless of financial need. The disability must not result from willful misconduct, and separation of the veteran from the service must have been other than dishonorable.

Actual monthly payment amounts depend upon the degree of disability as determined by the VA. Veterans whose disabilities were incurred during peacetime receive compensation equal to 80 percent of that of a veteran disabled during wartime.

PENSION PAYMENTS

Disability pensions are available to veterans who served in the Mexican Border disturbances of 1916–1917, either of the World Wars, the Korean conflict, or the Vietnam war and whose total and permanent disability did not result from military service. All veterans aged

65 and over are automatically considered "disabled" for the purposes of eligibility for disability pension payments.

Benefits depend heavily upon the annual income of the disabled veteran. All benefits are phased out, regardless of the number of dependents, when the veteran's income reaches a specified level. A veteran within the income limits who is deemed to need regular aid and attendance may receive additional monthly benefits. However, the pension may be reduced if the veteran is hospitalized, with the full amount resumed following release.

Upon the death of a veteran receiving disability pension payments, the spouse becomes eligible for a similar program. Under this program, the monthly payments are determined by the surviving spouse's income.

In contrast to compensation payments, the basis for disability pension payments is financial need.

Health Benefits

The availability of medical care in VA hospitals is one of the most visible benefits accorded eligible veterans. However, many additional types of medical care and services are also available.

HOSPITALIZATION

Any veteran whose discharge was other than dishonorable is eligible for hospital benefits. However, because of the possibility of shortages in available facilities, an order of priority for use of these facilities has been established. Top priority is given to veterans who sustained injuries or contracted diseases while in the line of duty in active service and who require treatment for such disability. Next are those veterans who were discharged from active service as a result of a service-related disability or who currently meet the requirements for disability compensation, but whose current disability or malady requiring treatment is not service-connected. Finally, the lowest level of priority is given to veterans who sustained no service-connected disability. Such veterans are given consideration only if it can be demonstrated that hospitalization is necessary and that they are incapable of paying for the required services elsewhere.

Veterans who are qualified for admission into a VA hospital are given all needed treatment at no cost. On occasion, otherwise unqualified persons may receive care in a VA hospital, but they are charged equitable fees for services performed.

OUTPATIENT TREATMENT

Veterans eligible for VA hospital care are also entitled to receive outpatient medical and surgical services for service-connected diseases and injuries at the expense of the VA. Such services may be performed at a VA hospital or by any physician approved in advance by the VA. Drugs and medicines are available without charge to qualifying veterans.

NURSING HOME CARE

Admission to a VA nursing home care unit involves roughly the same eligibility rules as does admission to a VA hospital. A service-connected disability is required. Where circumstances warrant, a veteran may be admitted to a private nursing home at VA expense.

DOMICILIARY CARE

The VA operates domiciliaries (rest homes) to provide ambulatory self-care facilities for disabled veterans who do not need hospitalization or skilled nursing care. Eligibility is restricted to veterans who were discharged for disability or who are receiving compensation for a service-connected disability, and who have no means of self-support.

OTHER HEALTH BENEFITS

In addition to the various inpatient, outpatient, and nursing facilities available to disabled veterans, several other types of care are provided. Extensive dental care is available to veterans eligible for VA hospital care, while others who qualify for only domiciliary care may receive somewhat less comprehensive dental care. In addition, any veteran who has received dental care as a result of a service-connected disability is eligible for free dental work when and if the original repair work becomes broken or otherwise inoperable because of legitimate wear.

Veterans who meet minimum standards for outpatient medical treatment, or who are receiving hospital or domiciliary care, are eligible for the fitting of necessary permanent prosthetic appliances such as artificial limbs. Included in this benefit is any required training in the use of such appliances, as well as any necessary repairs or replacements resulting from normal wear and usage.

Certain veterans with visual impairments may receive benefits such as electronic and mechanical aids for the blind or guide dogs, including the expense of training the veteran to use guide dogs properly. Eligibility is restricted to those blind veterans who are eligible to receive compensation for any service-connected disability or to those who are entitled to an increased pension based upon the need for regular aid and attendance.

BENEFITS FOR SURVIVORS AND DEPENDENTS

A wife or child of a veteran whose total disability is service-related, or a widow or child of a veteran whose death resulted from a service-connected disability, may be eligible for VA medical care. This care is usually provided at non-VA facilities and paid for by the VA, but VA facilities are used on occasion if they are specially equipped to provide the needed care.

Retirement and Death Benefits

Since retirement pensions to veterans are payable only to career members of the armed forces, they will not be considered in depth. Retirement benefits are quite liberal, generally requiring only 20 years of service, and are funded completely by the federal government. Further, they automatically adjust to rises in the cost of living. Military retirement benefits are supplemented by social security benefits. An important additional benefit available to service personnel drawing retirement pay is the continuation of free medical care, as if the veteran were still on active service.

Various death benefits are available upon the death of service personnel and veterans. Payment of up to $250 is authorized to defray the cost of burial. Educational benefits are available, under certain conditions, to widows or orphans of deceased service persons who incurred a disability while in service. Grave markers, American flags, and burial rights for family members are also available under certain conditions. Should death occur while the veteran is on active duty, active duty training, or inactive duty training, the veteran's family is entitled to an additional death benefit in the amount equal to six months' pay. Of course, the major death benefit payable to survivors of disabled veterans is the compensation payable to widows and dependents or the corresponding payments in the form of pensions discussed earlier in this chapter.

BENEFITS FOR CIVILIAN EMPLOYEES

As was discussed in Chapter 1, a major impetus for the origin of employee benefit plans was the realization by employers that a well-motivated, productive work force could not be recruited without making attractive fringe benefits available. The largest employer in the United States, the federal government, must also be competitive in its life and health insurance and retirement programs. The resulting benefit plans for federal employees, all administered by the Civil Service Commission, are outlined in this section.

Federal Employees Group Life Insurance

Determined to develop an efficient personnel program in his first administration, President Dwight D. Eisenhower outlined a nine-point proposal early in 1954 to eliminate inequities between federal compensation and that of private industry. One of the major points in his proposal concerned voluntary, contributory group life insurance for all federal employees. Partly because similar group life benefits were already available to millions of workers in private industry, the proposal met with little serious opposition. Less than six months after the

President's original proposal, Federal Employees Group Life Insurance (FEGLI) became a reality through the passage of Public Law 83-598. Approximately two million employees were covered initially.

Just as with all insurance plans, both public and private, the passage of time has seen broad changes in FEGLI since its inception. This discussion centers on the present program, with references to earlier provisions only for comparison.

ELIGIBILITY

Practically all full-time civilian federal employees are eligible to participate. The only notable exception is that of noncitizens employed overseas by the federal government. Even retired employees are eligible if they were covered while employed and if they meet other minimal requirements. Under no circumstances are there any age or health restrictions on those persons becoming eligible for the first time.

Employees are enrolled immediately upon becoming eligible, with no waiting period, for the full face amount for which they qualify. Those wishing to be excluded from the program must file the appropriate waiver forms on their own initiative. Persons who do so tend to be younger employees who have little or no responsibility for dependents.

Those who choose not to participate are not necessarily making an irreversible decision, however. Upon application, late inclusion in FEGLI is possible, but in no case may coverage begin prior to one year after written notice has been given that coverage was not desired. Further, evidence of insurability is required in all cases resulting from applications for insurance after such coverage has been initially rejected. Finally, the request will not be honored if the employee is 50 years old or older at the time of the request.

BENEFITS

The present benefit structure of FEGLI has three separate components: basic group life coverage, accidental death and dismemberment (AD+D) protection, and an additional amount of optional life insurance (the cost of which is borne entirely by the participants).

The amount of basic group life insurance coverage is determined by adding $2,000 to the participant's annual base salary and rounding the result to the next highest thousand dollars. The minimum and maximum amounts of insurance are $10,000 and $45,000, respectively. Accidental death and dismemberment is provided in the same amount as the basic coverage. Therefore, the maximum total benefit payable for an accidental death is $90,000. The loss of one hand, one foot, or one eye results in a payment of one half the basic amount. The full face amount is payable upon the loss of any two or more such members. Amounts of insurance change automatically when increases or decreases in salaries alter the amount brackets of individual employees.

Realizing that higher salaried federal employees were unable to obtain as much group life insurance as many of their counterparts in private industry, Congress passed a bill in 1967 permitting the purchase of additional optional insurance in the amount of $10,000. This optional coverage is available for the $10,000 amount for employees earning up to $55,000. Those with higher salaries are permitted to purchase the amount of additional insurance that will bring their total coverage up to the amount of their salaries. For example, an employee with a salary of $65,000 would be permitted a maximum basic coverage of $45,000 and optional coverage of $20,000. In all cases, additional AD+D coverage is granted in the same amount as the optional insurance.

Coverage for the basic amount continues until the employee reaches age 65 or the date of retirement, whichever comes later. Beyond such date, the face amount is reduced by 2 percent of the original face per month until only 25 percent of the original amount remains.

All AD+D coverage under both the basic plan and the optional plan is terminated at retirement. However, the optional life insurance may be continued on the same basis as the basic plan at no cost to the retired employee if the employee has been covered for the optional insurance continuously since the initial date of eligibility or if the employee has been covered for a period of at least twelve years' duration immediately preceding retirement.

PREMIUMS

When the premium basis for FEGLI was determined at the program's inception, a scale was adopted that was expected to be in line with group life premiums in private plans, with adjustments anticipated as experience developed. It was decided that the employee should bear two thirds of the total cost. That principle is still followed even though the scale itself was adjusted after the first 13 years of experience. The premium rate charged for the basic benefits is independent of the attained age of the worker. Employee premium payments cease at retirement; coverage is continued without cost to the retiree, subject to the decreasing face amounts already mentioned.

The premium scale for the optional insurance amounts differs in several respects from that for the basic life and AD+D coverages:

1. The entire cost of the coverage is born by the employee.
2. The premiums vary by five-year attained age groups, like premiums for commercial five-year renewable term insurance.
3. Premium payments continue until the later of age 65 or retirement, unlike the basic group life premium, which ceases at retirement regardless of age.

The setting of the premium rates upon the introduction of the optional insurance coverage represented a difficult task since the degree of participation was unknown. For two reasons, a significant degree of antiselection was anticipated in the beginning, and premium rates were set accordingly. First, nearly all the older, less healthy workers were expected to participate in the optional program. In addition, since optional insurance premiums are automatically paid on behalf of retired employees after the later of their retirement or age 65, those older persons who chose the extra coverage at the outset of the program stood to gain measurably from so doing, even if they were in good health.

Initial costs were high, as was expected. After experience began to stabilize, however, it was determined that premiums could be sharply reduced. The original scale was decreased in 1969, and at the same time the number of age-class cells was expanded from three to seven. In October 1973 there was a further reduction in premium rates.

OTHER FEATURES

Since FEGLI is a true group life insurance program, its provisions are similar to those described earlier as typical of group term life insurance. These include provisions for the naming of beneficiaries, the termination of coverage, and the temporary cessation of employment.

Conversion to a plan of permanent insurance is a key feature of FEGLI. Terminating employees retain the right of conversion for 31 days after their group coverage ends, or for 15 days after they have been informed of their rights by the employing office, if later. During this time, the employee must notify the Office of Federal Employees Group Life Insurance (OFEGLI) of an intention to convert. In turn, OFEGLI informs the terminating employee of the names of eligible insurance companies from which he or she may choose. The converted policy may be any nonterm plan of insurance regularly issued by the insurer, but without disability or AD+D benefits. The new policyowner pays the regularly charged premium for his or her age and risk class, but cannot be charged any additional amount because of physical impairment. The face amount of the converted policy may be any amount equal to or less than the sum of the employee's basic and optional insurance under FEGLI.

ADMINISTRATION

Between the passage of the original FEGLI legislation and the date of its implementation, the Civil Service Commission consulted with representatives of the group insurance industry. These representatives proposed that the Metropolitan Life Insurance Company be made the primary insurer under FEGLI since Metropolitan had the largest amount of group life insurance in force of all companies in the

United States. Metropolitan began the task of setting up the OFEGLI in New York City. This office represents the insurance industry in its dealings with the federal government.

A reinsurance agreement was established under which any U.S. insurance company with group life insurance on its books could elect to participate. More than 300 companies now participate in the reinsuring function. The total of all FEGLI business is distributed among these insurers according to a formula based on group life in force, with a slight preference given to smaller companies. Of course, a portion of the premium is allocated to cover risk charges and administrative expenses incurred by the companies participating in the FEGLI system.

SCOPE

At the end of June 1978, nearly two and one-half million employees and one million retirees were covered under FEGLI. Optional life insurance was being provided for about 685,000 employees and 62,000 retirees.[4] The FEGLI and SGLI plans represent the two largest group life policies in existence. The question of which is the larger at any specific time is largely determined by the size of the armed forces.

Federal Employees Health Benefits Program

A comprehensive means of providing health insurance protection for government workers came into being in much the same way as did group life insurance for these workers. The first Eisenhower administration was concerned about the lack of health protection for federal workers, especially compared with the availability of group health plans to employees in private industry. This disparity made government work seem less than ideal to many well-qualified individuals. Prior to Eisenhower's terms of office, Presidents Roosevelt and Truman had viewed national health insurance as the ideal vehicle to provide health coverage to all workers, public and private alike. However, the philosophy of the Eisenhower administration was that private health insurance plans were preferable to national health insurance and that civil servants could be covered most efficiently through the extension of voluntary health plans under government supervision.

Many legislative proposals were debated during the 1950s. The final result of these deliberations, the passage of the Federal Employees Health Benefits Act (FEHB), was not achieved until late in Eisenhower's second administration. On September 28, 1959, the FEHB Act was signed and became operative on July 1, 1960. Although several modifying amendments have been enacted since 1960, the format and general nature of the FEHB program remain essentially the same.

---

[4]Civil Service Commission, Washington, D.C.

ELIGIBILITY

Coverage under the FEHB Act extends on a voluntary basis to practically all full-time civilian employees of the federal government as well as to their dependents. Annuitants under the Civil Service Retirement system and their dependents may also participate. Coverage is available to qualified individuals regardless of whether they reside in the United States. Even workers on a contract or fee basis and those payable on a piece-work basis may be eligible under certain conditions. No restrictions are placed on age, sex, state of health, or degree of occupational hazard.

Coverage for employees may be elected on either a self-only or a self-and-family basis. When the self-and-family option is elected, coverage is provided for the spouse, unmarried children under age 22, and unmarried children over age 22 who became disabled prior to age 22 and remain incapable of self-support. Dependents' benefits are identical to employees' benefits. Self-and-family coverage is currently elected by approximately three fourths of eligible employees.

Health coverage may be continued beyond retirement for annuitants who either retire for disability or retire on annuity with at least 12 years of service. In either case, enrollment in the FEHB program must have been continuous for the five years immediately preceding retirement or since the first opportunity to enroll. Finally, survivors of a deceased employee or annuitant may retain coverage if they were previously enrolled as dependents.

PLANS OFFERED

Unlike any of the employee benefit plans thus far considered, the FEHB program incorporates several optional insurance techniques from which the eligible employee may choose. Three categories of health care plans with a total of some forty specific plans of insurance have been approved for inclusion in the overall program. These categories include:

1. Government plans open to all employees. Within this category are separate specific plans, one administered through Blue Cross-Blue Shield and offering service type benefits; the other administered through Aetna Life and Casualty Insurance Company (the resulting business is shared by a pool of other commercial insurers) and offering indemnity type benefits;
2. Employee organization plans available only to members of specific employee organizations such as the American Federation of Government Employees, the Government Employees Hospital Association, and the National Postage Union; and
3. Prepaid comprehensive medical plans (HMOs) available only to employees who reside in areas which have such an organiza-

tion. Both Individual Practice Plans such as the Hawaii Medical Service Plan and the Washington Physicians Group, and group practice plans such as the Kaiser Plans of northern California are included in this option.

The choice of plan is made by the individual employee. Although transfer from one plan to another is permitted at certain designated times, relatively few participants have chosen to transfer.

As of June 30, 1978, slightly under 4 million persons, including employees and annuitants (but not dependents), were covered under the FEHB program. Of these, approximately 54.7 percent were covered by the government-wide service benefit plan, 14.3 percent by the government-wide indemnity plan, 21.6 percent by the employee organization plans, and 9.4 percent by the combined group practice and individual practice plans. Approximately 90 percent of all eligible employees participate in one of the plans.[5] Not surprisingly, the FEHB program is the largest voluntary employer-sponsored health insurance program in the world.

Some of the plans, including both of the government-wide plans and most of the employee organization plans, offer their participants a choice between two levels of benefits. Referred to as high-option and low-option plans, they generally differ in the size of deductibles, the coinsurance provisions, or the overall maximum payable for a given illness or for a lifetime. The broader, or high-option, coverage, while more expensive, has proved by far the more popular. At the time of the initial enrollment procedure in 1960, the high-option coverage was chosen by 81 percent of the participants; in recent years a slightly higher percentage of participants has selected high-option coverage.[6]

COST

Deliberations prior to the passage of the FEHB Act in 1959 produced significant disagreement over the financing of the benefits. The end result was a provision that prescribed minimum and maximum government contributions for self-only enrollments, self-and-family enrollments, and for family enrollment of females with nondependent husbands. In no case, however, was the government contribution to exceed 50 percent of the lowest rate for the government-wide plans.

Several liberalizing changes in the determination of government contributions have been implemented since then. A change, effective on January 1, 1975, prescribed that the government share would be 60 percent of the average high-option premium for the six largest plans then in effect. Under no circumstances, however, could more than 75

[5]*Ibid.*
[6]*Ibid.*

percent of the premium of a given participant be paid by the government. Thus, whereas government contributions during the first ten years of the program averaged only slightly more than 30 percent, this figure rose markedly with the implementation of the new provision in 1975.

The series of increases in amounts payable by the government towards the health insurance coverage of its employees was clearly necessary to avoid having the burden of spiraling medical costs borne solely by the employees. The average overall annual premium in 1960 was $182. Ten years later, this figure had risen to $370, an increase of more than 100 percent.[7] The acceleration of this trend would have compounded the burden on the employee. However, the potential burden to the employees was eased by the increments in the permissible government contributions during the first half of the 1970s.

Retired Federal Employees Health Benefits Program

Passage of the FEHB Act in 1959 provided guaranteed health insurance protection for both present employees and future retirees. However, former employees who had retired prior to July 1, 1960, were not eligible to participate. In an effort to provide health protection for these persons, the Retired Federal Employees Health Benefits (RFEHB) program was implemented, becoming operative on July 1, 1961. The program was made available to survivors of retired workers as well as to retired workers and their dependents. It provides government contributions for persons who wish to be covered under a plan administered by a private insurer, under any qualified private health plan, or under Part B (SMI) of Medicare.

A detailed analysis of the RFEHB Program will not be presented because the program is relatively small and, as a result of the availability of the FEHB program, is getting smaller. Only about 138,000 enrollees were covered as of mid-1978, compared to 200,000 employees in mid-1974.[8] A 1975 Act permitted transfers from the RFEHB program to the FEHB program, and a significant number of such transfers has resulted.

Federal Employees Compensation Program

The oldest workers' compensation plan in the United States is the plan covering federal government employees. Enacted in 1908, the Federal Employees Compensation Act provides generally more liberal benefits than do the plans which operate under state auspices. The

---

[7]*Ibid.*
[8]*Ibid.*

program is administered by the Department of Labor, and covers all federal employees. The cost of benefits is borne entirely through congressional appropriations.

SUMMARY

Few of the benefit plans underwritten, administered, or supervised by governmental entities in the United States technically qualify as true group insurance. Group life insurance for members of the armed forces and for federal civilian employees are among the few exceptions. Yet government-related benefit plans have undeniably caused a ripple effect that is constantly being sensed and evaluated by the private insurance industry. Admittedly, the effect of government plans varies significantly in degree between that engendered by the mammoth OASDHI program and the most insignificant retirement plan covering the employees of a small municipality.

The effect of public plans upon the private insurance industry is clearly neither entirely favorable nor entirely unfavorable. Many plans directly complete with private insurance, such as certain features of OASDHI. Others have undoubtedly generated business for private insurers that would not otherwise have been written.

The advisability of the expansion or contraction of government activity into the insurance sphere largely depends upon the social philosophy of the observer. The most commen belief is that the economic security of individuals must be provided by a combination of individual initiative, reflected by personal savings habits and individually purchased insurance protection, by employer-sponsored programs, and through government programs. The proper mix of these three approaches may never be determined to the satisfaction of everyone. However, the rapid expansion of government into the arena of economic security in recent years seems to indicate that the prevailing trend is toward the increasing dependence of American families upon government for their protection against the many hazards that disrupt the orderly pattern of their lives.

This chapter has described a variety of government-related plans. The armed forces' and veterans' benefit programs of the federal government were described in detail (including the many life insurance programs), and the survivor, disability, health, retirement and death benefits were also outlined. Federal programs for civilian employees were sketched, including group life insurance, health benefits, and several smaller benefit programs.

CHAPTER 31

STATE AND LOCAL GOVERNMENT INSURANCE PROGRAMS

INTRODUCTION

The enactment of employee benefit legislation is not the prerogative of the federal government alone. State legislatures have also played an active role in promoting employee benefit plans.

No employee-related problem has been more universally addressed by state legislatures than that of the worker injured while on the job. Workers' compensation plans, offered in all 50 states, are among the most important of state-mandated benefit plans. This chapter begins with a discussion of these plans.

Five states, Rhode Island, California, New Jersey, New York and Hawaii, have enacted legislation mandating temporary disability income plans. Two states, Rhode Island and Hawaii, have mandated health benefit plans. These are briefly discussed.

State and local governments, like their federal counterpart, offer death, retirement, and health benefit plans to their employees. The scope of these benefit plans varies from state to state and municipality to municipality. The most generous of these programs, that offered by New York State, is described in this chapter.

WORKERS' COMPENSATION

A major developmental impetus in the origins of many types of employee benefit plans was the desire of employers to provide a benefit that would attract high-quality employees. Although each of these benefits was clearly desirable, few were as sorely needed as plans to protect the worker from loss of pay because of accidental injuries incurred while on the job. In fact, it has been argued that the

by
ROBERT W. BATTEN, FSA, *Professor of Actuarial Science and Head of The Actuarial Science Program, Georgia State University*

inability of injured workers to seek and receive compensation from their employers was one of the gravest social evils fostered by the rapid growth of industry in the nineteenth century.

The plight of the disabled worker before workers' compensation laws were enacted was sorry indeed. Though injured workers had the right to sue their employers, the legal odds were heavily stacked against the success of such action. A time-honored common-law principle asserted that employers were to be held liable only if disablement or death resulting from a work-related incident was caused by a negligent act by the employer. Yet the burden of proof of such negligence lay upon the employee. Not only was litigation time consuming and expensive to the plaintiff, who could seldom afford it, but fellow workers were often fearful of the consequences if they gave testimony supporting the wronged employee's contention of employer negligence.

In addition, three common law defenses often aided employers to avoid liability. These included:

1. The doctrine of contributory negligence, which held that an injured party should not be permitted to recover damages if he or she had contributed in any manner toward the injury, no matter how minor such contribution might have been;
2. The fellow servant doctrine, which denied compensation to an injured employee if any fellow employee contributed in any way to the injury; and
3. The doctrine of assumption of risk, which held that upon acceptance of a job by a worker, he or she entered into an implied contract under which the worker realized and assumed liability for any normal risk of employment.

Though the passage of employer liability laws in the first decade of this century modified the effects of the three common-law defenses, the situation was still far from ideal.

A 1902 Maryland law incorporating the concept of true and immediate employer liability, although later found unconstitutional, was a harbinger of future reform legislation. Under pressure from President Theodore Roosevelt, Congress in 1908 passed the Federal Employees Compensation Act. It covered federal employees only, but it paved the way for the passage of similar state plans. By 1925, workers' compensation plans had been established in 24 states. With the passage of legislation in Mississippi in 1948, all of the states had workers' compensation statutes. Workers' compensation plans were already operational in Hawaii and Alaska when they obtained statehood in 1959.

The philosophy behind workers' compensation is that industrial accidents and resulting medical costs and disability payments are a

cost of production, just as are raw materials and machinery. Therefore, these costs also should be borne in full by the employer, regardless of liability. Workers' compensation statutes are now on the books
in all 50 states, Guam, Puerto Rico, and in each Canadian province. In
addition to the Federal Employees Compensation Act, federal legislation extends to the District of Columbia and to employees in nationwide maritime work. This latter group, including both private and
public employees, is specifically covered by the U.S. Longshoremen's
and Harbor Workers' Compensation Act.

Specific provisions vary in each of the states or jurisdictions
having workers' compensation statutes. In addition, state legislatures,
aware of the ever-present possibility of federal legislation or supervision of workers' compensation, frequently update and liberalize provisions. However, the basic nature of the laws remains stable.

Types of Laws

State workers' compensation laws are either compulsory or elective. A compulsory law requires all employers within a jurisdiction to
comply with its provisions and provide the stipulated benefits for
eligible employees. An elective law permits the employer to decide
whether or not to be governed by its provisions. In reality, however,
little difference exists between states having compulsory and elective
plans since an employer who chooses not to comply with an elective
plan loses the three common-law defenses when sued by an injured
employee. Furthermore, an employer later found negligent under such
circumstances could well incur a much greater financial burden than if
the employer had absorbed the costs associated with participation in a
formalized plan of protection for the employees.

An employee may choose to elect out of the plan in an elective
jurisdiction. However, should that employee then lodge a claim against
the employer, the employer is entitled to the three common-law defenses. Rejection of the plan by employees is extremely rare.

Currently, all but three states, Texas, South Carolina, and New
Jersey, have compulsory laws. Since 1974, nine states have changed
their plans from elective to compulsory. The trend is to eliminate the
right of employers to choose not to implement workers' compensation
plans.

Types of Insurers

Workers' compensation benefits for employees are provided in
one of three ways. Six states and all Canadian provinces require
employers to be insured by a monopolistic state or provincial fund
(although three of these states permit self-insurance under certain
conditions). Twelve states permit employers the choice of insuring
their workers in a state fund or with a private insurance company. The

remainder have no state fund. All workers' compensation insurance in these states is carried with private insurers.

In addition, self-insurance of workers' compensation benefits is allowed in 46 states and the District of Columbia. Self-insurance is most suitable where the number of employees is large and the amount of annual incurred claims reasonably predictable. An employer wishing to self-insure must be able to assure state authorities of the financial ability to guarantee claim payments, and must in many instances post a bond with the state. Employers deciding whether to self-insure must weigh the savings in administrative costs (which would otherwise go to an insurer) against the expenses of administering claims, administering a safety engineering program (otherwise provided by an insurer), and securing the services of needed medical and legal personnel. In addition, the financial ability to absorb an unusually large number of claims in a given year must be considered by a prospective self-insurer.

Coverage and Benefits

Although every state has enacted a workers' compensation law, no single state law covers all forms of employment. However, the trend is toward wider coverage, probably because of the desire by state legislatures to comply with the spirit of the 1972 recommendations of the National Committee on State Workmen's Compensation Laws. These recommendations generally called for expansion and liberalization of coverages.

A distinction is made in most states between public and private employment, although near-total coverage of each is a reality in many states. Several states require coverage only for employers with some minimum number of employees, ranging from three to five. Persons in such occupations as farming and domestic work are excluded in some states, as are temporary or casual workers. Coverage for all public employees is compulsory in the majority of states. In most states, many employers who would otherwise be exempt from the law may choose to participate voluntarily. Even the self-employed are permitted to participate in workers' compensation plans in several states if they so desire. Several states have recently mandated workers' compensation for casual and domestic workers, implementing one of the principal recommendations of the National Commission's 1972 Report.

ELIGIBILITY FOR BENEFITS

Workers' compensation laws were originally enacted to protect employees from financial losses arising from work-related injuries. Thus, compensation benefits were typically limited to "personal injury caused by accident arising out of and in the course of employment."

Yet the true spirit of the various laws required that occupational illness and disease be compensable as well. Such compensation presented the problem of determining whether a given disease truly resulted from conditions related to employment.

An early approach to this problem was to enumerate those specific diseases that would qualify as work-related. Although such statutes simplified the legal process when a given illness was included in the list, they seemed unfair because the complexities of many industrial processes gave rise to diseases which, though not enumerated, should have been compensable. As a result, broad coverage of occupational disease is now provided in all 50 states. More liberal treatment of occupational diseases occurred, in part, because these diseases are numerically much less common than are industrial accidents.

Understandably, problems still remain in determining whether or not a given accident or disease is work-related and therefore compensable. The courts have consistently held that incidents must occur in the regular course of employment and that impairments must be directly linked to employment in a cause-and-effect relationship. However, interpretations remain cloudy in many jurisdictions. Uniformity from state to state is almost impossible because of the different language in the various statutes.

TYPES AND AMOUNTS OF BENEFITS

Benefits payable under workers' compensation statutes fall into three separate categories. Cash payments may be made to workers who have been injured or who have sustained a wage loss as a result of a physical impairment. Medical benefits are payable, often without limit, when impairments demand medical attention or hospitalization or both. Finally, rehabilitation benefits are available in all states, reflecting the philosophy that rehabilitative efforts are in the best interests of the employee and employer alike.

Income Replacement for the Disabled. The largest single category of cash payments consists of income replacement for the temporarily totally disabled. Persons entitled to these benefits are those who are totally unable to perform their usual employment for a limited period of time, but who are expected to return to work at full efficiency upon recovery. Disability payments to these workers are determined as a percentage of wages, with the average payment replacing slightly more than two-thirds of normal earnings. Most states specify both a maximum and a minimum weekly payment, and some specify a maximum aggregate amount payable for any single disability. A few limit the duration of payments to a fixed time period such as 500 weeks.

Many states have enacted legislation that automatically adjusts benefits annually, based upon the average weekly wage in the state.

Several states now permit weekly payments as large as 100 percent of the state average weekly wage. In addition, some states provide for additional weekly amounts, in excess of the stated maximum, for each dependent of the disabled employee. It has been estimated that compensation benefits replaced 75 percent of the average injured worker's net income as of early 1976, up from 63 percent in 1972 and 54 percent in 1960.[1]

Cash benefits for permanent total disability are similar in most respects to those for temporary total disability. The only significant difference is that permanent total disabilities are compensable for a longer period of time and thus have a higher aggregate payment amount than do those of the temporary total type. In addition, fewer states provide for a maximum aggregate benefit for permanent than for temporary disabilities.

Where disability is partial rather than total, distinctions are often made between disabilities that involve specific or "scheduled" injuries and those that are more general. Nonscheduled partial disabilities are generally compensable on the same basis as total disabilities. The appropriate percentage is applied to the difference between weekly earnings before and after the injury. Impairments to, or loss of, certain body members are compensable on the basis of specific schedules incorporated into state legislation. Such scheduled payments are often in addition to temporary total disability payments, although some states permit dual payments only for limited periods of time. Scheduled payments are usually based on a percentage of pre-injury earnings, with the duration of payments based upon the physical significance of the lost or impaired member. Typically, the greatest benefit is available in the case of the loss of an arm at the shoulder or a leg at the hip. The maximum amount of cash benefit payable in such cases may well be ten or more times greater than for the loss of a finger.

A final type of cash benefit is payable upon the work-related death of an employee. Payments to an unremarried spouse and dependent children are provided by the workers' compensation laws in each state. Benefits consist of a lump-sum burial allowance in addition to weekly benefits to the survivors. The lump-sum amount ranges from $400 to $1,800.

Cash benefits, other than those occasioned by the employee's death, are payable only upon the completion of a stated waiting period. The basic purpose of a waiting period, usually three to seven days, is to avoid payment for minor injuries that debilitate a worker for only a very brief period. In the case of a disability that extends beyond a given period, such as two or four weeks, disability compensation is

---

[1]U.S Department of Labor, Division of Workers' Compensation, Washington, D.C.

retroactive to the date of injury. For example, a typical statute might provide for no disability payments for the first five days of disability but, should disability extend beyond two weeks, benefits for the first five days would then be paid to the employee in a lump sum. Payment of any required medical costs is in no way affected by the existence of a waiting period.

Medical Benefits. After a slow start, payments for medical care have become a major feature of workers' compensation plans. Currently only three states place any limitation upon the duration of medical payments that may be made in cases of work-related accidents or diseases. Two states place a limitation upon the total amount of medical benefits that may be paid, but no state limits both duration and amount. Costs related to prosthetic devices are covered without exception.

Rehabilitation Benefits. In addition to cash payments for disabled workers and health benefits in cases of medical, surgical, or hospitalization expenses, each state provides some form of assistance to rehabilitate injured workers. Provisions vary widely from state to state, with some statutes spelling out the methods through which rehabilitation may be promoted, both financially and otherwise. Other states have made no provision for such benefits in their workers' compensation statutes; yet even these states promote the principles of effective rehabilitation through state boards of rehabilitation or, in some cases, state boards of education. In addition, each state is now eligible to receive federal funds through the Federal Vocational Rehabilitation Act to aid in the rehabilitation of the industrial disabled.

Financing

Since the large majority of employers provide workers' compensation benefits through private insurers, the plans' basic costs are simply the premiums charged by the insurers. Premiums are generally based upon experience statistics compiled by the National Council on Compensation Insurance, a council developed in the early years of workers' compensation to eliminate the necessity for each state to compute its own manual rates.

Large employers are almost invariably experience-rated when they purchase coverage through private insurers. They may also be granted quantity discounts from the manual rates. Smaller employers may be experience-rated as well, but with a much smaller degree of credibility accorded their experience.

The pricing structure of workers' compensation insurance illustrates a major reason why such plans are not generally considered social insurance. Premiums vary by the size of the group and by the degree of accident and sickness hazard. The experience-rating feature further separates such plans from social insurance in which the same ultimate premium rate is charged all participants. In addition, administration of workers' compensation plans is not always carried out by a government agency.

Sharp differences of opinion have arisen between those who favor the state fund approach and those who favor coverage by private insurers. Proponents of private insurance cite the higher loss ratios generally found in state funds and the smaller amounts expended for inspections and safety engineering by state funds. Further, they contend that state funds should not receive explicit or implicit support from general revenues, such as the according of tax-free status to premiums or the public absorption of the administrative expenses built into the premium structure of the private insurers. It is unlikely that the philosophical argument between the proponents of coverage through free enterprise and those who favor this type of government activity will ever be settled to the satisfaction of all parties.

SECOND INJURY FUNDS

One might suspect that employers would be hesitant to hire partially handicapped workers on the grounds that aggravation of an existing handicap might lead to a workers' compensation claim for permanent and total disability. For example, a worker whose loss of one eye had left him only partially disabled could sustain another injury resulting in total blindness, and hence total permanent disability. Such a claim could prove quite costly to an employer in the form of increased workers' compensation premiums.

To improve the chances of employment of the physically handicapped, nearly all states have instituted *second injury funds*. The effect of such funds is to make an employer, in whose employ a disability claim is incurred by a previously handicapped worker, responsible only for the disability resulting from the second injury. The disabled employee is entitled to benefits based upon the total disability, with the difference in cost being made up from the second injury fund. The funds are accumulated by various means in different states. A common method is an assessment in death cases where there are no dependents. In some states, a flat fee is assessed the employer or insurer for each workers' compensation claim that results in payment of partial disability benefit payments. Still other states tax insurers on the amount of premiums generated on workers' compensation coverage that year. In other states, all penalty fines assessed both employers and insurers are deposited into the fund.

RELATIONSHIPS WITH OTHER PUBLIC PROGRAMS

A consideration of workers' compensation suggests that duplication of benefits with other plans of insurance, notably the disability and survivor features of social security, may well exist. The same situation may occur with respect to short- and long-term disability plans issued by private insurers, private pension plans, and group life insurance.

Disability payments under social security are restricted in such a way that combined benefits payable under the two plans may not exceed 80 percent of a worker's earnings prior to disability. Although the Social Security Act, as amended, does not impose a similar restriction on payments to survivors, a small number of states have reduced workers' compensation payments to survivors by a fraction of the social security benefit. The majority of private insurance plans that incorporate monthly cash benefits have stipulated that benefits will be reduced by part of all of any workers' compensation benefits payable. A blanket statement about antiduplication provisions is impossible, however, because the myriad of private plans provide an almost endless list of types of benefits.

Outlook

The workers' compensation system has historically been a target of wide-ranging criticism. Much of this criticism is levelled against the state-oriented network of plans that necessarily provides more liberal benefits in some jurisdictions than others. Negative reaction has also been generated by the alleged slow payment of claims caused by time-consuming litigation. The failure of state plans to provide universal coverage has also been scored. As a result, many critics propose the creation of a federal system of workers' compensation that would, in effect, take precedence over state laws. Other critics of the present system prefer superimposing legislation upon state laws. Such superimposed legislation has in fact been introduced in the U.S. Senate. This legislation would set minimum standards and establish penalties for states not meeting these standards. One of its major effects would be to allow an employee to sue his employer in federal court if the applicable state law failed to meet federal standards. Though introduced in the Senate, no such legislation had been enacted as of the end of 1978.

Proponents of the state approach to workers' compensation point to the great strides made in recent years in coverage and benefits and to the tendency of the various statutes to become more nearly uniform. A comparison of the status of current workers' compensation plans with those of a decade ago seems to support this contention.

The future of workers' compensation in its present form seems to rest upon whether the U.S. Congress remains of the mind that workers' compensation is not an area in which federal intervention is justified. In turn, this position seems largely dependent upon actions of the states in providing equitable and adequate benefits for workers who lose their ability to earn an income as a result of an accident or disease that may arise in the course of their employment.

TEMPORARY DISABILITY INSURANCE

Members of the labor force in the United States are protected through several means from loss of income because of disability. The disability insurance feature of the social security system is largely designed to assist those workers whose disablement is serious and lasting. It is generally categorized as long-term disability protection. Workers' compensation benefits are designed to protect a worker against the economic effects of employment-related injury and disease. Such benefits are payable after only a brief waiting period and may continue for several years or even for the entire duration of the disability, which in many cases is the remainder of life. Thus, workers' compensation may be thought of as both short- and long-term disability coverage.

The only obvious gap in government-sponsored disability protection appears in the area of short-term, or temporary, benefits payable for nonoccupational disabilities. A basic philosophic conflict has arisen about whether a governmental body should legislate mandatory plans for such temporary disability. Those who answer this question negatively believe that the rapid growth of private plans, both group and individual, makes governmental activity unnecessary. Proponents of legislation providing for mandatory plans note that such private coverage is far from universal and that much of the growth of private plans has been fostered by the implementation of those government plans that do exist and by the threat of similar enactments in additional states.

At present, mandatory temporary disability insurance plans at the state level are not likely to become widespread. Five states have enacted such plans, but many other legislatures have considered and then rejected similar action. Four of the five state plans now in existence were established during the 1940s. Only Hawaii, in 1969, has been added to the list during the most recent quarter century. These plans are significant, however, because they cover the overwhelming majority of workers in New York and California, the two most populous states, and in New Jersey, a heavily industrialized state. The remaining two state plans, those in Rhode Island and Hawaii, are significant not because of the great numbers of workers covered but because of their unique features. The discussion here will focus on the general levels of protection provided and the overall means through which the provision of government-sponsored benefits for the temporarily disabled is effected.

History

Rhode Island became the first state to implement a temporary disability insurance program when, in the near-full employment war year of 1942, it decided to divert some of the surplus funds in its unemployment insurance plan to provide income for those workers who were temporarily unable to work because of a disability. California passed its law in 1946, and New Jersey followed two years later. These initial three plans integrated to a certain extent with existing unemployment insurance plans. In contrast, the New York law, passed in 1949, is structured more along the lines of extended workers' compensation benefits. These characteristics have been maintained to the present. The laws of the first three states are still administered by the unemployment insurance agencies, while New York's law is administered through its Workmen's Compensation Board. The Hawaii legislation followed neither pattern and bears little or no relationship to either unemployment insurance or workers' compensation. The history of the several plans has been spotted with wide financial fluctuations, but appropriate adjustments have been made as needed, and each state plan is currently stable and solvent.

Types of Insurers

As with workers' compensation, some states maintain their own funds while others rely more heavily upon private insurers and self-insurance among employers. Only Rhode Island requires that all employers insure with a monopolistic state fund, and only Hawaii has no state fund. The remaining three states have state funds that compete with private insurers. In these states, employers may (1) use a private insurer, (2) use the state fund, (3) self-insure under certain conditions. Private insurers have complained that genuine competition between themselves and the competing state funds has not existed, especially in California where a large proportion of the plans is currently carried with the state fund. Overall, the trend seems to be toward increased participation in state funds and less use of the private insurance mechanism except in New York where employers can generally purchase more protection from a commercial insurer than from the state fund.

Benefits

The specifics of benefit computation vary slightly from state to state. However, each statute attempts to replace at least 50 percent of lost wages. This figure may range as high as 66⅔ percent within specific minimum and maximum dollar amounts. The similarities of these benefits to those prescribed by workers' compensation statutes are obvious. California provides limited hospital benefits, but all of the other states limit benefits to income replacement through weekly payments.

The temporary nature of these benefits is evident from the limitations on the duration of the weekly indemnity payments. Each state provides payments for no more than 26 weeks. Nuisance claims and malingering are eliminated, or at least strongly discouraged, through the imposition of a waiting period of one week.

Benefits are available only to those workers who have satisfied a very liberal requirement for covered employment prior to disability. For example, Rhode Island requires that a worker must have earned $1,200 in the preceding one-year period, or at least $20.00 for each 20 weeks during that period, in order to be eligible for benefits. Under certain circumstances, however, payments may be available to unemployed persons who are prevented from seeking employment because of disability.

Financing

The Rhode Island state fund and the California state fund are supported by employee contributions alone. In each of the other states, and in most private plans in California, the cost is shared by the employer and the employee. In no state does the employer bear the entire cost. The degree of participation by the employer generally depends upon whether the plan being used provides more liberal benefits than the plan prescribed by the state.

Outlook

The superficial treatment accorded the five-state temporary disability insurance programs reflects the fact that expansion of the concept into new states is highly unlikely. Efforts of organized labor seem to be directed more toward private coverage of the disability risk through employer-sponsored plans than through a plan mandated by the state, probably because benefits under private plans are often more liberal and varied. Furthermore, labor groups seem to believe that a new employee benefit plan is more visible, and hence more appreciated by workers, when the plan is private rather than public.

The future of plans similar to the five currently in existence does not seem bright. Resources are limited, and priorities must be established. Liberals prefer bigger and better benefits at the federal level; conservatives emphasize the responsibility of individual wage earners to provide for at least a portion of their own economic security, especially for short-term risks that can be protected against with private plans or individual savings. In either case, it appears that the enactment of compulsory short-term disability insurance plans in additional states is not currently high on the priority lists of persons of any political persuasion.

OTHER STATEWIDE PLANS

Workers' compensation in all states, and temporary disability insurance in five states are generally cited as the clearest examples at the state level of government-sponsored benefit plans for employees. Another example is unemployment insurance, but this topic has been given only passing reference in this text because unemployment insurance plans are administered exclusively by state agencies, and the private insurance industry is not involved in any way.

Compulsory Health Insurance

Two states, Rhode Island and Hawaii, have recently implemented compulsory state health insurance plans clearly intended to guarantee universal health protection. Specification of certain minimum benefit levels may be considered by some critics as unwarranted invasion into the private affairs of employers. However, a clear precedent for such action exists for occupational injuries through imposition of workers' compensation standards. Since each of these two plans began operation on January 1, 1975, little experience has developed. Their degree of success or failure is yet to be evaluated. It seems likely that interested parties in other states will watch these plans carefully.

RHODE ISLAND

The Rhode Island legislation provides catastrophic health insurance coverage to all residents who have resided in Rhode Island for more than three months and who have not moved their residence to Rhode Island for the primary purpose of obtaining benefits. The catastrophe benefits are funded entirely through general revenues and are payable by the state to persons who demonstrate that losses have been incurred in excess of specific amounts.

The program is predicated upon the availability of private health insurance plans to all residents of the state. Each health insurer in Rhode Island is required to offer qualified plans containing coverage at least equal to that specified in the law to all persons and to all employers regardless of the nature of the employee group. To be qualified, a plan must be submitted to the state for certification. The state-provided catastrophic health benefits then serve as a layer of protection above and beyond that of the private plans.

The state plan reimburses individuals or families for their medical costs that exceed the stipulated "personal resource payment," or deductible. This deductible amount is determined in such a way as to encourage the purchase of private insurance plans with liberal benefits. For example, a family covered under a qualified private plan that includes major medical benefits is assigned an annual personal resource payment of the greater of $500 or 10 percent of income. Those families not covered by a qualified plan must bear the first $5,000 of medical expense or 50 percent of their income, if greater. Slightly different personal resource payments are stipulated for Medicare beneficiaries.

The program is administered by the Rhode Island Department of Health. Private insurers are used as intermediaries for the payment of benefits.

HAWAII

The compulsory health insurance legislation in Hawaii is strongly employer-oriented in the sense that employers are required to provide insurance against hospital and medical care costs for their employees after a four-week waiting period. Such insurance must meet minimum standards as prescribed in the law. Eligible workers are not given the right to waive coverage, although several categories of workers are expressly excluded from eligibility, notably government employees.

Benefits for State and Local Government Employees

Employees of state and local governments are often covered by the same generic types of benefit plans as federal government employees and workers in private industry. Generally, the benefit plans for these government employees are not as liberal as those for other workers, although there are exceptions.

There are approximately 2,300 retirement systems for state and local government employees in the United States. Many are quite liberal, while many others provide benefits that are considered insufficient. In addition, there are many other forms of benefit plans. Only a cursory survey of this network of diverse benefit programs is possible. Following this survey, a specific system, that of New York State, will be considered in detail.

HISTORY AND CURRENT STATUS

The history of employee benefit plans for state and local government employees closely parallels that of other plans. Many were implemented as a result of the same motivations that generated the rapid growth of employee benefit plans in general. Recent liberalizations in both coverage and size of benefits follow the same patterns as those of social security and private plans.

In 1857, New York City policemen became the first group to be covered under a public employee retirement system. Other plans were implemented shortly thereafter, but it was not until 1911 that an entire state (Massachusetts) provided retirement benefits for state employees generally. The development of plans in most states and municipalities has tended to result in separate plans for the fire fighters and police, for teachers, and for other state or local government employees. Often the most liberal of these three types of plans cover fire and police department personnel.

There has been little growth in the number of retirement plans during the last decade, but growth in the number of covered persons and benefit levels has been rapid. From 1962 to 1972, the number of plans actually decreased from 2,346 to 2,304, but the total coverage increased almost 70 percent to 9.1 million during the same period. The average monthly benefits paid under these plans rose from $137 to $233 during this period, an increase of 63 percent. While this increment is significant, it lagged behind increments in social security benefits and benefits increases in private plans.

Public employees were originally excluded from coverage under the Social Security System. The present situation, however, is different. Currently, employees of state and local governments with no retirement plans of their own may be covered if the state agrees. Where a retirement plan does exist, public employees may choose to be covered under OASDHI as well, if the state agrees and if the majority of employees so vote. Significant numbers of state and local government workers currently contribute toward social security benefits as well as to their own plans.

Workers' compensation plans now grant broad eligibility to employees of state and local governments, although this was not originally true for many of the state plans. Most state laws still exclude a few minor categories of state and local workers from compulsory coverage, but many of these states permit voluntary coverage of all such workers.

Unemployment insurance, traditionally offered to state and local government employees on a limited basis, has become more readily available to these workers in recent years.

Retirement plans for fire and police department personnel often provide for retirements for disability due to accidents in addition to the usual retirements. The accidental disability retirement benefits are often significantly more liberal than those for service retirements. These plans also often contain basic death benefits as well as additional accidental death benefits.

Except for a few of the very large plans, other benefits such as health insurance, life insurance, and disability insurance are ordinarily less generous than are those for employees of the federal government. Often, one or more of these benefits are available as a result of collective bargaining agreements between the employing unit and certain segments of the employee group.

THE NEW YORK STATE EMPLOYEES PLAN

Benefits available to employees of the State of New York are among the most liberal of all state and local employee benefit plans in the United States. The plan is huge, covering hundreds of thousands of workers. For these reasons, the New York plan may not be an ideal prototype. But its magnitude makes it important, and its liberal provisions were placed in the national spotlight in the mid-1970's because of the severe financial difficulties experienced by both New York City and New York State. Therefore, the reader must be cautioned against considering this plan as typical, while comprehending the scope and importance of the plan from an academic standpoint.

Normal retirements are permitted at age 55 with no service provisions. When combined with social security, retirement benefits under the New York plan are considerably larger than those available to federal civil service retirees. Disability retirees also receive benefits that are superior to those of federal employees when social security benefits are taken into consideration. However, New York requires ten years of service for disability retirement compared with only five years under the federal plan, one of the few provisions under which the New York plan appears to be less liberal. Another provision under which federal employees have an advantage is in cost-of-living adjustments to annuity payments subsequent to retirement which, under the New York plan, are applied only to the first $8,000 of an individual's retirement annuities.

A particularly generous feature of the New York retirement plan, mentioned earlier, is its noncontributory nature. This plan is one of the very few of its type that requires no employee contributions.

The health insurance benefits provided for New York employees are similar in several respects to those of the Federal Employees Health Benefits Plan. Both give participants the choice of the exact plan under which they will be covered. Aspects of the New York plan that are more liberal than the plan available to federal workers include a lower major medical deductible and the provision of a separate plan for dental care. On the other hand, surgical and maternity benefits are less generous than under the federal plan.

Health coverage for New York employees, including dental insurance, is funded entirely by the state. Further, 75 percent of the cost of dependent coverage is borne by the state. This feature is clearly more generous than that of the federal plan, under which the employing unit contributes only slightly more than half of the cost for the total health plan.

The area of life insurance is the major one in which employees of the state of New York fare poorly in comparison with other plans. New York State has no life insurance program for its employees. Although most other plans do provide some life insurance, life insurance benefits are generally less adequate for state and local government employees in comparison with the benefits available to federal employees and employees in private industry.

SUMMARY

The benefit programs of the various state and local governments vary in the scope of their coverage and the generosity of their benefit schedules. Most states and municipalities offer some or all of the types of benefit programs offered to privately and federally employeed individuals. All states offer workers' compensation benefits. This chapter discussed these plans in detail.

The chapter also sketched the mandatory health plans of Rhode Island and Hawaii. The general nature of state and local benefit programs was discussed. The point was made that with the exception of New York (which offers no life insurance benefits) benefit plans that state and local governments offer their employees are not as generous as those provided or administered by the federal government for its employees.

Index